The Frank Davis
Seafood Notebook

Also by Frank Davis
The Fisherman's Guide to Lake Pontchartrain

THE FRANK DAVIS
SEAFOOD
NOTEBOOK

Frank Davis

FOREWORD BY PAUL PRUDHOMME

PELICAN PUBLISHING COMPANY

GRETNA 1988

First printing, May 1983
Second printing, July 1984
Third printing, July 1985
Fourth printing, April 1986
Fifth printing, April 1988

Library of Congress Cataloging in Publication Data

Davis, Frank, 1942-
  The Frank Davis seafood notebook.

  Includes index.
  1. Cookery (Seafood)   2. Cookery, American—
Louisiana. I. Title
TX747.D279   1983   641.6'9   82-24679
ISBN 0-88289-309-2

Book design by Laura W. Neal

Manufactured in the United States of America
Published by Pelican Publishing Company, Inc.
1101 Monroe Street, Gretna, Louisiana 70053

To my wife Mary Clare and my daughter
Amanda, whose inspiration, patience, and
love were the ingredients that got this book
off the back burner and cookin'.

Contents

Foreword

I'd like to give you all the reasons that I can for using and enjoying this cookbook. I'm from Opelousas, Louisiana, and I've been a professional chef for the past 25 years. My wife, Kay, and I own and operate K-Paul's Louisiana Kitchen and Grocery in the French Quarter of New Orleans.

First, any book that you purchase is only as sincere and enjoyable as the writer. Frank Davis and I have had many conversations about food, while eating and while watching other people eat. My first recollection of Frank was watching him eat at my restaurant. I remember a man who talked excitingly with his friends and companions about food—not only what he was eating at the time, but what was cooked last night, and what he was to have for dinner that night.

The first time I saw Frank he was in a Louisiana Wildlife and Fisheries uniform (he spent many years as a magazine editor for that department). During that time, Frank learned about cooking fish and game as only a person devoted to preserving our bayous and wildlife and to appreciating the abundance of what we have to eat in Louisiana on a year-round basis can do. He is a man who cares about his family and his friends; he includes them in all phases of his life.

I watched the progress of his book and the anguish of testing and retesting recipes to make sure that they worked properly and had that great feeling and Louisiana taste that our state is so well noted for. I consider the book a valuable addition to the many books written on Louisiana food, and I consider Frank a number-one authority on cooking and eating the fresh fish and game of Louisiana.

I have every confidence that you will spend many hours of fun cooking and eating with *The Frank Davis Seafood Notebook*, as I know I'm going to do.

Chef Paul Prudhomme

An Open Letter
to Gourmets

Dear Reader:

It takes a lot of guts to publish a new seafood cookbook in South Louisiana. Where fixing fine foods is not only an art but an established way of life, and where one can find scores of Louisiana-style cookbooks at every turn, it might seem as if there would be nothing new to say, especially about seafood cookery. And yet it is not so.

Frank Davis has authored an exciting and different approach to the subject with his *Seafood Notebook*, a *narrative* digest of the tastiest aquatic treats this side of Bayou Teche. No dry, computerlike list of ingredients with minimal explanation in this book. Instead Frank *talks* you through each step, in plain language, right down to the finished product. The instructions are, in fact, so detailed you may get the feeling of standing next to the chef as he talks and works and carefully explains the entire operation.

In Cajun Country there is a word that means something extra, an unexpected and welcome addition to what you'd normally expect. That word is *lagniappe* (lán-yap), and it is in the lagniappe category that the genius of the *Seafood Notebook* becomes evident. In addition to basic recipes and their preparations, there is valuable advice on which recipe components may be safely substituted for others so as not to unbalance the taste. There are suggestions on how to add gusto to traditional dishes, how to brighten up leftovers (nothing is wasted), and how to do a little magic with sauces and fondue. You will see new recipes, very old ones like the 130-year-old recipe for turtle soup, oyster bread dressing, and recipes once passed on only by the spoken word.

But there is still more. The *Notebook* further recommends companion side dishes, vegetables, and even a compatible wine so that you may expand the entrée and experience the delicate weave of flavors that characterize a thoughtfully coordinated meal. Now *that's* lagniappe!

The *Seafood Notebook* is therefore much more than a cookbook. It is a sort of seafood novel, a learning experience, a personal guide to the preparation of seafoods, Louisiana style. As it teaches the basics of seafood savvy it leaves you worlds of room to create self-inspired variations. Once you have grasped the basics only your imagination will limit the mouth-watering masterpieces you'll be able to concoct.

One final thought in the interest of fair play and forewarning: The information within is not likely to favor any weight-loss regime you may presently be on or considering. On the contrary, you may find yourself toting about a few extra pounds after seriously practicing what this book preaches. Perhaps you can console yourself with the fact that there is no such thing as a Louisiana-style diet seafood dinner.

So now you have been warned. As one New Orleans gourmet—long since resigned to accepting an occasional pound of flesh as the price of his consuming hobby—was heard to say, "Forget about weight watching when you open up the *Seafood Notebook* . . . you can get fat just smelling the pages."

Bon appétit!

Dave John
Marine Biologist and Gourmet

Acknowledgments

The author wishes to thank the following persons for their support and assistance in putting this book together: Chef Paul Prudhomme, Jerald Horst, Jim Ledbetter, Tony Chachere, Dr. Mike Moody, Jean H. Picou, Rita Fitzgerald, and Carol Mura.

Special acknowledgment is made to the Gulf of Mexico Fishery Management Council, the National Marine Fisheries Service, and the Louisiana Wildlife and Fisheries Department.

The author also expresses sincere gratitude to Paul Arrigo of the New Orleans Tourist and Convention Commission for his continued assistance during chapter compilation, and to Frumie Selchen, whom I believe to be one of the best cookbook editors in the business, for withstanding the onslaught of this book's calorie-ridden pages way up in New Hampshire without gaining a single pound! Sincere thanks, too, to Dr. Milburn Calhoun, Wendy Long, and Kate Bandos of Pelican, the most patient publishers in the whole world!

Introduction

This book is the result of 18 months of testing, researching, compiling, rewriting, translating, and—best of all—*tasting* what I consider to be some of the finest seafood recipes of Louisiana. And it is done in a rather unique style.

In fact, it is not really a *cookbook;* I've always found cookbooks rather impersonal. I figured if I was going to write a book about cookery, it would be written for folks who would be happy to read what I had to write. They'd be able to use the material to create some really good dishes. The pages would contain *answers* to some questions they always wanted to ask. It would spell out in detail all the little things, including the kitchen trickery, that good cooks keep a secret and would-be cooks never think about. It would leave nothing to chance, appearing elementary in some places and quite complex in others. It would be a book for everyone who ever wanted to cook a good plate of fish, crabs, shrimp, oysters, or crawfish, just like those venerated dishes folks travel to New Orleans for from all over, just to taste.

But it wouldn't be hard to use. Because it would be scribed for "friends," wherever they might live, it would have a warmth, a conversational touch, kinda like we were together in the kitchen, side by side, whipping up some exciting new dish that we'd be proud to serve to anyone. So it would have to be a *fun* book, not some reference work that you'd stash away on a shelf. It would have to be entertaining. And it would, more than anything else, have to be as complete as I could make it. After all, isn't that what every good cook does—clip recipes from magazines, jot them down on paper bags, scribble new hints on scraps of paper, just to get all the possible answers to the questions posed by the art of cooking? I doubt seriously that there's one single cook who doesn't have a special notebook somewhere with all the little cooking tricks he or she has collected in it.

So that's what this is. I've simply expanded *your* notebook for you, particularly in the realm of seafood. And because I want you to be *creative*—a most important quality in a good cook—I wrote no recipe in these chapters that should be taken as gospel. They can all be altered (and improved upon!) to suit individual tastes. And I would be honored if your experimentation produced results superior to mine. If that happens I will have accomplished what I set out to do 18 months ago: convince folks that cooking, especially seafood cooking, is an art, is creative, and, most of all, is *fun*.

The recipes in these chapters come from many sources, but they are all truly representative of Louisiana, the Culinary Capital of the Universe. Quite a number of the recipes are originals I've created. Others have been gleaned from the ancestral traditions of the Acadians, the Italians, the Germans, the Creoles, and the mixed culture of old New Orleans.

My objective has been to put on paper, all in one volume, the best and most authentic recipes and the most important seafood information that characterizes Louisiana—and especially New Orleans—cookery. You will also notice that I've repeated certain techniques, cooking methods, helpful hints, and suggestions for emphasis. That's because I believe that cooking can be mastered only if it is repetitive.

In short, I've written this book so that, regardless of where you call home, you can fix seafood dishes and eat as if you were living in the historic French Quarter or in the heart of Cajun Country. And isn't that nice?

So *The Frank Davis Seafood Notebook* is your guide to fun in the kitchen. After you read through it several times—and I hope you will *read* all the way through it, 'cause there's some good stuff on these pages!—you should be ready to cook anything that lives in the water. Oh, it might not always turn out the way you wanted it on the first attempt, but at least now you won't be afraid to try.

Take the book and get into the kitchen!

CHAPTER ONE

It's All a Matter of Flavor

The Basics of Seasoning

LOUISIANA-STYLE FLAVORING INGREDIENTS

So that you will have a total picture of what goes into putting together Louisiana-style dishes, I've made this list of basic ingredients. If you prepare the recipes in this book, you'll find them used over and over again. You might want to add some to your shopping list the next time you're at the grocery. That way, you'll be ready to cook anytime!

Chives
Capers
Liquid Smoke (hickory)
Pitted black olives
Dill pickles
Philadelphia Brand Cream
  Cheese
Zatarain's Crab and Shrimp Boil
  (liquid)
Anchovies
Romano cheese
Prepared mustard
Contadina tomato paste
Yellow cornmeal
Unseasoned bread crumbs
Italian salad dressing
Pure horseradish
Cheddar cheese

Dry white wine
Dry red wine
Canned Mushrooms
Real mayonnaise
Imitation bacon bits
Pitted green olives
Tarragon vinegar
Tabasco Brand Pepper Sauce
Cornstarch
Process American cheese
Mozzarella cheese
Heavy cream (whipping cream)
Water chestnuts
Cream of mushroom soup
Cream of shrimp soup
Frozen lemon juice
Dry sherry
Zatarain's Fish-Fri (corn flour)

I also recommend that in order to fix Louisiana-style dishes, you keep on hand a good supply of rice, eggs, milk, half-and-half (breakfast cream), potatoes,

1

noodles, No. 4 spaghetti, cooking oil (preferably Crisco or Mazola), fresh bell peppers, celery, garlic, and white onions.

Let me also suggest you buy those specific brands I recommend in the list above (like Philadelphia Brand Cream Cheese, Zatarain's Crab and Shrimp Boil, and Tabasco Brand Pepper Sauce), and the brand names I list in the recipes throughout this book. I've tried many brands throughout the years, but in most instances the best overall results were produced with the products I've recommended.

When you can't find these brands locally, I heartily recommend you go with the *finest quality substitute* you can find. Don't skimp on quality! Because, as Pappy used to say, "You can't make chicken soup out of chicken feathers!"

Incidentally, Louisianians will be glad to ship our unique products (like Zatarain's) to cooks in other parts of the country. If you write to me, I'll be glad to furnish you with addresses and telephone numbers!

RECOMMENDED HERBS AND SEASONINGS FOR SEAFOODS

All kitchen shelves already contain salt and pepper, but to prepare the recipes traditional in French, Italian, Creole, and Cajun cooking it is essential that you have on hand a wide variety of seasoning herbs, spices, and condiments.

I've tried to make this a complete list of all the spices you're ever likely to use with seafood; I'd suggest keeping as many as possible as permanent stock in your pantry. You'll find that some of them are not mentioned often in specific recipes, but that doesn't mean you shouldn't use them. I want to encourage you to get familiar with them all and to use them when you think they'll add the kind of flavor you want in *any* recipe. Be *daring*, and let me know what you discover. Keep in mind that when you use these seasonings they should be added to your recipes gradually, in controlled amounts—*one-eighth to one-quarter teaspoon* at a time—and taste-tested between additions for flavoring.

● **Allspice:** Adds a unique flavor when sprinkled in water for poaching fish and shrimp, and gives a little extra zest to red gravy dishes used with seafoods. For the type of cooking this book recommends, your best bet would be to buy *ground allspice*. It tastes like a combination of cinnamon, nutmeg, and cloves.

● **Aniseed:** In seafoods, this spice should be used only in *dashes* or *pinches*. It should be an "enhancer," not a dominant seasoning. Use it only in poaching fish fillets, peeled shrimp, or shelled crab.

● **Barbecue Spice:** This is actually a dry *blended* seasoning that lends itself beautifully to seafoods, especially those prepared in butter bases. Italian-style shrimp, red piquante gravies, and broiled or grilled fish are all greatly enhanced by barbecue spices. To pick up the flavors in these dishes and to complement potato salads, casseroles, some gumbos, and cheesy au gratins, sprinkle some barbecue spice onto the ingredients. Usually barbecue spice is a mix of chili peppers, cumin, garlic, cloves, paprika, salt, and sugar.

● **Basil:** It is really difficult to overseason with basil—it is such a good herb. I can't imagine an Italian dish without it! So, when cooking seafood in tomato sauces—shrimp, fish, crabs, and so forth—if you want an Italian taste, be sure to toss in the basil. You should also simmer basil (about one-quarter teaspoon) in each stick of butter you melt as a baste for grilled or baked fish and shrimp. And if you want the baste even more flavorful, add a teaspoon of lemon juice.

● **Bay Leaves:** Should be put into gumbos, chowders, jambalayas, and other liquid-based seafood dishes, including stews and sauces (both tomato- and butter-based). It lends a mild, sweet richness that perks up these dishes and increases the flavor. Usually two or three leaves are all that is required.

● **Caraway Seed:** Used in Louisiana-style cooking only on rare occasions, caraway seed will add extra sparkle to shrimp, crabmeat, and fish casseroles. *Use it sparingly*, and remember that it resembles a combination of dill and anise.

● **Cayenne Pepper:** This is the mainstay of a number of "hot" Cajun dishes (sauce piquante, jambalaya, bisque) and a principal means of spicing up boiled seafoods. Cayenne is God's gift to Louisiana and is made from a variety of red peppers. So unless you're familiar with the brand you purchase there is no way to gauge its potency. This is one spice I suggest you add *a little at a time*. As a flavor enhancer, it is excellent, but too much can make a dish inedible. Nevertheless, never omit the cayenne, 'cause it ain't Cajun if there ain't cayenne in it!

● **Celery Flakes:** These are dehydrated flakes of the celery plant. I find them inadequate for most recipes I cook, and I recommend you use *fresh* celery instead.

● **Celery Seed:** Excellent for fish stuffings, crabmeat casseroles, and gumbo dishes when used sparingly. It is also good in shrimp stuffings for eggplants, mirlitons, and bell peppers. *Celery salt* is nothing more than celery seed combined with salt.

● **Chervil:** Not used all that much in Louisiana home cooking, but it is sometimes added to egg-based stuffings and sauces for fish dishes. You might also want to sprinkle it sparingly over casseroles, since it does serve to enhance other herbs when combined with them. Actually, I recommend you use parsley instead!

● **Chili Powder:** Another blended seasoning, not essential in seafood cookery. You would do better using barbecue spice instead—unless, of course, you're trying to make Mexican-Style Shrimp! Barbecue spice contains essentially the same ingredients as chili powder, without the allspice.

● **Cloves:** This spice really does wonders for certain sauce bases for seafoods. Sprinkled generously into dishes like Shrimp Sicilian and Barbecued Shrimp, cloves add mouth-watering flavor. As a Louisiana cook, you should keep both ground and whole cloves on your pantry shelf, using the ground product for stuffings, dips, and sauces while adding whole cloves to gravies and stocks. Note: Add cloves no more than *one-eighth teaspoon at a time* in the ground form, and no more than two or three buds at a time in the whole form.

● **Crab Boil (Crab and Shrimp Boil):** The principal Louisiana seasoning for boiling crabs, shrimp, and crawfish, crab boil is a blend of a variety of herbs and spices that produce the famous Bayou Country flavor that New Orleanians rave about. Crab boil contains whole peppercorns, bay leaves, red peppers, mustard seed, ginger, dill seed, allspice, cloves, coriander seed, and a few other secret goodies. It should be added to the water and "cooked in" before you add the seafood, and it should be supplemented with lemon juice, fresh onions, a couple of cloves of garlic, some chopped celery, and extra cayenne to really season boiled seafoods to perfection. Of course, salt should be added, too, according to individual taste.

● **Curry Powder:** Another blended seasoning that goes well in casseroles (especially crab and shrimp), chowders, and gravies, as well as in seafood dips made with creams and cheeses. Sprinkle it lightly into your sauces, too, for genuine Indian-curry flavor. Technically, the blend can contain as many as 20 different spices, including ginger, turmeric, cloves, cinnamon, cumin seed, black pepper, red pepper, etc. *Add curry powder only a dash at a time,* and taste before increasing the amount.

● **Dill Seed:** The seed of the dill plant is good poached with fish or blended lightly into sauces for fish and shrimp (especially cheese-based sauces). For seafood salads, I suggest you also stock your pantry shelf with *dill weed*, the leaves of the dill plant.

● **Filé:** This is what you add to your gumbo to make "gumbo filé." Filé is actually the ground-up leaves of the sassafras tree; it's used primarily as a thickener, but it does have a particular flavor all its own. One note of caution: Keep filé fresh and always add it to the *cooked* dish. Stale filé cooked into your gumbo will turn bitter!

● **Fennel Seed:** Excellent for bringing out Italian flavors in seafoods. You should add a pinch or two of fennel seed to crabmeat and shrimp dishes for just this purpose. But don't overuse it; fennel imparts a rather aromatic, sweet taste, somewhat similar to anise. Local Italians refer to it as "fenugreek seed" (pronounced fen-óke-kree), and use it in sausagé Italiano. Be certain you add a pinch of fennel to Shrimp Sicilian, Barbecued Shrimp, and all Italian gravies.

● **Garlic:** While the fresh product is always best (of course, that's a personal opinion!), it is possible to stock garlic products on your pantry shelf in a variety of bottled forms—garlic powder, garlic salt, garlic purée, and minced garlic. Garlic is an integral part of most styles of Louisiana cooking—Italian, French, Cajun, and Creole. So *add garlic!* You can use it in almost any seafood dish.

● **Ginger:** While not widely used in Bayou Country cooking, ginger makes all the difference in the world when you're creating Oriental-style seafood dishes. Sprinkled lightly over broiled shrimp or fish, or blended in butter for basting, ginger is a good spice to have in your kitchen. I recommend you stock *ground* ginger.

• **Herb Seasoning:** Can be found on most grocery shelves, but not essential to the cook who wants to be creative and learn to combine his or her own herbs and spices. While it can be sprinkled over poached fish, herb seasoning is principally used for salads and salad dressings, and those are the only things I recommend you use it for.

• **Italian Seasoning:** Unlike herb seasoning, Italian seasoning *should* be a regular part of your pantry stock. There are instances in preparing seafood sauces, dips, stuffings, gravies, and butters when you want only a *hint* of *Italiana*. At these times a dash or two of prepared Italian seasoning does the trick. You can also add the seasoning to the salads, vegetables, and canapes you serve with seafood. I do suggest, however, that you avoid using the prepared seasoning as a substitute for oregano, basil, garlic, etc. in full-scale Italian recipes.

• **Mace:** This is the fleshy growth between the nutmeg shell and its outer husk, and it closely resembles nutmeg in flavor. Mace is seldom used in Louisiana home cooking, and then only sparingly in fish casseroles and in sauces used as fish toppings. The one recipe in which you will want to include mace as an ingredient is oyster stew. It really heightens the flavor.

• **Marjoram:** Similar to oregano except in potency, marjoram is best described as a "mild oregano," while oregano is called a "concentrated marjoram." Just taste them and you'll see what I mean. Marjoram enhances the flavor of most seafoods, but is especially good in tomato-base dishes (jambalaya, shrimp creole, catfish courtbouillon, and so forth), rich cream sauces, and juicy casseroles made with fish or crabmeat.

• **Mint Flakes:** Mint flakes spice up the flavor of fish dishes. A pinch or two will do the same thing that lemon juice does to filleted trout and flounder. But for best results, make a mint-butter sauce (one-quarter teaspoon of mint to one stick of butter) and dab it lightly over the fish as a condiment. You might also want to add a pinch or two to your seafood cheese dips when you are preparing fondues for parties.

• **Mixed Pickling Spice:** While you won't use it that often, it's a good idea to have a bottle of pickling spice around just in case you want to fix pickled catfish, shrimp, etc. It keeps well on the shelf and can also do in a pinch to spice up a quick seafood sauce. Most brands contain mustard seed, bay leaves, black and white peppercorns, dill seed, red peppers, ginger, cinnamon, mace, allspice, and coriander seed.

• **Mustard:** One of the most versatile herbs for developing full-bodied flavors in seafoods, dry mustard (added to water and blended into recipes) can be an enhancer for crabmeat, shrimp, fish, oysters, frog legs, alligator, etc. It also lends a superb accent to deviled dishes, casseroles, and sauces. And you should always add a touch of mustard to cheese dishes, creamed seafood soups, cocktail sauces for shrimp, and Oriental seafood recipes. I have found that it's most convenient to use in the powdered form.

● **Nutmeg:** It doesn't have many uses in Louisiana seafood cookery, but nutmeg does add a unique taste to fish cakes or patties. I recommend you keep a can around the house and add a dash or two to your croaker patties, garfish balls, and old-fashioned codfish cakes. You might also want to toss in a pinch the next time you make fish stuffing.

● **Onion Flakes:** These dehydrated onions can be used in sauces and stews in seafood cuisine, but I recommend you use fresh onions whenever possible. I do keep a bottle of *onion powder* on my pantry shelf, however, and you'll find that it works well in touch-up situations when you need just a hint more onion. Onions themselves are mainstays of Louisiana cookery; use them whenever you cook any kind of seafood.

● **Oregano:** One of the basic flavoring ingredients in Italian seafood cookery. Oregano should be put in all tomato sauces, all cheese toppings, all stuffings, and all stews, regardless of the type of seafood you're using. And because of the amount of oregano you will use in Bayou Country cooking, I recommend you stock both ground oregano *and* oregano leaves. You might also want to prepare an oregano-butter (one-half teaspoon oregano to one stick butter) and use it to baste your shrimp and fish fillets. It's good stuff!

● **Paprika:** Paprika is a mild, sweet red pepper that is ground to a powder after all the seeds and stems have been removed. Contrary to popular opinion, it does add a mild flavor to foods and should be used as a garnish in crabmeat, shrimp, and fish dishes. It also goes well in seafood fondues and thick cream and cheese toppings.

● **Parsley Flakes:** While flakes are useful in a pinch, so to speak, I recommend you use *fresh* parsley whenever possible. It's a good garnish for most seafood dishes, and can be used to impart subtle flavors in gumbos, stews, and etouffées. Parsley should, however, be treated the same as filé, added only at the end of the cooking process. Otherwise, it can turn the dish bitter.

● **White Pepper/Black Pepper:** Absolutely essential in all seafood cookery to enhance taste and flavor as well as aroma. White pepper and black pepper are one and the same thing—the only difference is in the processing: white peppercorns are black peppercorns with the black outer sheath removed. For aesthetic reasons you should use white pepper in white cream sauces and black pepper in darker-colored sauces. But whatever you do, since pepper is pungent and aromatic, always keep a fresh supply on hand (don't stock up!) and grind it fresh from whole peppercorns whenever possible. I use both peppers in my cooking—I find black pepper a bit hotter than white.

● **Poppy Seeds:** Rarely used in seafood, except in casseroles. Sprinkle them lightly over noodles, cheese toppings, and cream sauces. Poppy seeds have a crunchy, nutlike flavor. The blue imported seeds from Holland are said to be the best.

● **Poultry Seasoning:** Actually, it could rightfully be called "Seafood Seasoning" as well, because it goes great with shrimp, fish, crabs, oysters, etc. This ground blend of sage, thyme, marjoram, savory, and rosemary can be sprinkled over seafood before cooking; it can be mixed into stuffings for bell pepper, eggplant, squash, and mirliton; or it can be added to soups, stews, gravies, sauces, and coating batters. Tip: For an extra treat, mix several tablespoons into plain flour and use the mixture to coat and dust trout fillets before you sauté them in butter.

● **Rosemary:** A touch or two in a recipe produces a fresh taste and a mildly sweet flavor. Rosemary is another herb that lends itself well to casseroles, poached fish, and baked seafoods. A pinch or two added to seafood stuffings also brings out locked-in flavors.

● **Saffron:** This is the most expensive spice on the market, but you use such minute quantities that it's worth having some around. Saffron is principally used to give food a succulent yellow color, but the taste it produces is also quite tantalizing. When preparing seafood, most cooks use saffron to spice up accompanying rice dishes, but it can also be added to fish and crabmeat sauces and to seafood stews. Note: *Use no more than a pinch at a time.*

● **Sage:** Rarely added to shrimp or crabmeat, sage is used primarily for baking and broiling fish. It can also be melted with butter and used as a baste for grilling fish fillets. It comes in three forms: sage leaves, rubbed sage, and ground sage. For seafood cookery ground sage is considered best.

● **Savory:** This herb yields a delicate, sweet flavor similar to that of thyme, and it also brings out the flavor of the herbs and spices it is combined with. In Louisiana, savory is used primarily in seafood sauces, but some cooks regularly add it to casseroles and baked fish. I would suggest you buy *ground savory*.

● **Seafood Seasoning:** According to most New Orleans cooks, this blend contains just about the same spices you'll find in crab boil, but in ground form. Obviously, then, if you find yourself in a situation where you're fresh out of crab boil or can't get a supply, seafood seasoning will do. Normally, however, you should use this product in other ways: in a stew base, in a sauce, in a gravy, in a chowder, as a sprinkling on raw fillets and peeled shrimp, and so on. It is excellent in sauces because the ground seasonings blend completely into the liquid, and it is super in gumbos and etouffées!

● **Seasoned Salt:** Fast becoming popular as an alternative to just salt and pepper, this product is replacing the familiar twin shakers on many Louisiana tables. The actual ingredients in seasoned salt vary according to the manufacturer, but each is basically a blend of herbs, spices, and salt. It can be used for any seafood.

● **Sweet Pepper Flakes:** Available dehydrated in bottled form, but a far cry from the fresh vegetable! Bell peppers are exceptionally well suited to a variety of seafood dishes; use them fresh-chopped or fresh-frozen whenever possible.

● **Tarragon:** Used in seafood recipes whenever a minty, aniselike flavor is desired. Most Louisiana cooks use tarragon in casseroles and heavy sauces, and in herb-butter bastes for fish, shrimp, and crawfish. It is also a popular ingredient in okra gumbo and pickled catfish. Should be used sparingly.

● **Thyme:** In Louisiana seafood cookery, thyme is as popular an ingredient as garlic, onion, celery, and cayenne. It is excellent in gumbos, jambalayas, etouffées, bisques, chowders, stews, sauces—you name it! And it goes well with just about every seafood, from amberjacks to alligators, from ling to lobster thermidor. Make certain your pantry contains thyme.

OTHER SEASONING INGREDIENTS

In order to cook Louisiana-style seafoods well, you must season them well. Herbs and spices in dried form can accomplish a lot of the necessary seasoning, but they can't do it all. *Vegetable basics*—of the fresh variety—build the foundations for most great Louisiana dishes. Very few Bayou Country recipes would be authentic without them.

For that reason, let me remind you that it is important to stock your refrigerator or freezer with **onions, garlic, shallots** (you might call them green onions), **celery, parsley, bell peppers, mushrooms,** and **fresh lemons**.

Chopped fresh, they are the finest ingredients you can possibly add for flavoring. But if it is impossible for you to keep a supply in the hydrator pan of the refrigerator, the next best thing is to chop a supply of each basic vegetable, package it flat in a Ziploc freezer bag, and freeze it until you are ready to cook. If you freeze the vegetables flat, you can break off just the quantity you need for the dish you are preparing.

In the final analysis, what you do when you season your seafood will make the difference between "something to eat" and that proverbial "meal fit for a king."

KITCHEN TERMINOLOGY

Dash	⅛ teaspoon (tsp.)
Pinch	less than ⅛ teaspoon
1 tablespoon (tbsp.)	3 teaspoons
2 tablespoons	1 ounce (oz.)
1 cup	½ pint (pt.)
2 cups	1 pint
4 cups	1 quart (qt.)
¼ cup	4 tablespoons

¼ cup	2 ounces
⅓ cup	5½ tablespoons
½ cup	8 tablespoons
½ cup	4 ounces
1 cup	8 ounces
1 pound (lb.) margarine or butter	2 cups
1 pound margarine or butter	4 sticks
1 cup margarine or butter	2 sticks
½ cup margarine or butter	1 stick
¼ cup margarine or butter	½ stick

Can Sizes Most Often Used

8-ounce	1 cup
#300	1½ cups (12 oz.)
#303	2 cups (16 oz.)
#2	2½ cups (20 oz.)
#3	4 cups (32 oz.)

Oven Temperatures, Degrees Fahrenheit

Low oven	250–300
Moderate oven	350–375
Hot oven	400–450
Very hot oven	500

Recommended Wines For Cooking Seafoods

Dry white Chablis	imported best, domestic good
Dry sherry	domestic suitable
Brandy	French preferred
Italian rosé	imported best

Actually, the philosophy among Louisiana cooks is that whatever wine you prefer to *drink* is also excellent to cook with. For example, if you plan to *drink* port with the meal, *cook* with port. If you will *drink* burgundy, *cook* with burgundy. Just don't cook with cooking sherry!

Several of Tony Chachere's prized recipes, originally printed in his *Cajun Country Cookbook,* appear in this volume by special permission. They are unique in southern originality and probably are without equal. I appreciate my old friend's courtesy, and I heartily recommend that you include his Cajun cookbooks in your culinary library if you want to have a well-rounded approach to Acadian cookery. He also developed Tony's Creole Seasoning, a product he formulated and has marketed for many years in the South; it is an ingredient that is called for in several recipes in this book. Found on most local supermarket shelves, it does the job of adding the right seasonings in the right proportions without your having to use guesswork. If, however, you live in an area where Tony's product is not available, you can write to David Forlani, Cajun Country Cookbook, P.O. Box 1687, Opelousas, LA 70507, and let him send you details on how you can put a new Acadian product on your pantry shelf.

CHAPTER TWO

All About Kitchen Utensils

In order to prepare good food, Louisiana style, it will be *essential* that you stock your kitchen with the right cooking utensils. As is the case with anything, if you invest in top-quality products the purchase becomes a one-time cost and, treated with proper care, what you buy will last a lifetime.

I recommend that whenever possible you avoid buying pots and pans—as well as accessories like spoons and whisks and knives—at your supermarket or department store. Instead, find a restaurant supply house that will sell to you retail and buy professional cooking gear. Oh, it won't have the pretty enamel outer coatings or the attractive space-age handles, but the enamel and the handles do not influence the flavor and texture of your dishes.

Buy good stainless steel. Buy good heavy aluminum. And get a set of cast-iron cookware and season it. You should have some of all three: the stainless, the aluminum, and the cast iron.

To direct you in your purchases, I've made a shopping list you might want to follow. Because of the cost, it takes a while to accumulate all of these items. So take your time; buy one piece at a time if you have to. Just remember, once you have everything on this list on the shelves in your kitchen you'll be able to cook anything your heart desires. Whatever you do, though, *buy top quality and nothing less*.

SUGGESTED POTS AND PANS

Quantity	Item
1	stainless-steel 10-inch skillet with tight-fitting lid
1	stainless-steel 12-inch skillet with tight-fitting lid
2	heavy aluminum 10-inch skillets with tight-fitting lids
2	cast-iron 10-inch skillets with domed evaporator lids
1	heavy aluminum 8-inch frypan with cover

1   heavy aluminum 1½-quart saucepan with cover
1   stainless-steel 1½-quart saucepan with cover
1   heavy aluminum 2¾-quart saucepan with cover
1   stainless-steel 3-quart saucepan with cover
1   heavy aluminum 4½-quart Dutch oven with tight-fitting lid
1   cast-iron 4½-quart Dutch oven with domed evaporator lid
1   stainless-steel 5½-quart vegetable steamer with basket
1   heavy aluminum 6-quart Dutch oven with cover
1   heavy aluminum 8½-quart stock pot with cover
1   heavy aluminum 12-quart stock pot with cover
1   heavy aluminum 20-quart shrimp boiler with cover
1   heavy aluminum 10-gallon seafood boiler with cover
1   stainless-steel 5/8-quart butter warmer
1   heavy aluminum jambalaya pan with cover (14½-inch diameter)
1   porcelain-coated 7-quart roaster pan with lid and rack
1   5-quart electric deep fryer with basket and crock
1   electric frypan with broiler lid and rack

Cooking Accessories

1   carbon-steel 10-inch slicing knife
1   carbon-steel 8-inch carving knife
1   carbon-steel 6-inch sandwich knife
1   8-inch chef's knife
1   6-inch chef's knife
1   carbon-steel 4½-inch paring knife
1   carbon-steel 3½-inch paring knife
6   heavy aluminum-alloy crab knives
1   carbon-steel 5-inch boning knife
1   carbon-steel 9-inch sharpening steel
1   Kwik-Sharp Crock Stick (black crock rods) for honing
2   Corning Ware 5-quart casserole dishes with cover
2   Corning Ware 3-quart casserole dishes with cover
1   Corning Ware 1-quart casserole dish with cover
1   complete set of wooden spoons
1   complete set of aluminum spoons
1   three-pronged testing fork
1   aluminum-alloy strainer-colander (12-inch diameter)
1   aluminum-alloy strainer-colander (9-inch diameter)
1   tea strainer (2-inch diameter)
1   food strainer (6-inch diameter)
1   carbon-steel 10-inch meat cleaver
1   carbon-steel 10-inch Chinese cleaver for chopping
2   stainless-steel whisks (one large, one small)

1   complete set of stainless-steel mixing bowls
2   General Electric slicing knives for fish filleting
1   Normark fish filleting board with hinge clip
12   stainless-steel skewers for seafood kabobs
1   complete set of Pyrex baking dishes
1   basting brush with nylon fibers
1   pepper mill for fresh grinding
3   stainless-steel spatulas, assorted sizes
1   stainless-steel strainer spoon
1   stainless-steel strainer ladle
1   long-handled stainless-steel seafood boiling spoon
1   oyster knife
1   4-quart pressure cooker
1   garlic press
1   Chinese wok (I prefer the nonelectric type)
2   soup ladles
1   stainless-steel double boiler
2   14-by-17-inch heavy aluminum cookie sheets (commercial grade)
2   heavy aluminum pizza pans (commercial grade)
1   plastic butter clarifier cup

I consider the items listed above *essential* to the preparation of good foods. Naturally, there are other gadgets and gizmos you might want to add to your kitchen collection, but they would be extras. Feel free to include anything that enhances your creativity and ease of preparation—after all, that's the name of the cooking game.

Before I close this particular chapter, there are a few things I feel need comment. First, about the pots. If you want your pots and pans to last a long time, avoid the various kinds of nonstick surfaces on the market. My personal experience with these coatings has been one of frustration. No matter which brand, mine have always *scratched*, even though the claims are that they won't. Some have *peeled off* (right in the middle of a delicious white sauce—you talk about yucky!). Others just didn't take the *high temperatures* well (and you must fry most seafoods hot). And most I've spent hard-earned money on seemed to last only a few months of heavy use at the most. About a year ago, I sold most of my pots and pans with nonstick surfaces at a garage sale, and I've been happy ever since!

You can get practically the same nonstick results by using either stainless steel or heavy-gauge aluminum and lightly rubbing a drop or two of corn oil (no cholesterol!) into the metal before putting it on the stove. And it saves you a lot of money in the process. I also don't use the nonstick sprays, not because they don't work, but because they cost too much and I can get virtually the same results with Mazola Corn Oil or pure olive oil and the proper cooking temperature. Try it.

Scanning the list, let me give you a few reasons for selecting the items I recommend for your kitchen:

1. You should have *stainless steel, aluminum, and cast-iron* pots in your kitchen because you'll have different uses for each of the three. Cajun dishes, for some reason or another, just seem to come out better in cast iron. Milk and cream products cooked into foods seem to cook better in stainless. And when even heating is necessary, I find that heavy aluminum consistently produces perfect results. Maybe, scientifically, I'm all wet, but for the past 25 years I've cooked successfully using these principles, so I pass them along and share them with you. Use them for what they're worth, and remember that I'm a cook, not a scientist!

I have learned, though, that cast iron will also give you even heating; the flat-ground bottoms assist in heat diffusion and stability. And cast iron is one metal that you can *pour the heat to* (almost unlimited temperatures for cooking!) and not have to worry about pots and pans burning. Heavy-gauge aluminum utensils also conduct heat evenly and efficiently and in most cases you can use low and medium settings to get good effects without spoiling the food with *hot spots*. If I had to recommend a brand to you, *Leyse* manufactures excellent quality cookware in aluminum. So does Magnalite. You can trust their products when the sauce must be perfect, the vegetables tender and crisp, and the seafood succulent. Stainless steel, of course, speaks for itself: it cooks well and it's a snap when it's time to clean up.

So much for the pots and pans—except for a note about sizes and covers. Different sizes accommodate different quantities, and if you want ease in preparation you should have a variety of sizes in your kitchen just to reduce "cook's frustration." More important is the need for covers. Even though you will do a lot of your seafood cookery uncovered, a number of recipes require tight-fitting lids, and a makeshift cover just won't do. So I suggest you have the proper cover for every pot and pan you buy. Try making Cajun jambalaya without a moisture-sealing lid. It flops!

2. Here's how to season cast iron: Take your new cast-iron pot or pan, wash it well with soap and water, then rinse it for what seems to you like a very long time, until you're absolutely satisfied that you've got all the soap out. Then rub it all over—inside and out—with lard (my preference) or vegetable shortening. Now you can either slow-bake it in the oven at 250 degrees until the shortening cakes on the pan, or—and this is what I'd suggest if you can do it—put it on an open barbecue grill or over an open fire (these can be *very hot*; in fact you can't get 'em *too hot*). Take the pot or pan off the fire (or out of the oven) after the first layer is baked on, cool it slightly (so that you can handle it), coat it again,

and repeat the process of baking and recoating at least half a dozen times, until there's a nice, thick black coating on the pan. You should follow the same procedure, separately, for the cover.

Once you season your cast iron, *do not wash it in soapy water*. Cast is a porous metal and it will pick up the soap in the pores. I guarantee you'll taste it in your next dish. Instead of using soap, wipe the pot clean with paper towels, scour it lightly with dry salt, rinse it gently in warm water, and dry it well by heating it on the stove before you put it away. That's all that's required with cast iron.

3. In addition to your steamer pot, you can also steam in your roaster pan. Most folks don't realize that a porcelain roaster can be used that way. It can; try it. It also makes a great oven poacher for fish, shrimp, and oysters.

4. As a Louisiana cook, I use conventional pots and pans for most of my dishes, and I recommend you do also. But you will sometimes find uses for an electric deep fryer and frypan, especially when you have a big meal going and you need just one more source of heat for cooking. I do suggest, however (since I believe in using crock pots for cooking, too), that instead of buying the deep fryer *and* the crock pot, you save money and get the combination unit: it's two cookers in one.

5. You will also find uses for the accessory *broiler rack lid* that some companies make for their frypans. The cover has a broiler element that fits into the lid, and it is extremely useful in providing a covered source of high-intensity heat for fish, shrimp, oysters, and a variety of other seafoods that you can fix right on your counter top. Works great.

6. Every Cajun kitchen should have a "super-skillet," which is why I've recommended the 14½-inch-diameter jambalaya pan. It becomes invaluable when preparing large quantities of food that can be cooked together as one-dish meals. But to ensure even heating with this oversized skillet, I do suggest you settle for nothing other than cast iron or heavy-gauge aluminum. And get a cover for it, too.

7. The most important items in the cook's kitchen (next to pots and pans) are knives. How many knives have you bought that you've cursed? Thrown out? Sold at garage sales? Could not keep sharp? Well, when it comes to your initial purchase, *invest only in top-quality carbon-steel knives*. Stainless is nice, but most stainless knives won't hold an edge for kitchen use. There is one rule of thumb you can go by when selecting a good set of kitchen knives: *If they rust, they're good for the kitchen*, and they'll last a long time. Of course, that means that to keep them from rusting you should dry them immediately after use and put them away.

8. To *sharpen* a knife, I recommend you use Kwik-Sharp Crock Stick blocks. These are various-sized wooden-base blocks that hold two angulated

crockery rods (the new black rods are fantastic!). Whichever size you choose for your kitchen (I recommend the large size), it should remain permanently on your counter top. You will never again have a dull knife in your house. And they are unbelievably easy to use! But watch your fingers—because they *do* sharpen knives.

Along the same lines, I recommend that every kitchen contain a butcher steel (the rod butchers use to keep the honed edge straight). And I suggest that every cook *use* it. The best way to keep your knife sharp is to ''steel'' and steel it often. Make four or five slices through fish or meats, then steel the blade. Your knife will *stay* sharp.

9. Before I get off the subject of knives, do invest in a *complete set* of kitchen knives (as well as oyster knives, crab knives, and filleting knives). Each knife is designed to perform a different task, and using a chef's knife to peel a potato or a paring knife to fillet a trout just never works. Get what you need. You'll find that the preparation of various dishes will be a whole lot easier if you've got the right tools.

And, folks, *nothing fillets fish better than an electric knife*. Trout, redfish, snapper, croaker, whatever—the job is done quickly and so easily with electricity and double-gyrating blades. I do recommend, though, that you buy the General Electric ''slim-handle'' model; the bulky handles on some electric knives will wear you out. And buy *two:* you'll have to alternate between them to allow the motors to cool when you've got lots of fish to clean.

10. For the rest of the list, explanations are simple enough. *Crab knives* make picking crabs a snap once you learn how it's done. *Corning Ware casserole dishes* are top-notch products and yield the best results. Have enough *spoons* to cook with ease; wooden ones are excellent for rice and pasta dishes. Have enough *colanders and strainers* around for steaming, straining, and making stocks. Use *whisks*, not forks or spoons, for mixing liquid ingredients and whipping sauces. And get into the habit of working first-class with *Pyrex baking dishes* and *stainless-steel mixing bowls*.

Spend a few additional dollars and pick up the extras you need to make cooking more fun: the butter clarifier cup, the strainer ladle, a couple of spatulas, a pepper mill for fresh grinding, good cookie sheets and pizza pans for broiling fish and shrimp. It will make all the difference in the world in your *enjoyment* of cooking. When you stop to consider that you spend more time in the kitchen than any other part of the house, shouldn't it be furnished, too?

So go shopping!

ABOUT BUYING A WOK

There are two kinds of woks available for the home kitchen. One is the conventional model used on top of the stove; the other is an electric model with the heating unit built in.

I recommend you stay with the conventional model, primarily because of its *temperature capability*. Wok cooking is usually *stir-frying*, where the foods are cooked at high heat very rapidly. My experience has been that, except for a few commercial grades, the electric units on the market do not produce the necessary heat levels. So if you plan to cook seafoods Chinese-style often, buy a conventional wok that you can fire up *hot!*

CHAPTER THREE

The Seafood Cook's Notebook
What to Cook and How to Cook It

Despite what you might think, when it comes to cooking, folks have more questions—and reservations—about seafoods than about any other main-dish foods.

It seems that anyone can follow a recipe and whip up a pot roast that tastes great. Pork chops, steaks, and sausage on the grill rarely cause any problems for cooks with some experience. And stews and goulashes, for the most part, are snaps even for novices. But seafoods—well, that's another subject altogether, even though it shouldn't be. Not if you remember that seafood cookery simply boils down (no pun intended!) to basic procedures and techniques, with a little bit of understanding thrown in for good measure.

Yet people generally *make* cooking seafoods difficult for themselves. They *create* problems; probably they're fooled by the simplicity of seafood preparation because they're expecting the work to be complex. And those who admit to the most difficulties are those who consistently tend to overcook their seafoods. I would venture to say that of all the sins committed in the kitchen, *overcooking* is the most lethal.

Well, this chapter is designed to clear up all the false assumptions, all the common misinterpretations, all the standard difficulties, and all the questions you ever wanted to ask about seafoods and seafood cookery. I've attempted to put down on paper—in one book!—detailed explanations dealing with choosing seafoods, handling them, and packaging them for the freezer; precooking preparations; nutritional values; and serving seafoods as entrées in finished dishes.

I hope that, because of this chapter and the ones that accompany it, you'll have no more problems with your seafood cooking. But just by chance, if I happen to omit a particular question you may have, I've included a mailing address at the end of the book. I invite you to write me. I guarantee you'll get an answer!

Use Only Top-Quality Fresh Products

Whether you catch your own seafoods or you buy them at the local market, insist only on the best quality and the freshest product you can find. Remember the old adage, "You can't make chicken salad out of chicken feathers!" And you won't make a gourmet dish using old seafood.

That's not to say I'm against using certain "canned components": always use a fresh seafood product, but if you don't have time to make the sauce that goes with it from scratch and you want to pour out a soup or a salad dressing as a base and doctor it up . . . go ahead! Remember, the whole purpose of this book is to encourage your creativity in the kitchen, and if you can take a bottle of salad dressing or a can of chicken soup, feel comfortable transforming it into a great sauce for trout or crabmeat, and have your family enjoy it—well, all I ask is that you send me the recipe so that I can use it, too!

Now, no matter what you have heard, you should not believe that *freezing* improves the tenderness of seafoods. It does not. The fact is you will lose a little quality naturally in the freezing process, and if you start with inferior grades, regardless of the kind of seafood, the loss will be even more pronounced.

I particularly like to live up to the slogan printed on the menu at Sartin's Restaurant in Sabine Pass, Texas. It reads: "This morning, the seafood you're eating now woke up in the Gulf of Mexico!" If you keep *your* seafood *that fresh*, you'll have an elegant dish 70 percent guaranteed.

If you catch your own seafood . . .

Be certain to maintain the freshness. Nothing is fresher than a fish or shrimp just out of the water, but if you allow your catch to remain unrefrigerated or uniced for any length of time, the *quality* is quick to go. And don't drive any distances from waterway to driveway without lots of ice in the cooler!

When you catch fish, shrimp, crabs, or crawfish, I recommend you ice them down immediately. The minute seafoods are removed from the water, bacterial and enzymatic changes begin in unsaturated oils and pigments. And once oxidation—which produces rancidity—starts in seafoods, it is almost impossible to stop. The result is strong taste and poor quality.

Carry plenty of ice with you on your trips. And *use* it. When fish come aboard, take time to put them in the ice chest. Don't toss them into the bottom of the boat no matter how good the action is at the rod and reel! Then, as you build layers of fish, make sure each layer has a bed of ice over it to promote uniform cooling.

It is also recommended that you either put a false bottom in the ice chest, to keep your seafoods from soaking in spoiled water, or leave the drain plug open on the chest to allow the excess water to leak off so that the freshness isn't tainted.

You won't find seafood fresher than what you catch yourself. Be careful not to lose that freshness through neglect.

If you buy your seafood at the market . . .

Buy only fresh-caught products. Let your nose be your guide. No seafood—fish, shrimp, crabs, or oysters—should be strong-smelling or "fishy" if it is fresh. Don't be afraid to smell what you intend to buy!

In fish, the flesh should be firm. The eyes should be bright, clear, and full. The gills should be red (not bleached pink) and free of slime buildup. The skin should be shiny, the colors unfaded. And the smell should be very faint and pleasantly fresh.

Shrimp purchased from the market should be almost translucent, extremely cold (to guarantee that they've been iced constantly), with no discoloration whatsoever. There should be no *deep orange* tinges inside the head, and the head should be firmly attached to the body part (not wilted and half falling off).

Crabs should not be purchased unless they are alive and kicking, and neither should crawfish! I also suggest that you discard all dead crabs and crawfish prior to boiling (unless you caught them yourself and they died on ice).

Oysters in the shell should be bought only from a reputable dealer, or from a supermarket that ensures a fresh product. Unshucked oysters should have tightly closed shells—open shells, even if they're only partly opened, should be discarded. You should also keep oysters constantly chilled, since they are alive inside the shells.

And after you've purchased it, get your seafood home and into the refrigerator (or into an ice chest) *right away*. Keep in mind that regardless of how you freeze it for storage or how you cook it for the table, *you cannot improve the quality if it's not there to begin with*.

About nutritional values

Without getting scientific, let's say that seafoods offer some of the greatest nutritional values of any foods we eat.

Fish is not only an excellent source of *good* protein, but of *easily digested* protein, because fish oils are polyunsaturated. Beef contains 13.5 milligrams of protein per 100 grams (or 3½ ounces), while fish contains 19.0 milligrams of protein per 100 grams. Nutritionists recommend that we include good sources of protein in every meal; *a 4-ounce serving of fish will provide a third of the daily protein requirement of an adult*.

Even though the protein levels are higher in fish than in beef, the *calorie levels* are lower because the fat content is lower. In one pound of beef there are 1,530 calories; in one pound of fish there are only 445 calories. In 3½ ounces of beef you get 30.1 milligrams of fat, while in 3½ ounces of fish you get 2.5 milligrams of fat. The differences are obvious—and significant.

Furthermore, fish provide high levels of vitamins and minerals. Fat fish such as mackerel are rich in vitamins A and D, and all fish (both fat and lean) contain good quantities of B vitamins. Fish contains more iodine than any other food, and provides traces of such minerals as cobalt and zinc and generous amounts of copper, iron, magnesium, and phosphorus.

Shrimp also contain large amounts of lean protein and very little fat. In fact, nutritionists agree that *one pound of cooked shrimp will provide one day's supply of protein for six adults!* The only problem with shrimp is their high cholesterol content. Individuals with cholesterol problems should limit their intake.

Like fish, shrimp are also good sources of vitamins and minerals, particularly iodine, copper, iron, magnesium, and phosphorus. Nutritional values of crawfish are comparable.

Oysters, in addition to supplying high levels of minerals, vitamins, and protein, are one of Mother Nature's richest sources of iron. The only acclaimed attribute of oysters that scientists have not authenticated is their aphrodisiac effect. In fact, my old Cajun friend Theophile Alphonse swears there's nothing to the aphrodisiac story—he says he eats a dozen oysters religiously every week, and can never get more than six or seven to work!

Crabs are high in protein, low in fat, and rich in minerals, like most other shellfish. Dieters, however, should be aware that while crabs are lower in protein than shrimp, their fat content, by percentage of weight, is considerably higher—18 percent in crabs compared to 9 percent in shrimp.

How much to buy, How much to serve

One big meal-planning problem is that only rarely does the cook know how much seafood should be planned for a meal, and how many people it will serve. Of course, certain families will eat more than others, but you can apply the following as a general rule of thumb:

Filleted fish	⅓ lb. per person
Whole fish	1 lb. per person
Shrimp (rough)	1 lb. per person
Shrimp (headless)	½ lb. per person
Crabs (boiled)	6 crabs per person
Crabmeat	¼ lb. per person

Oysters (on the half shell)........ 1 dozen per person
Oysters (meats only) .... 1 dozen or ½ pint per person
Crawfish (boiled)................... 2 lbs. per person
Crawfish (tails only).............. ½ lb. per person

To vary amounts according to individual needs, keep in mind that it takes 6 pounds of boiled crawfish to yield 1 pound of tails; 2 pounds of boiled shrimp to yield 1 pound of shrimp tails; and approximately 16 boiled crabs to yield 1 pound of crabmeat.

Preparing seafoods for the freezer

All seafoods must be *prepared* for freezing and storage. The one thing you don't want to do is "throw" seafood in some container and "toss" it into the freezer. Do so, and all that prime quality you paid for will taste no better than cardboard soaked in cod-liver oil.

Fish should be filleted, drawn and gutted, or scaled and steaked—and then *washed well*. When freezing whole fish, make certain excess slime and internal blood is washed away from the body cavity. Fillets, too, should be washed well. Do not skip or skimp on cleaning fish properly unless you like the flavor of rancidity.

Shrimp should also be washed well prior to being packaged for the freezer. Use lots of clean running water, and rinse them several times. The experts say that for a short period in the freezer you can leave the heads on. But if you plan to store large quantities for a long stretch, you should take the heads off and wash the tails thoroughly to preserve freshness.

Oysters can be frozen, but proper attention is necessary in the preparatory stage. Fresh-shucked oysters need not be washed in running water (in fact, you lose a lot of the salty flavor when you do this). You should, however, go through the oysters one by one to see that bits of shell are removed, and you should swish each one around in its own liquor. And *save the liquor*. You'll want to use it for stews, chowders, and stuffings.

Oysters bought commercially in jars are already washed. Keep in mind that because oysters are mollusks they will lose some quality in freezer storage—so, again, proper care in preparation for freezing is imperative.

Crawfish should be parboiled (dipped in boiling water for about a minute) and then deheaded in preparation for freezing, but only after they have been washed several times until clean. The so-called "purging process," in which crawfish are soaked in salt water to flush out the mud in their systems, is not only unnecessary—*it doesn't work*. There is no way the saline water will flush through the alimentary tract of the little crustaceans in such a short period of time. *All this process does is kill them.* Just wash your crawfish until the water runs clear—that's more than sufficient.

Crawfish can be stored in their tail shells or peeled, depending upon how you plan to use them in dishes. It is not recommended that you boil crawfish tails for a boiled crawfish entrée after they have been frozen; too much quality is lost in the freezing process. But you *can* use them with practically unlimited versatility in a number of dishes. One note: Peeled tails tend to turn blue after freezing because of the copper content in the crawfish meat. You can prevent this discoloration by adding a teaspoon of lemon juice to each pound of tails prior to freezing.

Crabs in their uncooked state do not freeze well enough to store for boiling at a later date. Whole crabs should be washed well in clear water and chilled in ice to make certain they are immobilized. Then you should remove the backs and clean them thoroughly. Remove the insides, the mouth parts, and the gills (usually called the "dead man") and split them into right and left parts.

Picked crabmeat, on the other hand, freezes quite well with very little preparation. Prior to picking, you should either boil crabs in *unseasoned water* or steam them for about 15 minutes. After years of trial-and-error investigation and experimentation, I've found that this priceless seafood meat should be stored only in the finest freezer bags available. I use a *double-layer* Seal-A-Meal bag for my crabmeat (one bag sealed inside another one).

Frogs, turtles, and alligators should all be thoroughly washed and cleaned (dressed for cooking with all the fat removed) prior to freezing. The cleaner the meat, the more choice, the more delicate the flavor—and remember that the so-called "gamy" flavors of these meats come not from the meat but from the *fat*. So strip all the fat away before you freeze. It's the only way to ensure quality and good taste.

What freezer materials to use

The only way to preserve seafoods by freezing—and to freeze them for lengthy periods—is to *freeze them fast, freeze them deep* (zero degrees or below), *freeze them in small packages*, and *freeze them airtight*. So choose the right material for freezing to conform to those criteria.

Cling wraps, such as *Saran Wrap* or *Handi-Wrap*, give good protection against oxygen and water vapor (keep in mind that oxidation produces rancidity and vapor loss gives you freezer burn). But they are good only for wrapping fish. Metal cans with snap-on lids and glass canning jars are also good protectors against oxygen and vapor, but they too are useful only for some kinds of seafood (like shrimp and oysters). Waxed and polyethylene cartons or waxed bags are useful, but they allow oxygen penetration and escape of moisture. And while polyethylene bags may be good moisture barriers, they may also permit oxygen to pass into the contents.

For those reasons, then, the best way most authorities over the years have found to store seafoods is *in water,* water that freezes into an impenetrable block of ice.

You prefer to use waxed cartons or leftover milk containers? Use them—but then fill them with water!

You like Ziploc bags? Use them—but fill them with water before you seal the tops!

Want to stick with Tupperware containers or ice-cream cartons? Go ahead—but fill them with water, too!

The block of frozen water keeps the moisture from escaping and keeps the oxygen away from the seafood. As a result, you'll have seafoods that will remain fresh 4, 6, 8, and even 12 months down the line.

But if you don't have space for bags or containers full of water, just *glaze your seafood.* Pack it the way you want to; then, after it's frozen, unpack it, dip it in ice-cold water, repack it, and freeze. The contents of your packages will then be covered with a glaze of ice that will work to prevent rancidity and freezer burn.

Fish, shrimp, crab, crawfish tails, frog legs, turtle meat, and alligator meat can be frozen or glazed in tap water. Oysters, however, should be frozen in waxed containers, plastic cartons, or jars and frozen in *their own strained liquor.*

Techniques for freezing your seafoods

Here are some techniques you might want to remember when freezing seafoods:

● Freeze seafoods only in deep freezers, especially if you plan to store them for a long period of time. Deep freezers (either chest types or uprights) are designed to keep temperatures zero degrees or below, and it takes a zero-degree temperature to retard bacterial and enzymatic changes. Refrigerator-top compartments barely get below 30 degrees, so they are suitable only for short-term freezing (two weeks or less).

● Freeze as quickly as possible. Remember that unfrozen foods absorb some of the cold from already-frozen packages around them, so the internal temperature of your freezer will rise when you add new packages. Also remember that the water content of seafoods will form ice crystals as the freezing takes place. These crystals could puncture the cells of the seafoods and result in flavor loss (called thaw drip) when the seafoods are defrosted. Fast freezing reduces the size of the crystals and the amount of cell puncture, thereby improving quality control.

● To ensure quick freezing, either pack smaller packages or turn your freezer to its lowest setting. Ideally, you should do both. Of course some deep freezers have a "flash-freeze" feature that blows cold air over the newly added packages, but if you don't have that feature on your unit you can compromise by placing a small battery-operated fan inside your freezer (the kind you see advertised for campers in most outdoor catalogues). This will achieve the same effect of blowing cold air over the packages.

● To further protect your seafoods, *master bag* your packages. In other words, whenever you use wraps, Ziplocs, or plastic bags, wrap small portions and then place several of those packages into larger plastic bags. But be sure to squeeze out all the air. Incidentally, *no package you home freeze should be more than a pound in weight.* So several pounds of individually wrapped packages should fit into one master bag.

● Seafoods to be stored for very long periods (three months or more) can be treated with antioxidants. Ascorbic acid—probably better recognized on the grocery shelf under the name "Fruit Fresh"—is a good antioxidant. So is cornstarch and water, and so is lemon juice. Four teaspoons of Fruit Fresh to a gallon of water gives you a .5 percent solution of ascorbic acid; all you need to do is dip the seafood in the mixture for about a minute. You can do the same thing by boiling six tablespoons of cornstarch in a gallon of water and using it as a dip. Or you can squeeze a squirt of lemon juice in the water you use to fill the plastic containers.

Just one note: Be sure to rinse away whichever antioxidant mixture you decide to use prior to cooking your seafoods, since leaving it on could occasionally cause an unpleasant off-taste to develop.

● Don't refreeze seafoods (or other meats, for that matter) once they have thawed completely. But notice that the key word is *completely.*

Let's say you take some seafood out of the freezer for a dish you plan to fix. You set it in your refrigerator to thaw, and then you change your mind about cooking it. Well—you *can* refreeze it *if* (1) it hasn't completely thawed, and (2) it still has noticeable ice crystals dispersed throughout the package. If thawing is complete, however, *don't refreeze it.*

Let me make one other point here. Suppose you thaw out too much seafood, more than you can use all at once. All you have to do is whip the remainder into a special dish—make a chowder, a stew, and au gratin—and then freeze that dish. The cooking process turns thawed seafoods into a whole new product. And it can be frozen again.

And speaking about thawing seafoods

Defrosting seafoods is probably as critical to the retention of flavor as preparing them for freezing. If you do not thaw seafoods properly, the taste and texture will suffer (again from bacteria and enzymes) and freshness will be lost.

All the experts say you should never thaw seafoods under hot water; the heat serves as a catalyst for chemical change. Neither should you defrost at room temperature, which is the way far too many folks defrost foods, because the surface area of the frozen package will thaw quicker than the inner areas and bacteria will form and reproduce rapidly.

There are only two ways to thaw seafoods to maintain quality and guard against the possibility of seafood poisoning. One is to *defrost in the refrigerator*. But that is time-consuming (it takes about 12 to 15 hours for fish that have been frozen solid). The other, preferred, method is to *defrost under cold running water*. It is faster, and it prevents bacterial and enzymatic buildup. And if you package your seafoods in water, as I've recommended, the process of defrosting is nothing more than that of melting the ice.

Once seafoods are completely thawed you should either cook them right away or place them immediately in the refrigerator. But don't leave them in the fridge unused for more than two days, and check freshness and quality when defrosting the same way you check when freezing: *smell the product*. If it smells fresh, has no pungent odor, no ammonia or strong iodine aroma, and doesn't smell "fishy," it's good!

But whenever in doubt . . . throw it out!

How long can you keep fresh seafoods frozen?

Generally, food experts recommend three to six months, if the seafood was purchased fresh and packaged in airtight containers. I've found, however, that if you freeze well below zero degrees and you package your seafoods properly *in water*, it isn't a problem to store fish, shrimp, crabs, and crawfish *for a year* inside a block of ice. Oysters deep frozen in their own liquor will stay fresh for about *eight months*.

METHODS USED IN COOKING SEAFOODS

It's no idle statement that when it comes to preparation possibilities seafood is the most versatile food in the world. You can do almost anything to it, and it will still come out tasty, full-bodied, and appealing. Most forms of seafood lend themselves to all the cooking methods: boiling, baking, broiling, poaching, sautéing, deep frying, grilling, braising, smoking, steaming, microwaving, stewing, and crock-potting. Only some of the oilier fishes, like mackerel, have limitations—they don't do well fried or baked in sauces because of their oil content. Otherwise, let your imagination be your guide . . . and create daringly!

For the sake of simplicity, the following tips have been put in note form for easy reference. You'll find additional notes on these methods in "Miscellaneous Notes About Fish Cookery" in the chapter on fish.

BOILING SEAFOOD

In Louisiana boiling may be defined as submerging seafoods in a large quantity of water to which a variety of spices, herbs, and other seasonings have been added. And while it might appear simple, there is a lot more to boiled seafood than just boiling water: the right seasoning, blending, preparation, and cooking time are all equally important.

Crabs, shrimp, and crawfish can be turned into delectable boiled treats with just a little bit of know-how—and the right recipe! Generally, with proportionate changes for different quantities, there is one basic boiled seafood recipe that is just about fool-proof.

To a 10-gallon pot, add:
   5 gallons water
   5 small to medium onions, coarsely chopped
   1 head garlic (each clove peeled, and coarsely chopped)
   6 lemons, sliced
   1 cup chopped celery
   6 bay leaves
   ½ cup liquid crab boil
   1 26-oz. box salt
   2 tbsp. cayenne pepper

Bring this mixture to a rapid boil and cover the pot with the lid for about 10 minutes until all the seasonings are cooked in. Then add your seafood. The water will stop boiling. At this point, you replace the lid and wait for the water to come back to a boil. When it does, start the timing process: 2 to 3 minutes for shrimp, 2 to 4 minutes for crawfish, 8 to 12 minutes for crabs. Boiling longer than this is *overcooking!* And if you overcook shrimp and crawfish, *the shells are going to set* and you won't be able to peel them.

After the cooking period, remove the pot from the burner and allow the seafood to *soak* so that the seasonings can be absorbed. For mild flavor, I recommend you soak for 15 minutes. For a more pronounced flavor, soak 30 to 45 minutes or longer. When the taste of the seafood is to your liking (and you must keep sampling every 5 minutes or so during the soaking period!), drain off the water and serve.

Let me pass along a few ideas on the subject of boiling seafoods:

1. Despite any explanations you've heard, it is not "stale shrimp," "shrimp caught during a full moon," or "shrimp that come from the Gulf" that make peeling difficult. Shrimp and crawfish that are hard to peel got that way because

they were *overcooked*. Among the purported remedies are *salting your shrimp after they are boiled . . . adding a few tablespoons of olive oil to the boiling water . . . and praying to your favorite guru.* Nothing works as well as avoiding overcooking. And if you make a concerted effort to follow the cooking times I've outlined above, your shells will not stick, I guarantee!

2. Adding the seasonings—especially salt and pepper—after the cooking process is completed so that your seafood picks up the flavor during the soaking process is perfectly acceptable. As I've just explained, the seasonings aren't absorbed during cooking anyway. It isn't until the soaking phase that they take in flavors.

The only difficulty with adding the seasonings after seafoods are cooked is *taste-testing the water:* it's a lot easier to taste water for salt and pepper content *before* you put the fire to it. But if you would rather do it that way, be my guest.

3. All this time I've talked about shrimp and crawfish. But crabs, too, are affected by overcooking. Crabs will become *mushy* if they're overcooked. So if you have ever eaten mushy boiled crabs, you now know the reason.

I suggest you boil your crabs for the time period I've indicated (sure, there are other recipes, but this one works and it's simple!) and soak them for about 30 minutes to get full flavor. They'll turn out perfect every time.

4. Except for small bayou crabs (and low-meat crabs, which are usually referred to as "clear" crabs), there is no maximum time restriction when it comes to the soaking process. I've soaked my seafoods for hours at times, even to the point of the water cooling down to room temperature. And they've still come out perfect. Ideally, though, you should find that if you've seasoned your water properly your boiled seafoods will be ready to drain and serve in about 45 minutes and have maximum flavor.

5. And finally: Seafoods tend to float on the surface after they are boiled because of air bubbles that get trapped under their shells. On the surface they do not absorb seasoning throughout. There is a trick, however, that you can use to get them to sink.

Instead of trying to weigh them down with wire screens, as some folks admit they do, simply pour about four cups of ice water (or two trays of ice cubes) over the crabs, shrimp, or crawfish. The sudden change in temperature forces the air out of the shell, draws in seasoned water—and down to the bottom sinks the seafood!

Toss extra goodies in the boil!

A favorite tactic in Louisiana whenever you're the host of a crab boil (shrimp and crawfish, too) is to toss *lagniappe*—that little something extra—into the boiling, seasoned water.

Whole, peeled baby onions . . . lengths of smoked sausage . . . corn on the cob . . . frankfurters . . . and about a dozen Irish potatoes go great in the boil. And they make up all the trimmings for what becomes a full meal instead of just a seafood snack.

Keep in mind, however, that since corn and potatoes usually take longer to cook than seafood, you'll have to add them to the boiling water *before* you add the seafood and cook them appropriately (about 8 to 10 minutes extra with shrimp and crawfish, 3 to 5 with crabs). The meats, on the other hand, can be added with the seafoods.

Try it, m'frien'. The extras really top off the feast, Cajun style!

What is "salt and pepper to taste" in boiled seafood?

In any other dish you create, "salt and pepper to taste" means exactly that—when it tastes seasoned enough *for you*, it's seasoned. But when you boil seafoods, you should use another technique.

Because your crabs, shrimp, and fish will pick up the seasonings from the water, the best method of preseasoning water for boiling is to make it *almost too salty* and *almost too peppery*. When you can honestly say to yourself, "Whew, that's salty and hot!", you'll have your water seasoned just right.

Recipes calling for "boiled" fish

Usually, Louisianians would rather do something other than boil their fish, but there are a number of dishes that can be made from boiled fish—fish salad, fish au gratin, flaked tuna, and even a mock crab meat. And preparation is not nearly so difficult as it may seem.

Certain fish species lend themselves to boiling: sheepshead, drum, redfish, and croaker, to name a few. This is because the texture of their flesh is well suited to recipes requiring firm fish chunks.

I recommend that whenever you boil a fish for preparation in another dish you fillet it completely, remove all the bloodlines and scales, and wrap it tightly in cheesecloth prior to cooking. Then allow it to cool thoroughly before you flake it. You get a superb product this way. (For more detail, see "Boiling Fish" in the chapter on fish.)

BAKING SEAFOOD

Baking means cooking in a pan inside an oven that ranges from low to very high heat. Seafoods can be baked both *covered* and *uncovered*, depending upon the recipe being prepared.

All types of seafoods can be baked: fish, shrimp, oysters, crawfish tails, or crabmeat (although whole crabs and cleaned crab cores are usually not baked except in a liquid).

Technically, fish like mackerel are best for baking whole, since their higher fat content eliminates the need for basting. I do recommend, however, that oily fish be baked on a rack placed inside the baking pan to keep an excess of fish oils from soaking into the meat.

When you bake leaner fish, it is a good idea to score the skin (slice in crosscuts) a couple of times and baste with lemon butter as it cooks. The same procedure should be used with heavy-bodied fish baked whole, such as red snapper, redfish, small grouper, or largemouth bass. Crosscutting not only allows basting juices to enter the fish; it also helps the fish to cook thoroughly throughout.

Some cookbooks suggest you bake only certain types of fish. I maintain you can bake *any kind of fish* if you bake it *properly*. Ideal baking temperature is 350 to 375 degrees.

BROILING SEAFOOD

Broiling involves cooking at very high temperatures (about 500 degrees), under a flame or broiler coil. The heat is usually applied to only one side of the food. Seafoods to be broiled should be basted frequently, and I recommend that you pay close attention to the broiling process since cooking time is relatively short.

Fish cooked under the broiler should be filleted (except in the case of small flounders and other small fish, which can be broiled whole and stuffed). Each fillet can be topped with a very thin slice of fresh lemon, and dabbed every few minutes with your favorite herb-butter mixture. Paprika sprinkled on before broiling also lends a nice color to broiled fish.

Oysters cooked under the broiler become delicacies when dressed with lemon, butter, bacon bits, and a sprinkling of parsley. Ideally they should be broiled in the half shell, but ramekins will do nicely also.

Shrimp can be broiled to perfection both in and out of their shells. In their shells, they should first be marinated in your favorite medium for about 3 hours (see the chapter on marinades and sauces), then laid in a single layer in a shallow pan under the broiler. Peeled from their shells, shrimp should be broiled in a single layer and continuously basted with your favorite seasoned herb butter. But keep a close eye on the cooking time—it doesn't take long. When they are pink and opaque, they're done.

Peeled crawfish tails can be broiled in a single layer and basted much the same as shrimp. I do recommend, however, that you butterfly and devein crawfish tails prior to broiling (this is not necessary with shrimp) to make them more appealing.

One more point: Broiled seafoods can be laid out in the cooking pan in attractive arrangements and placed directly on the table if they're garnished with a little creative flair. For example: In a pizza pan, place the peeled shrimp in concentric circles from the outside in by laying the shrimp so that they touch each other at the tail curvature. In other words, the top of one shrimp should fit against the bottom of the next shrimp, and so forth. Then separate every few circles of shrimp with circles of sliced mushroom caps, bits of bacon, pieces of onion, chopped bell pepper, or chunks of pimento. Top off with a sprig of parsley here and there, broil everything together, and you can serve right from the oven to the table. Just a hint, y'all.

One last hint, too: While *hard crabs* are not usually broiled, one of the most taste-tempting dishes you can fix under the broiler is *soft-shell crabs*. Marinated and constantly basted during the cooking process, soft-shells come out tasting like a treat from the gods. I do recommend, however, that you broil soft-shells on a rack inside a baking pan so that the water expelled during broiling doesn't dilute the basting sauces. And to produce a truly gourmet meal, whip up a batch of my shrimp sauce and ladle it over the broiled crab when you serve it. Oh la la!

POACHING SEAFOOD

Poaching is a variation of boiling, but better because it usually involves cooking in a flavored stock. The actual amount of water used is minimal.

Every kind of seafood can be poached—fish, shrimp, crabs, crawfish, oysters, scallops, etc. The secret to good poached recipes is *bringing the stock to a boil before adding the seafoods, then reducing the heat to simmer for the actual cooking.* Recommended poaching stocks include chicken broth, shrimp broth, fish broth, wine, soups, vegetable liquors, and milk.

Poaching is a great way to reduce calories in a dish while still keeping all the gourmet flavor. And in certain dishes, like casseroles and stuffings, it adds even more flavor than the dish would otherwise contain.

Just keep in mind that seafoods cook quicker than usual when poached in stocks, so as soon as the seafoods go in the heat must be reduced—especially with fish—or the seafood will fall apart. To keep this from happening, handle the seafood as little as possible (this can be accomplished by adding just enough stock to completely cover the seafood being cooked).

BRAISING SEAFOOD

Braising is nothing more than *baking with some kind of stock or liquid*. What we normally refer to as "baked redfish in tomato sauce" is really *braised* redfish. Louisiana's famed barbecued shrimp is really braised when it is done in an oven. Oysters smothered in mushroom and bacon sauce are really being braised if they are cooked in an oven.

PANFRYING SEAFOOD

Panfrying or sautéing means frying foods gently in only minimal amounts of oils, as opposed to frying them submerged in deep fat. The one thing you want to remember about panfrying or sautéing is that since the cooking temperatures are usually low, you want to avoid heavy batters on your seafoods because they will get gummy and gritty. Panfried foods should be only lightly dusted with the coating of your choice. And for the best taste, they should be sautéed in an equal mix of butter and cooking oil (one tablespoon of oil to one tablespoon of butter).

Panfried seafoods come out best if they are ice-cold when added to the pan. The sudden change in temperature sears the outside of the seafood and seals in natural juices.

There's one important point I want to make right here, though. Don't confuse sautéing (panfrying) with frying in an electric frypan half-filled with grease. That's equivalent to deep frying. Of course you *can* sauté in the electric skillet—it's a great device and offers that capability. But you can deep fry too. But I didn't want you to be misled: *a frying pan in the kitchen doesn't mean you automatically "panfry."*

All seafoods can be panfried, but fish should be handled gently or they will break up as they do in poaching. Use a wide-blade spatula to flip fillets (and incidentally, fillets cook better sautéed than do whole fish, however small). Flip them only after the side closest to the heat is just about thoroughly cooked (it should be golden brown and opaque). And to keep the fillets in one piece, you should make only *one flip*. If you use two spatulas instead of one (one for the "up" side and one to slide under the fillet), the flipping procedure will be easier.

You need not be so fussy when sautéing oysters, shrimp, or crawfish. They will not break apart and can almost be *stir-fried*. In fact, you might want to use both a spatula and the *agitation method* of sautéing for these seafoods (that's when you shake the pan briskly back and forth across the burner to move seafood around). It helps to distribute the heat more evenly, and prevents sticking.

Soft-shell crabs, on the other hand, should be handled much the same as fish fillets. Just keep in mind that if you want "sautéed crabs," you should panfry. And panfry on both sides, flipping them over only after each side is just about cooked. If you want thick-batter, ultracrispy soft-shells, fry them in an electric skillet in deeper oil or *deep fry* them.

One caution about soft-shell crabs: Because of the high water content of this seafood, you should cover the sautéing pan with a splatter screen; soft-shells tend to "pop" when cooking. Watch that you don't get burned!

DEEP FRYING SEAFOOD

Deep frying means frying hot—at 400 to 500 degrees—in deep fat to get extra crispness into seafoods. All seafoods, including hard-shell crabs, can be deep fried.

Some recommendations for deep frying:

1. Use fresh oil each time you cook, regardless of what you've heard about using oils over and over again. The quality diminishes, especially in seafoods, whenever you try to use oil two or three times.

2. Make sure the oil is at the proper temperature (with the basket in the cooker) before adding seafoods for deep frying. Putting in your fish, shrimp, or crabs before the oil is hot enough will cause them to absorb oil and come out greasy. (Hint: If a pinch of sliced bread fries instantly when dropped into hot oil, your oil is hot enough!)

3. Fry *hot*—and add the seafoods *cold* (not at room temperature). This is what ensures crispness in the batter and coatings. Ever eat gummy oysters? The reason is the oil was too cool to crisp them up.

4. Add seafood *one piece at a time*. And don't use the basket as an "adding container." As explained in more detail in next chapter, the baskets that come with most deep fryers are generally used incorrectly. Many people believe they are intended to be used as devices to load up with fish, shrimp, oysters, or whatever, then dropped into the oil in bulk. That's wrong! If you deep fry this way, you'll end up with greasy seafood and big gobs of coating floating around in the oil because the temperatures were too low to fry.

That basket is designed only to help you *remove* the seafood *from* the oil, not to put it *into* the oil! It should be inside the oil as the fryer heats up, and should be the same temperature as the oil before the seafoods are added.

For superb, crisp fish, shrimp, and oysters, drop individual pieces of fish, two or three shrimp, and one or two oysters at a time into the basket, watching all the time to make sure that the oil continues to bubble rapidly as the pieces are added. This will prevent the lowering of the oil temperature, and the coating will stick to your fried foods. And don't overload the fryer, either. Add just enough pieces to allow for frying room. It's better to make an extra batch than ruin the quality of the whole batch.

5. Remove the seafood when it floats. Don't overcook. In deep oil, seafood is done when it rises to the surface and floats easily. This is when you lift out the basket and drain off the hot grease. I also recommend you further drain your

seafood by placing it on several thicknesses of *highly absorbent* paper towels. The added flavor far outweighs the cost of these extras.

One more point concerning temperatures and seafood pieces: When deep frying, you'd do better to cut fish fillets in finger steaks rather than fry them whole. The crispness is greater and the cooking times are shortened. But if you'd rather prepare your fillets whole in the deep fryer, you must be aware of temperature adjustments you'll have to make. If your frying pieces are small—shrimp, oysters, crawfish tails, chunked fish—fry at 450 to 500 degrees. The small areas will all cook equally and thoroughly throughout. If, however, the fillets are whole (or you're frying jumbo shrimp), reduce the heat on the deep fryer to 400 to 425 degrees. The lower temperature is necessary to prevent the outside areas from becoming overcooked while the inside portions are still raw.

6. Use good-quality oils and ingredients for the coating mixes. Since all fried seafoods are usually coated with either flour, cornmeal, or corn flour, you will be risking loss of flavor and texture if you cook with poor grades of mix products. Of all the products on the market, I use Crisco religiously as an all-purpose oil. But I also recommend peanut oil and corn oil for seafoods if you want that little something extra in flavor and lightness.

7. Coat your seafoods properly before deep frying. That usually requires two types of coatings—*liquid coating* and *meal coating*. The liquid coating should contain two raw eggs beaten well into one cup of milk or beer. The meal coating I've found works best in the deep fryer consists of two cups of cornmeal, two cups of corn flour (commercial Fish-Fri), and one cup of corn starch, all blended together and seasoned to taste with salt, cayenne pepper, and fresh-ground black pepper.

The technique I suggest to you in preparation for deep frying is: (1) dip the seafood into the meal coating and shake off all the excess; (2) dip it into the liquid mix and drip off the excess; and (3) dip into the meal again, shaking off the excess and *dropping immediately into the deep fryer*. The resulting batter is not extra thick, but it does have body and seals in the seafood juices. For a thick batter, mix the meal with egg and milk until you produce a sticky paste, roll the seafood in it, and fry at about 400 degrees.

Understand that if you prefer to leave the salt and peppers out of your meal coatings and to salt and pepper your seafoods directly instead, that's perfectly acceptable. This is a matter of choice. Both seasoning methods work equally well.

GRILLING SEAFOOD

You can grill or barbecue seafoods over an open grill to bring out extra natural flavors, or to add smoked flavors. Just about all types of seafoods can be grilled, but most should first be soaked in a marinade or basted throughout the cooking process.

Among the grilling recipes I recommend to outdoor gourmets are: Grilled Fish in Scales, Barbecued Trout, Barbecued Shrimp a la Bourbon, and N'awlins Smoked Barbecued Oysters. Of course, there are hundreds more; the number extends as far as your creative talent. At this point let me give you a couple of general tips that will make the barbecuing process easier:

1. Thin cuts of filleted fish should go close to the heat, and thicker cuts should be grilled further from the heat source. The principle behind this rule is the same one that governs baking and frying times; lower temperatures prevent the thicker cuts from drying out on the outside while the inside portions stay raw. Using lower heat for thicker pieces allows uniform cooking throughout.

2. Ideally, fish you want to barbecue "right on the grating" should be cooked in their own skins. This, of course, will take some planning during the cleaning process (you'll have to clean the fish, but leave the skin on), but it is the best way to prepare grilled trout, snapper, redfish, flounder, and so forth. And to achieve even better effects, leave the scales on as well. The scales serve as a natural "platter," holding the juices and keeping the meat together.

Simply remove the head, the entrails, and the belly fins and tail; then run the knife blade alongside the backbone of both fillets and *remove the backbone*. This will give you both side slabs connected together in a triangular piece. Wash it well, salt and pepper it generously, and marinate it in the refrigerator in milk, Italian salad dressing, Liquid Smoke, or all three for 4 hours or more. Then place it on the grill *scales down* and cook it on medium heat, *covered*, until the meat begins to flake. Baste constantly and you'll have a dish fit for a king!

If you choose not to leave the scales and skin on your fish, you can either change to smaller grill mesh or grill in aluminum foil to keep the fish from falling through the grating after it cooks. When you've cooked it—whichever way you choose—baste it a few more times with the basting mix you've prepared, and serve it up on a heated platter. (Incidentally, fish grilled in scales can be scooped right out of the scales with a spatula.)

3. All lean fish (speckled trout, croaker, flounder, sheepshead, etc.) should be continuously basted with some type of sauce. Fatty or oily fish (Spanish mackerel, king mackerel, bluefish, tuna) may be grilled without basting, since the natural oils self-baste as the fish cooks, but I generally baste all fish, lean or oily, for extra flavor.

4. Shrimp can be grilled both in and out of their shells on the barbecue pit, but they must first be marinated, then basted during the cooking process. The best way to get the flavored seasonings inside the shells (for shrimp cooked with the shells on) is to perforate the shells with the tip of an ice pick prior to

marinating. Because the actual shrimp tail—the edible meaty portion—will render some natural juices and shrink away from the shell as it cooks, there will be succulent juices trapped inside the shells when the shrimp are done. Ideally, you should cook only extra jumbo shrimp (16 to 20 to the pound) in their shells and leave the heads on, but this recipe is so good it's not uncommon to find smaller shrimp cooking up on the grill! Note: If leaving the heads on disturbs you, don't fuss about it—just take them off. But you'll have to baste more frequently since the natural juices will drip out.

Shrimp cooked on a grill out of the shell must be basted very frequently. Keep a close eye on the little critters; it doesn't take long for them to cook. Over a good bed of hot coals, *5 minutes* should more than do it. (When they turn pink, they're done!)

5. Because each crawfish shrinks down into a little ball of meat after it's cooked, crawfish should be grilled on a sheet of oven-thickness aluminum foil. The foil also permits you to baste the tails quite easily; I'd whip up a basting brew of butter, lemon, garlic powder, and fresh-ground black pepper. I recommend you grill crawfish tails on a low fire—it keeps them more tender.

6. Crabs have to be handled in a special way if you want to grill them (and you should, because they're excellent grilled!). You must remove the backs from the raw crabs and thoroughly clean them (gills, insides, fat deposit, etc.), cut them into right and left halves, and soak them in a marinade *in the refrigerator* for 6 hours or more. Then, when you want to grill them, simply place them directly on the barbecue pit rack (about six inches from the coals), lower the cover on the grill, and cook them for about 20 minutes or until done (the meat will pull out of the shell in chunks easily when cooked). All you do is pick the crabs just as you would pick them boiled. And let me suggest you learn to use a *crab knife*—it makes eating hard-shell crabs a real joy. (For more about crab knives, see the chapter on crabs.)

7. Oysters grilled on the open pit should be cooked in their half shells, in their own liquor, until the edges curl. One of the best ways to fix grilled oysters is to set them on the grill, sprinkle them lightly with a dash or two of Tabasco sauce, squeeze a little lemon juice into the shell, add one or two drops of Liquid Smoke, and top with a dab of horseradish. When the edges curl up, place the sizzling hot oyster on a buttered cracker and have at it!

SMOKING SEAFOOD

Smoking is the cooking and preserving of fish and other seafoods either in a commercial smoker-cooker or in a smokehouse. Generally, only fish and oysters are smoked by most southern cooks, but there are also mock-smokery recipes that involve crawfish, shrimp, and crabs.

All fish can be smoked, even though you may hear that only the more oily species are palatable. It is an art that is rapidly being revived, what with all the home-use smoker models turning up on the market these days. Smoke-cooking not only preserves food, but also heightens and improves the flavor of the finished product. In an elaborately built smokehouse out back, a commercial model (and I prefer Mr. Meat Smoker), or even a unit refashioned from an old 55-gallon drum, you can turn out delicacies that will amaze you! But it is a slow process that can't be hurried.

Technically, you can hot-smoke fish *whole* (scaled with the skin on), *halved*, *filleted*, or *in chunks* (tuna, for example), and no special brining or dry-curing is necessary. All you do is prepare your fish the same way you'd fix it for baking in a conventional oven. Stoke up the smoker, create a medium density of smoke (preferably hickory), and preheat the oven to 185 degrees.

While the smoker is heating, make a basic smokehouse seasoning mix as follows:

1 26-oz. box table salt	**4 tbsp. black pepper**
1 tbsp. onion salt	**4 tbsp. cayenne pepper**
1 tbsp. garlic salt	**2 tbsp. dill salt**
2 tbsp. celery salt	**4 tbsp. granular sugar**
2 tbsp. paprika	

Mix together well, place in vapor-lock jars, and set in hot water in the sink for about 2 hours prior to use so that the flavors blend. (The mixture can be stored for future use in cool, dry places.)

When the smoker-cooker is at the right temperature, sprinkle the seasoning mix over the fish and pat it into the skin and meat with your hands. Then set each piece of fish on the racks in the smoker, replace the cover, and time the process the same as you would in your oven if it cooked at 185 degrees. Oily fish need not be basted, but lean fish should be brushed periodically with vegetable oil as they cook to keep the smoke from drying them out.

Thin fillets will cook rapidly and you'll have no problem deciding when they are done. Within several hours you should notice the meat beginning to flake. Whole fish are cooked when the temperature at the center of the fish reaches 140 degrees.

Oysters should be smoked at the same temperature as fish, but they can be smoked either in the half shell or on a stainless-steel cookie sheet placed in the smoker. For best results, I recommend you limit the amount of seasonings placed on your oysters. A light sprinkling of the basic seasoning or an occasional dab of melted butter will produce a nice flavor. Your oysters will be done when they curl at the edges.

Keep in mind, also, that—like every other method of preparing seafoods—smoking can't improve quality that isn't there to start with. So smoke only the finest product available.

I also suggest that you wrap individual serving-size pieces of smoked fish in several layers of Saran Wrap or Handi-Wrap and refrigerate them as soon as they have cooled to room temperature. The smoked product will remain fresh in your refrigerator for up to 4 weeks, and it can be frozen for up to a year for later use in dishes calling for smoked seafoods, with only a slight percentage of texture loss.

Cold-Smoke Variation: There is also a technique you might want to use if you have a homemade smokehouse and you want to "hang" larger chunks of fish on wire racks. Here's how it works:

Fire up the smoker and stabilize the temperature at 115 degrees in dense hickory smoke. Put in the fish and cook it at that temperature for 2 hours. Then add more chipped hickory to maximize the smoke and raise the temperature to 170 degrees. Continue cooking the fish *until all dripping ceases*. When no more liquids come from the fish (about 8 hours), it's done. Then prepare the fish in wraps for the freezer. Excellent!

CHAPTER FOUR

Cooking with Trickery

A wise man once said: "God created the universe with the right tools and a few little tricks." Would you believe these are the same tactics most good cooks use to create the dishes that win them acclaim?

Preparing good dishes requires some basics: fresh ingredients in the proper amounts, attention to cooking times, and the experience of repetition. So in essence, *anyone can cook.* You may have to follow a cookbook to the letter, but you can cook.

The creative cook, however, goes beyond just cooking with recipes. Deep-seated interest in the art of cooking—and it is an art, make no mistake about it—prompts good cooks to add trickery to technique, resulting in greater ease of preparation, dishes with finer texture, and cuisine with unequaled flavor. It is an interest in cooking that produces menus anyone would be pleased to serve to the most sophisticated of VIPs. But it's the trickery that makes it all happen!

This chapter is designed to reveal some of that trickery—the oft-hidden secrets of some of the best cooks in South Louisiana. The tips themselves, some so important that they're repeated elsewhere in this book, should make your cooking more *fun*, to say nothing of the compliments you'll receive—and the money you'll save!

When freezing or cooking fish fillets

If you cut your fillets into three-inch-wide chunks, you can cook or freeze meal-size portions that are all the same thickness. This means that pieces will all get done at the same time in the cooking process, preventing thin pieces from becoming tough and dry while you're waiting for thick sections to cook all the way through.

How to keep the claws on your crabs

One of the most discouraging results you can encounter when boiling crabs is finding that claws have settled to the bottom of the pot instead of staying attached to the crabs. This need never happen if you prepare your crabs prior to boiling using this little bit of information: Crabs snap off their own claws when they hit boiling water alive (it's a shock reaction). To keep it from happening, all you have to do is chill the crabs before you drop them into the hot water. Simply put them in an ice chest or cooler while you're waiting for the water to come to a boil, and cover them with a bag or two of crushed ice. This method will produce crabs with virtually every claw intact!

Submerge your seafood to pick up seasonings

This is such a helpful trick that I had to repeat it in case you missed it.

Whether you are boiling crabs, shrimp, or crawfish, after the boil is completed you will find most of the seafood floating at the surface of the pot. This happens because, as water boils, tiny air bubbles collect inside the shells and create buoyancy. When suspended on the surface of the liquid, seafood cannot absorb seasonings that the soaking process is intended to provide. So you must *sink* your crabs, shrimp, and crawfish.

Some folks attempt to push the seafood down with a spoon or to find a weight large enough to force the seafood below the surface. This isn't necessary. All you have to do after the boil is completed is pour about a quart of ice-cold water (or two trays of ice cubes) over the seafood, stir it around for a second or two, and—presto! The shrimp, crabs, or crawfish will sink like bricks!

This process is the result of thermal change. But who cares why it works? It works, and that's all that counts, huh?

Add extra kick to your seasoning flour for sautéing

When most folks get ready to sauté seafood, they dust the seafood in plain flour spiced only with a small amount of salt and pepper. It's good, no doubt, but to *really* perk up the flavors of food from the sea, try this:

To *one cup of flour or cornmeal*, add one tablespoon salt, ½ teaspoon white pepper, ¼ teaspoon cayenne, ¼ teaspoon McCormick lemon pepper, a pinch of powdered mustard, ½ teaspoon celery salt, one teaspoon onion powder, and a dash of mace.

Then dust the fillet of fish, the oysters, the deveined (butterflied) shrimp, or whatever in the mixture and shake off the excess. Dunk it in a cup of milk and dip it in the coating flour again. Then fry immediately in a small amount of Crisco oil combined with about one pat of unsalted butter. The resulting flavor is rich and superb.

Beer as a seafood marinade

I'm no chemist, nor am I a brewmaster, so I can't tell you why it works. But I can tell you that in Louisiana one of the most popular marinades for seafood (especially for fish and shrimp) is *beer*. A can of beer poured over a bowl of filleted trout, redfish, or croaker produces the most flaky texture imaginable. It also seems to lock the natural juices inside fried shrimp. Note: The seafood should be allowed to soak in the marinade, *in the refrigerator*, for at least an hour before cooking.

Make sure your fried seafoods come out crisp

A well-blended coating mixture—and I recommend you use equal parts of *cornmeal* and *corn flour*—will give your fried fish, shrimp, and oysters a succulent crispness when cooked at the proper temperature (at least 400 degrees). But for added texture that provides moistness on the inside and crunchiness on the outside, I suggest you always fry your seafoods when they are *ice-cold*. Add them to the oil *one piece at a time*, directly from the refrigerator. When the cold seafood comes into contact with the sizzling oil the juices will instantly be sealed in, and golden browning will occur without overcooking.

The principle of adding one piece of the seafood at a time applies not only to panfrying but to deep frying as well. Just remember that if you cool the oil too rapidly, the seafood will soak up the grease and taste greasy.

About deep frying in the basket

Ya know them li'l baskets that come in deep fryers? Well, they're probably the most misused devices ever invented! This is another trick I'm going through again to make sure you use it.

First, most folks heat the oil in the deep fryer *without* the basket in the oil. That's wrong! Leave the basket inside the deep fryer so that both the basket and the oil reach at least 400 degrees Fahrenheit. A cold basket immersed in hot oil will bring your oil down to an incorrect temperature for frying seafoods and your seafoods will get awfully greasy tasting.

Second, most folks also think the basket is designed to be a device to lower all the seafood at once down into the oil. That's not only wrong—it should be considered a mortal sin! Can you see now what happens when you put six fish fillets or two pounds of peeled shrimp in a *cold* basket and lower it down into 400-degree oil? Right! The thermostat indicator light flashes on instantly. And it takes about 5 minutes before the seafood even begins to fry. Try this with oysters (God forbid!), and it's like eating cotton balls dipped in cod-liver oil.

The basket is designed *only* for removing fried foods from the deep oil, and it should remain in the fryer until that point in the cooking process arrives. Gently lower fish fillets into the basket. Add butterflied shrimp no faster than *two* at a time. Drop in oysters (because of their high water content) *one or two* at a time, and count to three before dropping in the next two. And don't try to fill the basket to the brim! Two or three fish fillets, a dozen or so oysters, and about two dozen 40-count shrimp are just right. You'll find that you'll fry the batches much faster with less in the basket because the oil will retain the proper temperature.

And everything will come out picture-perfect, crisp, and golden brown. Or as the Cajun cooks say, "No more of the greasies!"

The right temperature for panfrying (sautéing)

Let me suggest, even though it is common to sprinkle a few drops of water into oil to test the temperature for frying, that you try this instead: *When you think the oil in your sautéing pan is hot enough to begin frying, test it by dropping a pinch of cornmeal (or sliced bread) onto the surface. If the fat is ready, the cornmeal (or bread) will sizzle and turn golden brown.*

Water sprinkled into hot oil will splatter and could cause skin burns. And the other suggestion you often hear, dipping a match in the oil until it lights, could be just as dangerous; it could set the pan of oil on fire! I've used the cornmeal technique for years, and it always works well.

Italian salad dressing as a flavor enhancer

One of the best marinades you can get for seafoods (especially fish with low oil content, like trout and croaker) is Italian salad dressing. Simply place your seafood in a bowl, pour a 16-oz. bottle of dressing over the pieces, cover with Saran Wrap, and refrigerate for about 2 hours. Then cook the seafood as planned—fried, baked, broiled, etc. Note: This is exceptionally delicious when you're planning to grill seafood over an open flame.

One more suggestion: Save the dressing. It can be used again for other seafoods, since it keeps well in the refrigerator for up to 3 weeks. And it makes a good basting agent to brush on seafood as it cooks.

Italian salad dressing is a versatile mix for cooking. You might want to use it as the essential base for marinated crabs (just drop pieces of boiled crab into the dressing and let stand a few hours). You'll find that a few drops placed over oysters enhance the flavor of the oysters when eaten raw. Soaking raw oysters in Italian salad dressing for about an hour, then replacing them in their shells also prepares them succulently for broiling. Boiled, leftover shrimp become a whole new number when peeled and soaked in the marinade and served up as canapes with Ritz crackers and Philadelphia Brand cream cheese.

There's no end to the creative ways to use it—whether you're an Italian or not!

Making roux bases in advance

The old Cajun expression "First, you make a roux!" is as much a part of Louisiana cookery as red beans and rice on Mondays. Virtually every familiar

Acadian dish starts with this subtle browning of oil and flour. Yet there are even some Acadians who reluctantly admit that they just can't make a roux. So for the sake of simplicity, let me go through the process with you.

The best rouxs are made in direct 1:1 proportions of flour to oil. For example, add *one tablespoon* of flour to *one tablespoon* of oil; *one cup* of flour to *one cup* of oil. Amounts should always be equal (although there are some cooks in Louisiana who use twice as much oil as flour).

I suggest you make your rouxs in heavy pots (either black cast iron or Club aluminum) because the heat distribution is more even in a stout cooking utensil. And since you will constantly be stirring a roux, try to avoid Teflon-coated skillets to keep from marring their surfaces.

Incidentally, if you're on a low-fat diet and need to avoid oil as much as possible, you can make a pretty decent roux by browning your flour in your oven under the broiler without fat and adding it to a little beef or chicken bouillon. Just spread the flour out evenly in a baking pan and stir it often to disperse the heat. It certainly isn't authentic, but it tastes good.

Start a Cajun roux by heating your oil to medium hot, then sprinkling the flour into the oil evenly, stirring all the time. Watch it closely because it will first turn beige, then brown, then dark brown. Stop it at this point; *otherwise it will burn, and taste burnt*. The best way to stop a browning roux is to toss in a handful of minced onion and remove the pot from the fire. As soon as the onions are stirred into the flour, the browning process will stabilize.

You'll notice that most Cajun rouxs contain chopped onions, minced garlic, celery, shallots, and other vegetable seasonings. Once you get used to browning flour, it is possible to toss everything in the same pot. But until you do, I recommend you sauté your vegetable seasonings in a separate skillet in about two tablespoons of butter or margarine, and then add them to the browned flour, along with a cup of water to simmer them in. You'll find that this technique, although it's not conventional, lends more distinctive flavor to the base. Try it and see what you think.

A couple of notes here:

1. Browned flour has the capacity to expand when water is added to it; that fact is the basis for most brown gravies. So you should begin adding water as soon as the browning process is completed. But add it in *small amounts, and while stirring constantly*, until the desired consistency is reached. Good roux bases (gravies) should be simmered for at least 10 minutes before the other ingredients (fish, chicken, etc.) are added. Salt and pepper go in after the simmering process; that's the only way to balance the taste.

2. If you want to have a *supply roux* on hand for instant gravies, simply brown the flour and oil to the proper texture, then add the sautéed vegetable seasonings and just enough water to maintain the thickness of paste. Then pack the paste

down in a Mason jar or empty Coffee Mate bottle and store it in the coldest part of your refrigerator. It will keep for months—and it will be ready for all your favorite dishes.

3. Roux is excellent for adding to all liquid-base dishes: gumbos, stews, gravies, etouffées, soups, sauces, and whatever else calls for a Cajun stock or a thickening agent. Just stir two or three tablespoons into a cup or two of water, depending upon how rich you want it; put it on the fire; and let it go. You'll swear your family name is Boudreaux!

Smoked seafood mockery

Thanks to a commercial product found on just about every grocer's shelf, you can turn out some of the finest hickory-flavored dishes imaginable *without a barbecue grill or hickory chips.*

It's called "Liquid Smoke" on the label, and it generally contains water, vinegar, dissolved hickory smoke, and a few stabilizers. Several suppliers make this condiment, but I've found *Woody's* to be more concentrated and flavorful than some of the others.

Let me caution you, though, to use the preparation very sparingly until you become familiar with its enhancement properties. Just a few drops in a butter and lemon baste or in a light coating brushed on as a topping will season oven-baked or broiled fish as if it had been suspended in a smokehouse for days. Because it is an *additive* seasoning (meaning you can still add it to your foods up to the time of serving), you can increase the amount if necessary later in the cooking process.

Barbecued fish done on a grill, baked beans as a seafood accompaniment, the sauce used for dipping oven-baked shrimp, and broiled oysters in the half shell should all contain a few drops of liquid smoke. What it does for the flavor I can't begin to describe!

Extending the life of dried herbs and spices

A wide variety of dried herbs and spices should be permanent stock on your pantry shelves. It is the spicy seasonings that give seafoods their traditional Louisiana tastes. But occasionally, in Louisiana's humid climate, the ground leaves and powders are not used quickly enough to remain fresh, and they become aged and clumpy.

When this happens—whenever you feel your herbs and spices are getting old on the shelf—don't throw them away. Simply take them, dump each spice into a tight-lidded Mason jar, pour either vegetable oil or water over them, and store them away in your refrigerator. Some noted New Orleans cooks even keep two sets of jars, one for oil-flavored spices and the other for water-based spices. That way, when you need garlic flavoring, for example, and the dish calls for an oil, you can use the spiced garlic oil. If the dish is light and water additives will do, add the water-spiced product. Virtually all herbs and spices can be treated this way, and putting them into solution will eliminate wasting aged seasonings.

Handling seafood cheeses

So many shrimp, crab, and fish dishes are highlighted with cheeses that it would probably take an entire book to treat the subject fully. But suffice it to say here that you should always have cheddar, colby, Swiss, and mozzarella cheeses on hand if you plan to prepare succulent, gourmet menus.

But what do you do with cheeses that you can't store in the refrigerator because they tend to mold? You grate them by hand, run them through your blender, or chop them very finely in your food processor; package them flat in Ziploc bags: and *freeze them*. Cheeses for cooking keep well in your freezer and are ready to sprinkle liberally over most dishes (or into them) in the grated form.

Another note: If you have a party or get-together and put cheeses out as appetizers, pieces left on the serving trays should be placed in airtight containers, stored in your freezer, and used for cooking. Several cheeses blended in the same dish (mozzarella, cheddar, and Swiss together, for instance) will go nicely into an au gratin.

And when you have a block of cheese in the refrigerator that begins to mold, *don't throw it out*. Just trim off the mold with a sharp knife, grate the remaining part, and freeze it.

Speaking of blocks of cheese, you should always buy your cheese in blocks (rather than grated or sliced) for cooking. It's a relatively simple procedure to grate, shave, or chip cheese. And you will be amazed at the difference in price.

I recommend that on your next trip to the grocery store you pick up one block each of mozzarella, colby, cheddar, and Swiss, just for cooking purposes. Then grate them, pack them flat (so you can break off just what you need from the freezer package), and keep them handy at zero degrees. And the next time you want to add zest to a broiled fish fillet, a little kick to baked shrimp, some tang to a crabmeat casserole, or some sparkle and flavor to steamed vegetables or side dishes, grab a handful of grated cheese and simmer it in or melt it over the dish. It's good stuff, cher—and you're limited only by your imagination!

How to get the most juice out of a lemon or lime

You just can't beat fresh lemon and lime juice for bringing out hidden flavors in seafoods. Many of New Orleans's most famous restaurants wouldn't dare serve a seafood that wasn't first highlighted in some fashion with a sprinkle or two of lemon juice.

But there's a way to get the maximum amount of juice from citrus fruits, especially lemons. *You drop the unpeeled fruit in boiling water for about 10 minutes.* The process tends to burst every pulp sac, and releases the fluids inside the peel. Citrus fruits can even be processed like this and stored in your refrigerator.

In fact, for home use you can simply poke a little hole in the top of the lemon and pass it around to be squeezed at the table, or you can render out the juice conventionally in a juicer. Either way, you'll get more juice than you ever imagined was in one lemon!

More about your food processor

I'd venture to say that the food processor is one of the greatest devices the housewife has on her counter top. And for Louisiana folks—and folks who want to cook like Louisianians—it is almost a do-or-die essential!

The whirling blades of the processor have made quick work of chopping vegetables for gumbos, stews, soups, chowders, jambalayas, and casseroles. They have made seafood dressings a pleasure to prepare, eliminating all the time it formerly took to cut up oysters and slice shrimp. And when it comes to getting seasonings ready for the freezer, well, they are worth their weight in bullion!

You've no doubt seen a product on the market (in the freezer section) called "Chef's Seasonings." It consists of a frozen tablet of chopped onions, garlic, celery, parsley, and some other goodies. When I first began buying the product for making rouxs and gravies, I bought it for about 29 cents a pack. Today, the very same pack retails in most places for about $1.39. And you must be satisfied with what the manufacturer puts into the blend.

Suppose, though, you want to save a bunch of money—and who doesn't? And suppose you'd like the option of adding exactly what *you* desire in the way of spices to your seafood dishes—more onions, less garlic, etc. With a food processor, you can do both these things. All it takes is a fresh supply of seasoning vegetables, a box of the large-size freezer-type Ziploc bags, and your trusty processor. Go ahead, buy bulk quantities. As long as you have room for your chopped ingredients in the freezer, you can stock up.

Mark each bag with the seasoning and the manner of processing. For example: "ONION—CHOPPED FINE" or "GARLIC—SLICED THIN." A permanent marker is excellent for writing directly on the heavy plastic bags, but you should mark the bags while they are empty and dry. Then chop up your onions, garlic, bell peppers, celery, parsley, green onions—whatever—any way you want them, and bag them separately. The only care you have to take is that you package the seasonings so that you can flatten them out in thin sheets inside the bag. That way you can easily break off just the portions you need for each dish. Do not *fill* the bags; you don't want solid blocks. Just small amounts, smashed out flat and frozen.

You'll always have fresh onions, fresh garlic, fresh celery, and so forth. And by buying slightly wilted vegetables from the produce manager (they're excellent for cooking) you can save money on your fresh seasonings and all but eliminate the need for some of the more common dried seasonings.

One note here, though: You cannot substitute a blender for a food processor. *Blenders* tend to liquefy foods, regardless of the speeds you select. *Processors* slice, shred, and chop, and by regulating the running time in the "on" position you can produce virtually every consistency from rough-coarse to extra-fine.

Do yourself a favor and buy a food processor if you don't already have one!

Cook with real butter

To add richness to your seafood dishes, you'd do best to cook with real butter rather than margarine whenever possible. But it is important that you treat butter with appropriate care so that the best flavors will be emphasized in the finished dish.

Because it is a creamery product, butter will *burn quickly* and get an off-taste if too much heat is applied to the sautéing pan. So keep all dishes requiring sautéing in butter at *medium to low* heat and watch the pan carefully (especially on electric ranges).

There is one little gizmo you can buy that makes it a snap to clarify butter (i.e., take the heavy cream residue out). It's called, oddly enough, a "butter clarifier," and it looks like a measuring cup with a spout on it—only the spout connects at the bottom of the cup instead of at the top. When your butter is melted, the cream residue falls to the bottom and you pour it off, leaving the clear butter in the container.

In seafood cookery, *flavored butters* are important for enhancing fish fillets, oysters, shrimp, crawfish, crab, and other entrées. You can make your own very easily in a sautéing pan. For example: For a rich lemon butter, just clarify the butter and add a few drops of lemon juice over a low heat. Brush it over the fish fillets; this technique produces a more uniform taste throughout the fish than just buttering and sprinkling juice indiscriminately. If you want an oregano-flavored butter, clarify the butter and add about one-quarter teaspoon of oregano over low heat. When making broiled oysters, you can combine parsley and garlic and spoon them into the shells with clarified butter for a most distinctive taste.

The combinations are endless. And once you learn to mix flavored butters, you'll add a whole new dimension to your culinary prowess.

Incidentally, you can prepare flavored butters in advance and keep them in plastic containers in your refrigerator for up to 2 weeks.

Use potatoes as a seasoning extractor

Have you ever noticed that when you boil crabs or shrimp and add potatoes and corn the potatoes and corn usually come out saltier and hotter than do the crabs or shrimp?

That's because potatoes are seasoning extractors—neutralizers of sorts. This characteristic, fortunately, has salvaged a lot of overseasoned dishes and prevented a considerable amount of embarrassment among cooks. The extraction principle can be applied to many dishes in need of salvage—gumbos, stews, etouffées, soups, sauces, entrées, etc.—anything where stock or liquid bases cook in the seasonings.

All you do is dice up some raw potatoes (or cooked ones, in a nearly finished dish) and add them to the overseasoned liquid base. Stir them around thoroughly to make certain they are evenly dispersed, and simmer them for about 15 to 20 minutes. The starch in the potatoes, being highly absorbent, will usually extract most of the excess salt, pepper, herb, or spice—at least enough to make the dish edible. Occasionally you may have to add a second helping of potatoes if the overseasoning was extreme. But generally this technique will prevent your having to chuck the whole dish.

Understand, though, that once the potatoes have done their bit, you must remove them from the dish. Again, dig out a Mason jar, 'cause you don't have to throw the potatoes away! Just refrigerate them in the jar and add them sparingly to future dishes. Your flavorings will already be "in content," as they say, and you'll come out of the whole episode smelling like a rose!

Use whole milk to remove pungent odors and tastes

Every now and then a piece of fish will be *fishier-tasting* than usual. Occasionally shrimp will have a strong *iodine aroma*. And, more often than not, exotic dishes like *alligator stew* or *frog legs etouffée* will be pungent if the meat was improperly cleaned before cooking.

Well, there's something that virtually eliminates those unpleasant tastes and aromas: *whole milk*. When you add a half-cup or so of the dairy cocktail to the dish during the cooking process, unwanted "flavors" seem to disappear almost magically.

Just as a quart of milk left open in the refrigerator picks up traces of onion, bell pepper, and other aromatic foods, milk will soak up unwanted tastes in seafood cookery. Not to mention making the overall dish richer. Just remember that the trickery works in any recipe in which you can add milk without altering consistency. (By the way, whole milk also removes the so-called "wild" tastes from game.)

Milk as a marinade for seafood

Italian salad dressing, beer, wine, vinegar, and a host of commercially prepared concoctions are all used from time to time as marinades in Louisiana cookery. But one of the most effective marinades you can use for seafoods is *whole milk*.

Soaking shrimp in milk before cooking seems to make them juicier. Basting fish in milk overnight makes the fillets flakier. Chilling crabmeat in a small amount of cold milk produces a certain succulence you can't obtain otherwise. And to think that there was a time in New Orleans when folks were told not to drink milk and eat seafood at the same time or risk getting sick!

To get that special goodness only milk can give you, you should marinate your seafood (any kind) for at least 4 hours, preferably in the coldest part of your refrigerator. Then, when it's time to cook, just pour off the excess fluid and prepare your seafood as usual. Nothing to it, huh?

Keep ice trays around for stocks and rouxs

Earlier in this chapter I mentioned storing prepared roux in a Mason jar in the refrigerator. Well, if you know you're not going to use it quickly enough to keep it in the fridge, pack it into conventional *ice-cube trays* and freeze it. When you're ready to cook, it becomes a simple matter of breaking out two or three cubes.

Ice trays—and you can occasionally buy extras on sale for about 30 cents apiece—also make ideal devices for storing stocks and broths: chicken, beef, oyster, shrimp, mushroom, onion, whatever. It is no secret that many of New Orleans's best cooks add various stocks *instead of water* to a whole variety of dishes to bring out those special flavors. In fact, whenever someone tells you that his ingredients for flavor richness are a secret, you can just about bet that the secret is a stock of some sort.

It is relatively simple to make your own stocks. All you do is boil down the substance you desire in unsalted water seasoned with onion, celery, and carrot pieces (about a handful of each). For the best stock, boil for about 20 minutes.

A good *shrimp stock* can be made by boiling the shells of peeled shrimp. (Many folks peel shrimp for frying and then toss out the hulls. Boil them instead!) Along these same lines, instead of dumping out the water you use to boil crabs, shrimp, or crawfish, save a gallon or so and freeze it in ice-cube trays as stock. Then add the crab stock to crab dishes, crawfish stock to etouffées, shrimp stock to stews and soups and gumbos. Every seafood dish will come out richer tasting, from the simplest sauce to the thickest chowder.

Chicken fat can be boiled in water for a rich stock and used in practically any seafood-based dish. One suggestion, though: To eliminate all the fat in chicken stock, it is best if you first run the broth through several thicknesses of cheesecloth. Oh, if you boil the neck, heart, liver, and gizzard in the stock and then chop them up finely in the food processor, the stock becomes even richer! *Make no mistake about it, chicken stock forms one of the finest bases in seafood cookery.* It seems to enhance the seafood properties, lay a foundation for other flavors, and give full body to the finished recipes. The Orientals discovered this "secret" eons ago.

Oyster water, the by-product of shucking the tasty critters from the half shell, can be strained and mixed half and half with water to lend a subtle Cajun taste to many dishes; freeze it and store it in ice-cube trays. Keep one important thing in mind with oysters, however. When you cook with oyster stock, *be careful about adding salt* to the dish. Most Louisiana oysters are naturally salty anyway—that's the reason we are so proud of them! So be careful.

I could go on and on about stocks; the possibilities are endless. Many of them we never stop to consider as cooking mediums: the bell-pepper water that's left after parboiling peppers for stuffing, the water remaining after fish are poached, even the water used to boil rice for all the southern dishes rice accompanies (it can be used as a natural thickening agent for stews and gumbos!).

So get yourself a supply of extra ice-cube trays and begin "stocking" up!

About freezing rice—and boiling it, too

There is nothing like a big bowl of fresh-cooked rice. I doubt that you could name a seafood that wouldn't go well with it. Without rice, a gumbo isn't a gumbo, an etouffée is not an etouffée, and there would be no such thing as jambalaya! In fact, you could probably say that rice is the mainstay of Acadiana!

I never could understand why folks complain about boiling rice; some say it is difficult, while others flat out admit they can't do it. Sure, there are panels on the packaging that tell you "add a cup of rice to two cups of water, and when the water is absorbed the rice is done." And there is a device that automatically times your rice and rings a bell when it is supposed to be cooked. In all honesty, I've found that these methods produce gummy rice that sticks together in globs. And nothing is more tasteless than a gummed-up ball of congealed rice!

Let me suggest you try this method next time. I guarantee your rice will come out grain for grain, firm but cooked, and free of excess starchy residues. Here's what you do:

Take a 6-quart Dutch oven (stainless steel, Club aluminum—it doesn't matter!) *and fill it with 14 cups of water* (a 1-gallon plastic milk jug will hold 16 cups). Then bring the water to a boil and add 2 teaspoons of salt. When the water is boiling rapidly, pour in *up to 4 cups* of rice and wait for the water to come back to a boil again. Notice I said *up to 4 cups* of rice; you can boil a half-cup or 4 cups, it makes no difference. But don't alter the water volume: *keep 14 cups of water* regardless of the amount of rice up to 4 cups.

Rice is a carbohydrate and starchy, and unless you have a saturation medium (a lot of water) to dilute the starch factor, you'll never get grain-for-grain rice. It is just that simple.

When the water comes back to a boil, reduce the heat somewhat to keep the water actively bubbling, and begin to consider your cooking time. It should take no more than 15 minutes for your rice to be completely, perfectly cooked.

At this exact point, spoon out a couple of grains and *taste* them. Make certain they are tender all the way through—no hard centers. Don't let it go past the "tender" point, or the rice will begin to overcook and get gummy and soft. When it *tastes* cooked to you, take it off the fire *immediately,* pour it into a colander, and rinse it well in hot water. Drain it, and your rice will be nonsticky, done to the proper texture, with each grain separate from the rest.

Don't be afraid to cook more rice than you need (unless you are a purist and insist on freshly cooked rice for each dish), because rice freezes well after it is cooked, especially if you use this method to remove the starches. Just take a freezer container or a Ziploc bag, fill it with the cooked rice, seal it up, and stash it in the deep freeze. When the time comes to serve up rice, just dump it in a colander and run hot water over it. When the temperature is right, drain it and serve; it will taste fresh cooked.

Just two more points concerning cooking rice: (1) as it cooks, you should continue to stir it every 2 or 3 minutes to distribute the heat, and (2) you need not cover the pot while the rice is boiling.

How to remove burnt tastes in foods

Every now and then we cook a sauce or a roux just a little too hot and it burns slightly. The milk sticks to the bottom, the flour blackens, the gravy clumps up. Most folks spew out a select number of old Navy expressions and promptly toss the whole dish out!

Well, while I'm not saying that this works in all instances (because there's little you can do with a really badly burnt dish), on occasions when only a little damage has been done you might try removing the pot immediately from the heat source and setting it in a sink full of cold water. There are Louisiana cooks who swear that the sudden change in the temperature *removes the burnt taste* from the food. Nobody knows how it happens, but it works! And anything is worth trying to salvage an otherwise good meal.

And speaking of scalding milk

One of my neighbors in New Orleans told me once that you won't ever scorch the bottom of a pan while you're scalding milk if you first rub margarine all over the bottom. I was surprised, as you will no doubt be. Because it does work! Try it.

Yes, Virginia, there is a microwave roux

While the idea is generally frowned upon by most folks of Cajun ancestry, it is possible to make a quick roux in the microwave oven. All you do is mix your oil and flour together (two parts oil to one part flour) in a Pyrex bowl, and slide it into the microwave. Set the timer for about 2 or 3 minutes at full power and cook the mixture until proper consistency and color is obtained.

I suggest you cook in *quarter-minute* intervals, stirring well every 15 seconds in order to get quality control.

Microwave rouxs are lifesavers when you've added too much stock or water to a dish for the roux you initially prepared. Rather than make do with a thinner gravy, go to the microwave and whip up a quickie. No one will be able to tell the difference in the finished recipe—and that's what kitchen trickery is all about.

What to do with unsalty oysters on the half shell

I don't believe there is anything more embarrassing than inviting guests over for oysters on the half shell as appetizers and serving them milky, unsalty oysters. But since you can't fool Mother Nature, there's nothing you can do about it. Right?

Wrong!

The next time you open a sack of oysters and find they are lackluster, tasteless, and anything but salty, try this. As you open the sack, place a large pan under the shells and collect the natural oyster liquor. Set aside the oyster meats in a separate container and select shells for each one (you'll place the meats back on the shells later).

When you're finished shucking, strain the liquor to remove grit and shell fragments and gradually stir in small amounts of salted water (one quart of warm water with a couple of teaspoons of table salt added) until the oyster liquor tastes as salted oyster water should. Then pour the liquor back over the oyster meats and place the container in your refrigerator for about an hour. You must remember that oysters are alive when you extract them from the shell, and during the hour they are in the liquor in the refrigerator they will "pump" the salted water you added through their valves (or at least some of it).

Then, just prior to serving your guests, place the meats back on the half shells you selected and set the shells on a bed of crushed ice. As your guests will confirm, it *is* possible to fool Mother Nature, because the meats will taste as though you reaped them from the choicest and saltiest grounds in Louisiana.

Leftover oysters and other stew

One of Dixie's most delectable dishes is broiled oysters (in or out of the half shell). They can be fixed "plain vanilla" (without any condiments on them), or liberally dressed with everything from cayenne pepper to bacon bits to chipped parsley to lemon and garlic butter. And they are succulent, m'frien'!

Usually, especially among the folks I know, there are no broiled oyster *leftovers*. But should this phenomenon ever occur, it will give you the perfect opportunity to whip up the best-tasting oyster stew you ever had. And it's simpler than making a snowball!

All you do is take the leftover broiled oysters (and I hope you sprinkled them liberally with parsley, lemon butter, and bacon bits), put them in a sautéing pan, and add just enough milk to simmer them gently. While they are simmering, boil a couple of potatoes, dice them up, and toss them into the pan. Then poke the oysters full of holes with a fork to release the juices, stir and simmer for another 5 minutes, and spoon out a generous helping in a soup bowl. Serve with Old London Bacon-Flavored Melba Rounds, cher, and you can't beat it!

Brown bag your fresh seasonings

Earlier in this chapter I explained how to run a variety of fresh seasoning vegetables (onions, garlic, celery, parsley) through the food processor and store them in your freezer. But how do you keep fresh seasoning vegetables "fresh" in your refrigerator?

Generally, a stalk of celery or a bunch of parsley—even in the hydrator pan—will begin to wilt after about 4 or 5 days in the refrigerator. For some reason or other plastic wraps and bags do little to prolong this period.

Brown bags, however, are another story. The best way to keep refrigerator vegetables crisp is to store them in *brown Kraft bags* (the ones you bring your groceries home in)! Apparently the paper holds in the moisture it is supposed to hold in, and absorbs the excess moisture from the outside. But regardless of what it does or how, celery stays fresher, chopped onions don't wilt nearly so quickly, parsley stays dry and firm, garlic retains its flavor, bell peppers and cucumbers stay green, and so forth. Even lettuce stays much crispier than it would in a so-called "lettuce crisper."

In fact, this method could double refrigerator storage time. Try it. It has virtually eliminated spoiled vegetables at my house!

Collect seafoods for gumbos, Tupperware style

If you have a freezer, it is a relatively simple matter to keep a good supply of seafoods on hand for gumbo. Of course gumbo seafoods should be uncooked, but that presents no problem if you follow this little bit of Cajun trickery.

All you need is a *family-size Tupperware bread box* (that's the one that has a tight-fitting lid and holds a long loaf of bread) stocked permanently in your deep freeze.

It then becomes a simple matter of depositing in the box all the extra seafoods you don't use at meals or the mixed catches you make on poor fishing trips. How many times have you gone fishing and come home with only one trout, croaker, or redfish? Three crabs? Less than a pound of shrimp? Well, with a *gumbo box* in your freezer, these skimpy catches aren't wasted. You simply *clean the shrimp* (remove the head and shell), *pick out the crab* (take off the top shell, remove the insides and gills, and split in halves), and *fillet the fish* (keeping only the bone-free chunks). Then toss them in the box and cover with water to prevent freezer burn.

And you can keep on adding bits and pieces of seafoods periodically, too. Just toss them on top of the previous layer and cover with water, making certain the airtight lid is replaced snugly.

When it comes time to whip up a big gumbo, just melt the ice surrounding the seafood you need to cook with and drop it in the pot. Whatever you don't need can be placed back in the Tupperware and refrozen.

And then the process begins all over again!

Be sure you label your frozen seafoods

Because seafoods should be rotated in your freezer to keep stock fresh, no package should be stored away without a date on the label. That way, when you make a new catch it can be packaged and stocked so that the older product is the one you use first.

Labeling and rotating stock will practically eliminate loss of freshness and texture. This practice should apply to all types of seafoods, from fish to oysters.

About refreezing seafoods

You've heard that you *cannot refreeze seafoods.* For the most part, the statement is correct. But there is a reason for the rule and an exception to it you don't often hear about. You *should not (not cannot!)* refreeze seafoods because once refrozen the seafood product loses a great deal of taste and texture and comes out yucky when cooked. But it is still safe to eat. The one time you can refreeze and still have a good product when you cook is when there are still ice crystals present in the semithawed product. As I said earlier, I do recommend that if your seafood has thawed completely you *do not refreeze it.* Cook it!

Do you know your shrimp "counts"?

More often than not, the person you buy shrimp from will sell you the product by the "count"—16–20s . . . 43–50s . . . 70–100s. Do you know what that means?

Well, when someone refers to the count of a shrimp, they're actually talking about the *number of shrimp to the pound.* And whether you're a consumer or a novice trawler, you'll need to know how these counts break down into *sizes*.

The National Marine Fisheries Service has established a standard reference for shrimp *sizes* in relation to *counts*. The figures are for the raw, headless product. And while they are not absolutely accurate, if you are familiar with the numbers you can be somewhere in the ball park when it comes to looking at shrimp.

Size	Count (number per lb.)
Extra colossal	1–10
Colossal	10–15
Extra jumbo	16–20
Jumbo	21–25
Extra large	26–30
Large	31–35
Medium Large	36–42
Medium	43–50
Small	51–60
Extra small	61–70
Tiny	Over 70

Note: I recommend you order or buy your shrimp by the count, rather than by a description of the size. What one person refers to as "large" might be "medium" in someone else's judgment.

And examine that sack of oysters before you buy!

Too many folks make a critical mistake when buying oysters by the sack. They believe that just because the oysters are sacked and tied, they can't check the quality. Well, you can—and you most definitely should!

Don't be reluctant to ask the seller to open the sack so you can see the product. If they're too small for your liking, don't buy them. If you want to taste the oysters, ask the seller to go ahead and shuck one for you to eat. If the quality is not what you want, *don't buy them!* After you get home is no time to check the product; do it before you hand over the cash. And don't be embarrassed about being choosy. You deserve the best!

CHAPTER FIVE

Seafood Sauces

Traditional gourmet-style cooking has always involved the use of rich-bodied sauces that complement dishes and enhance their flavors. And just as certain sauces top off beef, veal, and poultry, there are certain sauces that seem to make all the difference in the world when it comes to seafoods.

This chapter, therefore, deals with *seafood sauces*—how to make them, which dishes to use them with, secrets to good blending, and other tips. So whenever a recipe in this book refers to a sauce, turn to this chapter for preparation directions.

But do yourself a favor: Learn to be daring, to be creative. Instead of using the same sauce over and over again, prepare a variety of sauces and use them on your meals. Try derivations from the recipes I've given you; make some *new* sauces. After a while you'll be surprised at how easy it is to come up with tasty concoctions.

Also included in this chapter are *spreads* . . . *dressings* for salads . . . *dips* . . . *gravies* and *rouxs* . . . and a few other items you might find interesting. Learn to use them, too!

Mustard Butter Sauce (Excellent with shrimp or crawfish.)

1 stick butter	½ tsp. garlic salt
4 tbsp. prepared mustard	dash cayenne pepper
2 tsp. lemon juice	

Melt the butter (but don't let it bubble!), then add the remaining ingredients *one at a time,* stirring constantly until smooth. It comes out better if you add the ingredients over low heat. Serve hot.

Note: You can use mustard butter sauce as a seafood dip, or you can bake seafood in the sauce.

Baste for Barbecued Fish (Brush on while fish is cooking.)

---

4 tbsp. olive oil	**1 tsp. Liquid Smoke**
4 tbsp. lemon juice	**½ tsp. basil**
½ tsp. paprika	

Blend all the ingredients together and allow to stand at room temperature for at least 20 minutes so that the flavors mix well.

Note: Right-out-of-the-bottle Italian salad dressing also makes a great baste for barbecued fish.

Basic White Sauce (Pour this over most any seafood dish.)

---

2 tbsp. butter	**¼ tsp. salt**
2 tbsp. flour	**dash of white pepper**
1 cup warm milk	

Melt your butter, but don't let it bubble; use low heat for best results, and keep on stirring. Then gradually add the flour and stir it in well. If you add too much flour at once, it will lump and your sauce won't be smooth. Slowly blend in the warm milk and continue stirring until your sauce reaches the thickness you desire. Just before you take the saucepan off the heat, sprinkle in the salt and white pepper and stir lightly.

Heavy Cream Sauce (Good for seafoods and creamed vegetables.)

All you do is make a basic white sauce (see previous recipe), but instead of using milk substitute *half-and-half cream* or whipping cream. (When using whipping cream, omit the flour.)

Note: This is what you make when you want to create "special sauces." For instance, if you want a cheese sauce, make the basic heavy cream sauce and add grated cheese a little at a time until you get the texture you want. You do the same when adding shrimp (very finely chopped), crabmeat (finely flaked), mushrooms (slivered or minced), hard-boiled egg yolks (minced), etc.

Learn to make a basic heavy cream sauce and then get as creative as you want. You'll do very few things that won't come out right. Just remember to *simmer it slowly* over *low heat*.

Remoulade Sauce (A legendary New Orleans sauce for cold shrimp.)

4 tbsp. Creole mustard
4 tbsp. tarragon vinegar
2 tbsp. catsup
2 tsp. horseradish
2 tsp. paprika
½ cup pure olive oil
2 hard-boiled egg yolks

1 rib celery, finely chopped
2 tbsp. finely chopped green onions
2 tbsp. mayonnaise
¼ tsp. thyme
1 tsp. garlic powder
salt and cayenne pepper to taste

Put all the ingredients in a blender (or use the mixing blade of your food processor) and fold together well. Then place the sauce in your refrigerator and chill for about 2 hours before serving.

Note: This is as close as you'll come to Remoulade sauce, since the original recipe is a closely guarded secret in New Orleans.

Mornay Sauce (Excellent sauce to serve over trout, bass, etc.)

2 tbsp. butter
2 tbsp. flour
1 cup hot milk
¼ tsp. salt

dash white pepper
Plus
½ cup sharp cheddar cheese

Simply make the basic white sauce and then gradually add the cheese, melting it down a little at a time and stirring to keep it smooth. Try this—the taste is superb!

Meunière Sauce (Excellent sauce for trout, shrimp, crabmeat.)

½ cup butter
1 tbsp. finely chopped parsley
1 tbsp. finely chopped green onions
2 tbsp. lemon juice

½ tsp. salt
pinch cayenne pepper
dash Tabasco sauce
dash Worcestershire sauce

Melt the butter over low heat and add the remaining ingredients *in order, and one at a time*. Stir continuously. The secret to meunière is to get it smooth and unseparated!

Italian Gravy (Tomato sauce for basting fish, sautéing shrimp.)

4 tbsp. olive oil	¼ tsp. oregano
1 medium onion, finely chopped	2 bay leaves
1 12-oz. can Contadina tomato paste	¼ tsp. basil
	2 cloves garlic, pressed
2 cans water (use paste cans)	¼ tsp. Italian seasoning

Brown the onions in the olive oil until they become tender, then add the tomato paste and fry it down for about 5 minutes. Next, pour in the water and stir everything together well. Add the remaining ingredients and simmer the sauce on low heat for about 2 hours.

Note: Any recipe calling for Italian gravy can be put together using this basic sauce. This mix can also be used as a basting spread.

French Roux (Forms the base for gumbos, many stews, etc.)

1 cup flour
1 cup Crisco oil

As simple as it sounds, there are cooks who have a difficult time making a roux. Actually, all that's involved is browning flour in oil. But where the problem comes in is in browning to the point just short of burning. Two hints that might help: Preheat the pot before adding the oil so the flour won't stick, and sprinkle the flour into the oil instead of adding it all at once. It is also important that you stir *constantly* and remove the pot from the fire as soon as the flour turns the color you want it.

Note: Usually roux is combined with onions, celery, garlic, and parsley. They form the basis for Louisiana-style seasoning. I take these ingredients one step further and add bell pepper. You might want to consider making a batch of roux to keep in your refrigerator. For instance, instead of 1 cup of flour to 1 cup of oil, fix 5 cups of roux (5 cups oil to 5 cups flour) and store it in a Mason jar. That way, it's ready when you want it!

Louisiana Cocktail Sauce (For dipping shrimp and raw oysters.)

1 cup tomato catsup
1 tbsp. lemon juice
1 tbsp. horseradish
1 tbsp. Worcestershire sauce
¼ cup very finely chopped
  celery

2 tsp. Tabasco sauce
¼ tsp. garlic powder
salt and cayenne pepper to taste

Put all the ingredients simultaneously in a blender or food processor and fold them all together on the "mix" cycle. Then set the sauce in your refrigerator for about 30 minutes to chill before serving.

Hint: For a slightly more unusual flavor, substitute tarragon vinegar for the lemon juice.

Hollandaise Sauce (Exquisite over most seafoods and vegetables.)

4 egg yolks
2 tbsp. lemon juice
¼ tsp. salt

dash white pepper
2 sticks real butter

To make a good hollandaise sauce the old-fashioned way, you need a double boiler and a wooden spoon. Start by "superheating" the water but *not boiling* it—if it's boiling the temperature will be too high and your sauce won't be smooth. After the heat is adjusted properly, break the yolks in the top of the boiler and beat them together with the wooden spoon. Blend in the lemon juice and add the salt and pepper.

Then, a *pat* at a time, start adding the butter and whipping it around with the spoon. You *must* keep the sauce moving constantly or you won't get hollandaise consistency.

It is possible to keep the sauce warm in the double boiler by reducing the fire to simmer. However, if your hollandaise separates into layers, simply add ¼ teaspoon of *boiling water* to the sauce and whip it again until it re-forms.

Note: If all this is too complicated for you, you can always try making the Easy Blender Hollandaise that follows. It's good, too.

Easy Blender Hollandaise Sauce (For hollandaise in a hurry!)

4 egg yolks
¼ tsp. salt
pepper to taste
4 drops Tabasco sauce (optional
  enhancer)

1 tbsp. lemon juice
1 tbsp. water
½ cup melted butter

Break the eggs and drop the yolks into your blender. Get the butter foaming hot (without burning it) in a saucepan.

Remove the top from the blender and add the salt and pepper and Tabasco, if desired, to the yolks. Then, *for about 3 seconds,* whip up the yolks at high speed. Add the lemon and water.

When your butter is ready, turn the blender on again (at *high speed*) and in a thin, steady stream begin adding the hot butter until it's all poured. Immediately remove the sauce from the blender vessel. Note: Blender hollandaise must be used *immediately.*

Shrimp Marinade Bruscato (Excellent precooking marinade for all kinds of shellfish.)

½ cup pure olive oil
4 tbsp. chopped parsley
6 tbsp. freshly squeezed lemon
  juice
3 cloves crushed garlic

2 tsp. salt
1 tsp. dry mustard
½ tsp. white pepper
dash cayenne pepper

In a saucepan, *simmer* all the ingredients together over low heat until they are well blended. Then pour the mix over your shrimp, crabs, crawfish tails, etc. For best results, you should cover the seafood and marinate it in the refrigerator for at least *3 hours.*

To maximize the enhancement effect, seafoods marinated in this mix should be either grilled over charcoal or broiled under the broiling element of your oven. Incidentally, you may save the excess marinade and store it in your refrigerator for future use. It will keep fresh for up to 3 weeks.

Italian Salad Dressing Sauce (An easy-to-prepare sauce for shrimp, crabmeat, or fish.)

---

1 16-oz. bottle Kraft Zesty Italian Salad Dressing
1 tbsp. finely chopped green onions

1 level tsp. flour
2 tsp. grated Parmesan cheese

This topping is exceptionally simple to prepare, yet it adds a gourmet touch to seafoods. All you do is pour the bottle of salad dressing into a saucepan and simmer it gently over low heat until you can no longer detect the aroma of vinegar—it *will* cook out in about 8 to 10 minutes. Then, still on low heat, add the green onions and simmer them until tender. Next add the flour, which should be stirred into the dressing a little at a time so that the sauce comes out smooth. When you are ready to serve the sauce over your seafood, add the cheese and stir it in gently as you carry it to the table. *Don't cook the cheese.*

Italian Salad Dressing Marinade (Really improves the flavor of all seafoods.)

Some of the best Louisiana cooks use bottled Italian salad dressing all by itself—no doctoring necessary—as a marinade. Although you could make your own homemade dressing, I've discovered that you won't quite match the quality of the prepared dressing, with its ingredients perfectly *married* in the mixture. It can be poured over fish fillets, cracked and cooked crabs, crawfish tails, shrimp, etc. Soak the *raw* fish, crawfish, and shrimp in the marinade about 45 minutes before cooking (and try the dressing without added salt and pepper). When cooking crabs, you should lightly boil or steam the cleaned parts before using the dressing as a marinade.

Dishes made with this marinade are hailed as gourmet concoctions, but using it requires little or no extra effort.

Frank's Slivered Shrimp Trout Sauce (This ought to be poured over every piece of fish you ever serve!)

¼ cup water or shrimp stock	2 tbsp. butter
2 cups coarsely chopped raw shrimp	1 oz. Velveeta cheese
½ cup half-and-half	dash marjoram
½ tsp. flour	dash rosemary
	salt and white pepper to taste

Take a saucepan large enough to hold the chopped shrimp and put it on the fire at medium heat. When a drop of water dropped into the pan dances and sizzles on the surface, pour in the water or stock and the chopped shrimp and begin stirring vigorously. When the shrimp pieces turn a uniform pink, gradually add the cream and mix everything together well. Continue stirring and work in the flour a little at a time, until the consistency is smooth. Then remove the pan from the heat.

Put the entire mixture in your food processor (a blender will suffice, but a processor works better). Using the cutting blade, chop up the shrimp pieces until you have nothing but *slivers* showing in the mix. But *don't overchop.*

At this point, pour the sauce paste from the processor back into the saucepan, turn the heat up to *medium,* and begin recooking slowly, stirring all the while. When the mixture begins to steam, add the butter and blend it in. Then add the Velveeta and dissolve it in the mix. Go ahead and sprinkle in the marjoram and rosemary, and season to taste with salt and pepper.

The trick to making this sauce topping is simple: Once you pour the mix back into the pan from the processor jar, *never stop stirring.* If you're cooking the sauce over too high a heat, the mix will thicken too much. Correct this by stirring in extra cream until you get the consistency you desire. Ideally the sauce should come out rich and creamy—*but not pasty!*

I worked weeks to perfect this one—it's super over pan-sautéed trout or broiled shrimp.

GOT SAUCE LEFT OVER?
WANT A NICE TOUCH FOR SNACKS?

You can take my Slivered Shrimp Trout Sauce, pour it back into the food processor, add about a tablespoon of chopped shallots and 3 or 4 tablespoons of creamed cottage cheese, and create one of the tastiest dips you've ever eaten!

Or take the dip, add more cream a little at a time until you get a suitable consistency, heat it up in a chafing dish, and you've got one heck of a fondue!

All the creativity is up to you!

Basic Cajun Sauce (Excellent for casseroling or stewing shrimp, crawfish tails, flaked fish, or picked crabmeat.)

1 tbsp. flour	**4 cups water**
1 tsp. tomato paste	**1 tsp. lemon juice**
3 tbsp. finely chopped onions	**1 tsp. Tabasco sauce**
½ tsp. minced garlic	**½ tsp. crushed bay leaf**
1 stick margarine	**salt and pepper to taste**

Gently fry the flour, tomato paste, onions, and garlic in the stick of margarine until cooked—about *5 minutes*. Then begin adding the water half a cup at a time, stirring continuously to get good blending, and turn the heat up to medium. After all the water is added, you can toss in the remaining ingredients and stir them together. Then reduce the heat to *low* and let the sauce cook for about 15 minutes, *covered*.

When the time comes to add the seafood to the sauce, or the sauce to the seafood—depending upon whether you're going to stew or casserole—*taste your sauce* and make any ingredient corrections you think you want. If you'd like more onions, toss in another teaspoon or so. If you need more salt, or if you want more cayenne, toss those in, too. And when everything is the way you want it, add your seafood or pour the sauce over your seafood.

Hint: If you want to thicken the sauce, stir in half a teaspoon of arrowroot at a time until you get the consistency you want. If you want a thinner sauce, stir in some whole milk. Simple!

Grilled Redfish Sauce (Actually, this is a great sauce not only for redfish but for any fish fillet you cook over an open grill.)

1 cup Italian salad dressing	**1 tsp. minced garlic**
1 tbsp. Liquid Smoke	**1 tbsp. Jack Daniel's black label**
3 tbsp. barbecue sauce with	**whiskey**
onions	**salt to taste**
¼ cup mushroom stems and	
pieces	

This is simple to prepare. All you do is pour all the ingredients into a blender or food processor and whip them around until you have an homogeneous mixture that you can brush over your fish fillets. Then baste with the mix while the fish cooks.

Hint: If you want a spicy taste, add Tabasco or cayenne to taste.

Frank's Homemade Tartar Sauce

Nothing is tastier as a dip for seafoods—all kinds—than a good homemade tartar sauce. Try this one and see if you don't think it gets the job done!

1 cup real mayonnaise	1 tsp. pure horseradish
1 tbsp. prepared mustard	1 tsp. lemon juice
4 gerkin-size sweet pickles	dash thyme
8 pimento-stuffed green olives	dash Worcestershire sauce
2 hard-boiled eggs	dash Tabasco sauce
3 tbsp. chopped white onions	salt to taste˙
1 tbsp. chopped parsley	

In your blender (on "mix") or using the pastry blade of your food processor, combine all the ingredients, turning the machine off only when the consistency is smooth and pasty.

Pack the sauce into a fresh Mason jar, cap it tightly, and store it in the refrigerator for at least 4 hours. Keeps fresh for up to 3 weeks.

My Crescent-City Seafood Sauce

The next time you're fixing grilled shrimp or boiled shrimp and you need a great dippin' sauce, try putting this recipe together. A cross somewhere between the famous Remoulade and Arnaud's sauces, it tastes so good you'll even enjoy spreading it over melba toast and snacking on it! I'm proud of this original.

1 stick margarine, melted	1 tsp. Tabasco sauce
½ cup mayonnaise	2 tbsp. freshly squeezed lemon juice
¼ cup tomato catsup	
4 tbsp. chopped onion (white or yellow)	1½ tsp. salt (more if you like it saltier)
1 tbsp. chopped garlic	1 dash thyme
2 tbsp. Worcestershire sauce	1 hard-boiled egg
1 tsp. liquid crab boil	
3 tbsp. Creole brown mustard (or Dijon)	

All you do is throw everything into your blender and turn it on high speed, letting it run until the texture is smooth and uniform. Then spoon the sauce out into a bowl, cover it with Saran Wrap, and chill it in the refrigerator for a couple of hours.

When you're ready to eat, just dip fried shrimp, boiled shrimp, fried oysters—whatever—into the sauce, and enjoy! (The sauce also keeps well in the refrigerator for about 3 weeks.)

EASY CANNED SOUP SAUCES

Thanks to the Campbell Soup Company and the manufacturers of food processors, you can now make a vast array of seafood sauces and sauce concoctions with just a little doctoring up! With the right ingredients added in the right proportions, they come out pretty good, too.

For that reason, I recommend that all seafood lovers stock their pantry shelves with such products as cream of chicken soup, cream of mushroom soup, cream of shrimp soup, and cream of onion soup. As bases for baking, broiling, poaching, and marinating, they lend considerable flavor to just about every type of seafood.

But don't be satisfied with the familiar "dump-and-cook" practice many folks are guilty of. Use the soups as *bases*, and learn to stir in a sizable helping of creative flair!

For instance, in everything but the cream of onion soup, go ahead and chop up some onions or bell peppers and simmer them down in the soup base. Add other enhancers as well: fresh minced garlic, a dash of thyme, some green onion, a sprinkling of basil or oregano, several pats of butter, a tablespoon or two of white wine, some crumbled bacon or black olives, a few pinches of fresh parsley, a half-cup of grated cheddar cheese, or a little Romano. Let your taste buds be your guide—and learn to cook *by taste instead of by recipe*.

It's relatively easy to do, and you'll be surprised how little time it takes to master the technique. You simply cook everything *one step at a time*. For example, the next time you prepare a sauce don't toss in all the ingredients at once. Go *ingredient by ingredient*. And after each one is added, simmer it into the mix for about 3 minutes, then *taste it*. Try to memorize the flavor. Try to discern what flavor changes the ingredient produced in the mix—made it *salty*, made it *peppery,* made it *nutty*, made it *sweet*, made it *tart*, etc. Once you learn to do this (and it only takes about a half-dozen taste tests), you'll be quite good at tasting a finished dish and determining immediately what seasoning is lacking.

I also recommend you study the chapter on seasonings in this book and learn to use new herbs and spices. I emphasize the word *study:* don't just read the chapter, *study it!* Commit the herbs and spices and their uses to memory, and experiment with them in new dishes. Use the same sampling technique I've just described—stir in the herbs or spices one at a time and taste the flavoring after each addition. Most folks let seasonings scare them; you shouldn't! And you won't ever overseason if you add your ingredients *a quarter teaspoon* at a time.

Sample Soup-Base Sauces

To 1 10¾-oz. can cream of shrimp soup, add:

½ tsp. flour
3 tbsp. finely chopped celery
1 tsp. finely chopped garlic
½ tsp. coarsely chopped green
    onions

½ cup whole milk
2 tbsp. butter
salt and white pepper to taste

Simmer all the ingredients together (do not add water to the soup) and pour the mixture over your favorite seafood. Or cook your favorite seafood in the mixture, either in a saucepan or a casserole.

To 1 10¾-oz. can cream of mushroom soup, add:

1 tbsp. minced bacon, crisply
    fried
2 tbsp. finely chopped white
    onions
2 tbsp. butter
¼ tsp. very finely chopped
    parsley

2 Velveeta cheese slices
½ cup whole milk
¼ tsp. thyme
1 tbsp. white wine

Simmer all the ingredients together (do not add water to the soup) and use the sauce as a baste over your favorite seafood. Or cook your favorite seafood in the mixture, either in a saucepan or baked in the oven.

CHAPTER SIX

Fish
Species and Recipes

The approach taken in this book to the various species of fish (and the recipes in which they are featured) is unique: as far as I know, it has never been used before. But it is also a very simple format, and I am certain it will open a whole new world of fish cookery to persons seeking exciting new ideas.

Just about everyone has heard of "Trout Amandine." But what about "Croaker Amandine"? Or "Snapper Amandine"? Or "Bass Amandine"?

You've no doubt tried "Redfish Courtbouillon." It has become a standard Deep South delicacy. But have you eaten "Catfish Courtbouillon"? Or "Sheepshead Courtbouillon"? Or "Channel Mullet Courtbouillon"?

I'll bet that at some time during your kitchen experiences you've prepared "Baked Snapper in Crabmeat Sauce," huh? But why haven't you fixed "Baked Drum"? Or "Baked Crappie"? Or "Baked Walleye"?

Are you beginning to get my drift? All I'm saying is that because of effective culinary promotions, semantic traps, indoctrination by restaurateurs, and just plain lack of perspective, we've been conditioned to think that only trout should be put into a meunière or an amandine! That only redfish deserves to be baked or broiled! That it's a mortal sin if you do anything to largemouth bass other than deep fry it!

I'm here to tell you that the first thing you should learn is that *all fish* (with the exception of a few listed later in this chapter) can be prepared in all the so-called standard—and succulent!—ways familiar to gourmets. And if you don't fix them *all*, you're severely limiting your creativity as a cook, you're missing out on a lot of seafood flavors, and you're spending a lot of money on specific species when you could be using substitutes instead.

So this book *will not* list several hundred pages' worth of arranged-by-species fish recipes. Sure, there will be some I'll want to go into in detail because of methodology. But, generally, you will find *standards:* an amandine . . . a courtbouillon . . . a meunière . . . plus more frying, baking, pan-sautéing, broiling, grilling, and barbecuing instructions.

Then you can use those instructions and directions and apply them to any fish that fits the recipe criteria and suits your taste.

God made thousands of species of freshwater and saltwater fish, and, with the exception of a very few that are poor in food quality, they are all high in protein, low in fat and cholesterol, and rich in taste. Don't limit your culinary efforts to trout, flounder, redfish, and bass!

TABLE FISH CHECKLIST

The following listing gives the names of the edible fish found throughout the United States, rates their value as table fare, and suggests proper preparation techniques.

As a general rule of thumb, fish are classified as lean, slightly oily, medium oily, and oily. Lean to slightly oily fish can usually be fried satisfactorily. But those in the medium oily to oily category usually don't lend themselves well to frying. Of course, that's a rule of thumb, and it doesn't always apply. For example, even though the smelt is classified as an oily fish, it does fry quite well and imparts a sweet taste rather than the heavy, greasy taste of a fried tuna.

For that reason, I have taken pains in this section to avoid generalities and to be specific about each species and its preparation. You should refer to this list whenever you're in doubt as to how to fix a particular species, or when you're planning to substitute one species for another in a particular recipe.

● **African Pompano:** Very good eating, but because of the high oil content the fish should be grilled, broiled, poached, smoked, or baked. I do not recommend frying.

● **Albacore:** Most valuable of tunas because of its white meat. Albacores "can" well, but they are also delicious baked, broiled, grilled, smoked, or poached for use in salads. Medium oily, so not ideal for frying or sautéing.

● **Alligator Gar:** A slightly oily fish with a soft flesh texture that is often coarse. Does not bake, grill, or broil well. I recommend you poach the fish slightly, form the ground meat into patties, and deep fry or pan-sauté. **Do not eat gar roe—it is toxic.**

● **American Eel:** Probably the oiliest fish in the ocean. People do occasionally grill or fry eels, but I suggest you use them to make jellied fish or smoked eel and nothing else.

● **American Grayling:** Excellent fish with firm, white, delicate meat. Classified as medium oily, it's good fixed any style, including poached or in a courtbouillon.

● **Arctic Char:** Another excellent fish with yellow-white to fiery red meat, depending upon where it is caught. Generally regarded as a delicacy, it is best when smoked, grilled, or broiled. Does not lend itself well to frying.

● **Atlantic Cod:** A lean fish, excellent prepared any style. Filleted and whole fish can be fried, baked, broiled, grilled, poached, and sautéed.

● **Atlantic Croaker:** Lean to slightly oily, depending upon where caught, these fish lend themselves to almost any kind of preparation; the meat is firm, white, and flaky. They fry exceptionally well.

● **Atlantic Halibut:** Medium to lean, they are excellent fixed any style. The best ones are those under 20 pounds.

● **Atlantic Herring:** All herring are oily fish (in fact, they are classified as very oily by most experts). They are best smoked or slow-grilled. Do not fry them or cook them in sauces.

● **Atlantic Manta Ray:** Definitely edible, although usually not eaten. The young fish are tender and flaky and can be fixed broiled, grilled, baked, or deep fried. The larger ones are generally tough and stringy, and are good only when slow-grilled or smoked.

● **Atlantic Permit:** Related to the pompano, and classified as a medium-oily fish. Good flavor, but I would recommend you grill or smoke the larger ones, and broil or bake the smaller ones. Do not fry permit.

● **Atlantic Sailfish:** Oily and only fair as a table food. I suggest you smoke sailfish; the meat is tough fixed any other way.

● **Atlantic Salmon:** Oily, but a gourmet treat nevertheless. Can be canned, smoked, grilled, or broiled on a rack. Only the very young fish can be fried satisfactorily.

● **Atlantic Spadefish:** Oily, but excellent in flavor. Bake, grill, broil, or smoke.

● **Atlantic Tomcod:** Excellent table fish fixed any style. Low to medium in oil content.

● **Atlantic Wolffish:** Medium oily. Very good when steaked and grilled, but also delicious when marinated and smoked. Does not fry well.

● **Barjack (Skip):** Firm, white meat, but rather high in oil content. Best smoked or grilled.

● **Barn-Door Skate:** Member of the ray family. Lean in oil content. Good poached, sautéed, broiled, grilled, and smoked, but can also be chunked and deep fried like scallops.

● **Bigmouth Buffalo:** A medium-oily fish with white flesh and delicate flavor. When fried, it usually comes out dry and cottony. But when baked, broiled, or poached in stock, it's delicious. Also a very good smoking fish.

● **Big Skate:** Another ray with delicate meat. Best cooking methods are poaching and deep frying the "wing" chunks to resemble scallops. Usually low in oil content.

● **Billfish:** This group includes the sails, marlins, spearfish, and swordfish. All are high in oil content and best when smoked or grilled. Many species can also be used for sashimi (raw fish), and some do grill, broil, and bake well. See the individual species listings for specific details.

- **Black Bass:** Lean fish that can be prepared any style. Excellent flavor.
- **Black Bullhead Catfish:** Lean to medium oily, depending where caught, but exceptionally well suited to practically any kind of preparation. When the meat is yellow, grill or broil it; when the meat is white, deep fry or pan-sauté it.
- **Black Crappie:** Medium-lean fish that lends itself to any style of preparation. Called *sacalait* ("sack of milk") in Louisiana, named for the succulent, white, flaky flesh. Outstanding panfried.
- **Black Drum:** Small ones are excellent in flavor and texture; larger ones are often infested with parasitic worms (which are harmless if eaten) and very coarse and tough. Drum up to 10 pounds can be prepared any style. Medium oily.
- **Blackfin Tuna:** Very oily, but excellent flavor. Best when smoked, grilled, or poached. Do not fry.
- **Blackfish (Tripletail):** Medium oily, but makes excellent eating any style. Best when baked, broiled, or pit-grilled. To fry, cut into finger steaks.
- **Black Grouper:** Low oil content, excellent panfried, deep fried, grilled, baked, or fixed any style. A truly succulent table fish.
- **Black Marlin:** Medium oily, fine white meat, excellent steaked and deep fried, poached, broiled, grilled, or baked. Makes good sashimi.
- **Black Perch:** Low to medium oil content. Fair flavor. Can be fixed any style.
- **Black Rockfish:** Fair eating, but soft meat. Do not allow to stand unrefrigerated for any length of time; it's very oily and will turn rancid in a hurry. I recommend only smoking or pit-grilling.
- **Black Sea Bass:** Excellent, white, firm, and delicate flesh. Lean to medium oil content. Fix any style.
- **Black Skipjack:** Very strong-tasting because of the ultrahigh oil content. The meat is dark red. Good only smoked. I don't eat these, period.
- **Black Snapper:** Like all snappers, has low oil content. Fix any style. Excellent flavor.
- **Black Snook:** Oily tissue is just under the skin pads; remove the skin before preparing. I suggest you limit preparation to baking or broiling.
- **Blue Catfish:** Medium oily, but excellent any style. Exceptionally good in courtbouillon.
- **Bluefin Tuna:** Oily fish that tastes best when grilled, broiled, or smoked. This is the best tuna for boiling in seasonings and flaking for salad. Do not fry.
- **Bluefish:** Either excellent or terrible, depending on where it's caught. Southern fish have a strong oily taste; nothern-caught fish are mild, delicately flavored, and excellent prepared any style. Most southerners do not eat bluefish. I suggest you bake, broil, or grill them.

- **Bluegill:** Succulent medium-oily panfish, excellent any style. Super when coated in light cornmeal and panfried.
- **Blue Marlin:** An oily billfish, but has excellent flavor when baked, broiled, grilled, or smoked. This species also makes good sashimi. It can be chunked and deep fried, but the flavor is only fair.
- **Bluestriped Grunt:** Excellent any style. The meat is white and firm, with medium oil content, highly prized throughout Florida. Very good panfried.
- **Bonefish:** Lots of bones, but worth the trouble. The meat is firm, white, and nutlike in flavor. Even the roe is excellent. I suggest you marinate bonefish in lemon and bake in foil; to do anything else would be a sin!
- **Brook Trout:** Excellent table fish. Medium oil content. Flesh varies in color from white to orange, depending on the habitat; the more orange the color the higher the oil content. Still, brook trout can be prepared any style.
- **Brown Bullhead:** Medium oil content, but good fixed any style. The absolute best way to prepare this fish is to fillet it, dip it in heavy batter, and deep fry, but other methods are also delicious.
- **Butterfish:** Very oily. Should only be smoked or pit-grilled. Do not fry.
- **Cabezone:** Very popular along the Pacific coastline, with a fair-to-good flavor rating. I recommend you do not fry cabezone, but rather broil, bake, poach, or grill it. **Do not eat the roe—it's toxic!**
- **Caesar Grunt:** Very good, lean fish that can be fixed any style. Best pan-sautéed with sliced onions.
- **California Halibut:** Low-oil table fish, excellent any style.
- **California Skate:** The "wings" of this ray are best when poached in a stock, but they can also be chunked and deep fried. I don't recommend broiling or baking.
- **California Grunion:** These famous little fish should be deep fried, even though they are high in oil content. The meat is sweet and delicate. Also excellent smoked and grilled.
- **California Yellowtail:** Good taste, rather high in oil content. Best when smoked, grilled, or broiled. Also a good fish for canning. I do not recommend frying.
- **Carp:** Very good for smoking because of the oil content, but the dark meat along the bloodline should be removed, since it imparts an unappetizing flavor if it is cooked with the fillets. Do not fry carp—they become dry and cottony.
- **Chain Pickerel:** Medium-oily fish that has a good taste when prepared properly. The Y-shaped bones that run down both fillets are difficult to remove, so the best method of dealing with them is to cut crosshatches down the fillets, deep fry them very crisply, and eat them, bones and all. Suitable only for frying.
- **Channel Catfish:** Excellent, medium-oily fish, good any style. Super in courtbouillon.

● **Chum Salmon:** Very high oil content, so ideally suited for smoking. In fact, I suggest you use this fish only for smoking or grilling. Do not fry.

● **Cobia (Ling):** One of the finest saltwater fish you can put on your table. It is commonly referred to as "lemonfish," because it has a lemony flavor. Medium-low oil content. Can be prepared any style.

● **Cod:** Very fine-grained, flaky, white meat that is low in oil content. Good any style, including fried, baked, broiled, poached, and caked for patties.

● **Coho Salmon:** Medium-oily fish that is excellent prepared in just about any style. This is one salmon that can even be steaked in "fingers" and panfried because its fat is sweet and light. But nothing beats smoked coho!

● **Corvina:** Related to the weakfishes, so can be prepared any style because of the medium oil content. A great substitute for speckled trout when preparing the popular fish-with-sauce recipes.

● **Cottonwick Grunt:** A good eating fish that can be fixed any style. Because of the medium oil content, it fries up flaky and light and also smokes delicately.

● **Cunner:** Excellent table fish served any style. Medium-low oil content. Delicious panfried.

● **Curlfin Sole:** Like all the flounders and flatfishes, this sole is excellent both in flavor and texture. The meat is white and can be fixed any style. Low oil content.

● **Cutthroat Trout:** Excellent any style. Medium oil content. But this is also one of the trout that hot-smokes really well, and one you can wrap in foil and bake to succulence.

● **Diamond Turbot:** One of the only flounder-flatfishes that does not fry well, because of the unusually high oil content. I suggest you limit your diamond turbot cookery to smoking. The taste any other way is, at best, only fair.

● **Dolly Varden Char:** An oily fish with pink to red meat. I recommend you do not fry it, but it is superb when baked, broiled, grilled, or smoked. Smoked char provides one of the best tastes you can find anywhere.

● **Dolphin:** The fish—not the mammal—is excellent prepared any style. It can be fried or smoked because of the medium oil content, and it comes out extremely appetizing almost any way. One recommendation: To preserve the quality, use lots of ice on your dolphins once you get them out of the water.

● **Dover Sole:** Despite the slimy covering, they are excellent flatfish with medium oil content, which means you can fix them any style. Stuffed with crabmeat and baked is my favorite way.

● **Flathead Catfish:** Also known in Louisiana as the "Opelousas" and "Tabby" cat, this is one of the best eating catfish you'll find. It has a medium to high oil content, but the oils are sweet. Can be fixed any style, but is best "fingered" and deep fried or baked in tomato sauce.

- **Flathead Chub:** A fair-tasting food fish with a high oil content. I suggest you grill or smoke it for best results; any other cooking yields unimpressive results.
- **Flier Sunfish:** A low-oil bream with excellent flavor. Don't do anything but panfry this little critter!
- **Florida Largemouth:** Slightly oily bass. Superb any style.
- **Florida Pompano:** High-oil fish that is best when broiled, grilled, or smoked. Do not fry pompano!
- **Flounder:** Excellent any style, but stuffed with crabmeat and baked or broiled it's a taste treat with few equals. Medium-low oil content.
- **Freshwater Drum:** Commonly known in Louisiana as the gaspergou, this fish has commercial value but isn't that great as gourmet table fare. Medium to low in oil content, it tends to dry out when cooked unless it's prepared in a stock of some kind. Do not fry this fish—it gets tough and cottony. I suggest you poach it.
- **Gafftop Catfish:** While many persons discard these fish because of their slimy covering, they are excellent prepared any style, especially after the lateral bloodline is removed. The meat is white, tender, and flaky, with a medium oil content. Gafftops can be succulent treats when fried or chunked for courtbouillon.
- **Golden-Eye:** With its high oil content, this fish is important commercially, but not appealing to most seafood cooks because it is soft-textured and unattractive. It is best smoked, and I do not suggest you fix it any other way.
- **Golden Trout:** Considered a prime table fish. The meat is medium oily, firm, white, and fine-grained. These fish can be fixed any style, but most experts agree that grilling, broiling, or hot-smoking are the tastiest methods of preparation.
- **Gray Snapper:** Low in oil content and excellent panfried when small. Larger ones can be steaked and deep fried, baked, grilled, broiled, poached, or fixed any style. Excellent flavor.
- **Greater Amberjack:** Edible, but certainly not among the best of table fishes. Be certain to check with fishermen in your region before eating the greater amberjack; in certain waters it has been credited with causing ciguatera (nerve poisoning) in humans. Usually those caught in Louisiana are not suspect. I suggest that if you eat amberjacks you grill, broil, or smoke them. The fish is medium oily, the flesh is rather coarse, and the larger ones are usually wormy. But their flavor is fair.
- **Green Jack:** Fair eating, but coarse flesh. I suggest you grill, broil, or smoke these fish. They are medium high in oil content.
- **Green Sunfish:** Excellent any style, highly prized in the western United

States. Medium-low oil content, which makes them tasty panfried as well as prepared any other way.

● **Grouper:** Medium low in oil content, all groupers are excellent served any style. Their meat is very flaky, firm-textured, and ultrawhite.

● **Haddock:** Low in oil content, haddock are excellent just about any way you fix them. While they are best cold-smoked, they are members of the cod family and can be steaked and fried, baked, broiled, poached, grilled, and microwaved. Smoked or salted and marketed under the name "Finnan Haddie," which commands top price on the commercial market.

● **Halibut:** Excellent table fish with succulent, tender, flaky flesh. All species can be fixed any style because of the low oil content.

● **Hickory Shad:** Fair quality with medium oil content. Best only when pickled or smoked. I do not recommend you broil, bake, or fry hickory shad.

● **Hogchoker:** A small fish, but with excellent flavor. Like most flounder types it is suited to filleting, frying, baking, broiling, and other methods of preparation. Oil content is low to medium.

● **Jewfish:** The largest of the groupers, it is excellent any size and prepared any style. The meat is usually white, flaky, and medium low in oil content. I can't think of a single method of fish cookery that couldn't be successfully applied to jewfish.

● **Jolthead Porgy:** Excellent taste and firm meat, moist, and white. Medium oil content makes the fillets ideal for panfrying, broiling, baking, grilling, smoking, and poaching. But the best taste results from slow-grilling over charcoal.

● **King Mackerel:** Extra-oily fish that is excellent when open-grilled, broiled, or smoked, but does not fry well. The meat tends to be slightly gray in color, but it is firm, and it does cook well over a charcoal fire. Mackerel can either be filleted or steaked. It should be refrigerated quickly after removal from the water so that it doesn't spoil.

● **Kokanee:** A very oily fish that is good principally when smoked. Because of the mushy texture of the meat, I suggest you ice the fish immediately upon removing it from the water. Not recommended for frying, baking, or broiling.

● **Lake Trout:** Extremely oily; should be cooked over a grill, barbecued with stock, or smoked. The meat of the lake trout spoils easily, so it should be kept refrigerated until you're ready to cook it. Do not fry.

● **Lake Whitefish:** An excellent fish for hickory smoking; in demand all over the world. It has a medium oil content and is also delicious when broiled or baked. Frying is not recommended.

● **Lane Snapper:** One of the best-tasting fish in the snapper family. The low oil content makes it suitable for any kind of preparation. I especially recommend you fry the "cheeks" and the "throat" sections of the lane snapper.

- **Largemouth Bass:** Low to medium oil content makes this fish ideally suited to any style of preparation. It is best filleted and panfried.
- **Little Snook:** The skin tissue is very oily, even though the flesh is only medium oily. For best results, remove all the skin prior to cooking. The best way to fix it is baking, broiling, or poaching in stock.
- **Longfin Smelt:** Even though it is slightly oily, the smelt is one of those fish that defies the rules of thumb. It can be fixed any style and is quite delicate in flavor when pan-sautéed.
- **Lookdown:** Usually frowned upon by most anglers as trash fish, the lookdown has outstanding flavor when filleted. I've fixed it in every conceivable manner, and have yet to find one that isn't delicious. It is slightly oily.
- **Mako Shark:** Almost a delicacy in fishing circles, this shark is excellent in flavor and texture. Try it any style. It is similar in texture to swordfish, and the oil content is low.
- **Mountain Whitefish:** Very good, especially in winter. You can fix this medium-oily fish any style and still have a delicate, subtle dish. All accounts, however, indicate that the best method of preparation is poaching in wine or smoking over hickory chips.
- **Mullet:** An overlooked and underutilized species that can furnish a source of iodine nearly 1,000 times greater than the best cut of beef, to say nothing of the richness of the mineral content. Depending upon the species, mullet can be either oily or lean. But regardless of oil content, it can be fixed any style. And smoked mullet is a superb taste treat. Incidentally, even the roe is classified as gourmet eating.
- **Muskellunge:** Fair to good eating, especially when baked or broiled in lemon butter. Oil content is medium to slightly high. I do not recommend frying muskies—unless they're baked on a rack or broiled, they are generally rated as poor table fish.
- **Mutton Snapper:** One of the best saltwater fish you can eat! The meat is firm, white, ideal for baking or broiling, and can be delicately deep fried in chunks or fingers (especially the cheeks and throat). The bones and skin make an excellent fish stock. Oil content is low. Prepare any style.
- **Nassau Grouper:** An excellent food fish, but only once the skin is removed—grouper skin has a strong taste in the Nassau species. The fillets are firm and white, and the fish can be prepared any style. Medium low in oil content.
- **Northern Pike:** Fair in food value, medium in oil content, and suitable for preparation any style. I suggest grilling, broiling, or baking for best results.
- **Northern Puffer:** The flesh is good, but the skin and the roe are *toxic*. I would fry or broil this fish for best results, but *be sure you make certain it has been cleaned properly*. Oil content is low to medium.

- **Northern Redhorse:** A sucker fish, this species is the best-tasting of the lot. Very oily, it is outstanding smoked over hickory or pecan. It is also delicious slow-grilled over an open pit. I do not suggest you fry the redhorse.

- **Northern Sennet:** Excellent any style, but best when broiled or grilled. It also smokes well because of the medium-high oil content. If you fry it, be sure you fry hot and quick! Related to the barracuda, but rarely toxic.

- **Northern Squawfish:** Very bony, but good when smoked. I do not suggest you fix it any other way. Very oily.

- **Nurse Shark:** The flesh is extremely tasty and the fins are regarded as a delicacy for shark-fin soup. Can be fixed any style. Medium oil content. Slightly dry when fried.

- **Ocean Perch:** Very commercial species with a strong fishy flavor, but good for baking, broiling, and grilling. Also fairly good smoked. I do not suggest you fry the fresh fillets because of the high oil content.

- **Ocean Sunfish:** Edible, but very oily and good only smoked.

- **Opaleye:** Fair to good food fish, but because of the texture and the oil content I suggest you only bake, broil, or grill this species. It tends to be rubbery when fried.

- **Pacific Amberjack:** Fair as a food fish. Larger species tend to be tough and coarse. I suggest you do not fry this fish, but rather bake or poach it in a courtbouillon. I would also marinate it in milk prior to cooking to remove some of the oils from the meat.

- **Pacific Barracuda:** Not like the other 'cudas! This one is rarely suspected of carrying ciguatera (nerve poisoning). It can be steaked, fried, filleted, baked, broiled, grilled, poached, smoked, etc. Flavor is excellent. The roe is highly esteemed.

- **Pacific Cod:** A fish with low oil content, suitable for baking, broiling, grilling, poaching, and panfrying in filleted form. And even though the oils are absent, the cod is one species that is superb when smoked, primarily because of the flaky meat texture.

- **Pacific Halibut:** Excellent any style, but best baked in butter, lemon, and garlic. Oil content is low.

- **Pacific Herring:** High oil content, but good for canning and smoking. The fish also responds well to slow-grilling and broiling.

- **Pacific Jack Mackerel:** Good only smoked or grilled in fillets. Much too oily for any other kind of preparation.

- **Pacific Ocean Perch:** Good grilled or broiled, but has a very "fishy" taste. Remove all the skin before you cook. Not at all good fried if you prefer delicate, subtle flavors. The smoked product is fair, but rather chewy. High oil content.

- **Pacific Permit:** Excellent, though slightly oily. For that reason, instead of frying this fish, prepare it broiled, grilled, or smoked. You might also try it en papillote (baked in a paper bag).

- **Pacific Sailfish:** Excellent when smoked, but generally tends to be too tough for other methods of preparation.
- **Pacific Sand Dab:** Like the other flatfishes, it is low in oil content and can be fixed practically any style. The best way is to split down the dorsal, stuff with lump crabmeat, and broil.
- **Pacific Tomcod:** Good virtually any style. Medium oil content. Suited to frying, baking, broiling, poaching, grilling, etc. I like this fish best smoked.
- **Paddlefish:** Extremely oily, but one of the best fish you can find for smoking. Flesh texture is ideal and the oils are sweet. The absence of bones in the fillets also makes it ideal for feeding to children and elderly people.
- **Pinfish:** Edible, but not very good quality. Best prepared panfried or broiled in lemon butter. Medium oil content.
- **Pink Salmon:** Superb. Best when smoked, but also delectable in salads after poaching. When available in fresh fillets, can be prepared any style in spite of the high oil content.
- **Pollock:** Low to medium oil content makes this fish suitable for any style of preparation. Fillet for frying, steak for grilling and broiling, and chunk or leave whole for smoking. Fresh pollock can also be used for specialty baked fish dishes.
- **Pompano:** One of the most exquisite fish ever to swim in saltwater. High in oil content, the pompano should not be fried, but it is outstanding when baked, broiled, grilled, poached, microwaved, and smoked. One of Louisiana's most acclaimed dishes is Pompano en Papillote (pompano baked in a parchment bag). Superb!
- **Pompano Dolphin:** Excellent food fish. Firm, white, flaky meat. Medium oil content makes it good any style, but when smoked it's a delicacy.
- **Porbeagle Shark:** Oily flesh, but good smoked or grilled. The texture resembles that of swordfish. I don't recommend that you fry this shark.
- **Porcupine Fish:** This little critter is hard to clean and its internal organs have been reported to be poisonous at times. But the skinned fillets, properly cleaned, are said to be delicious. Lean in oil content, they are best panfried or broiled in butter.
- **Porkfish:** Good any style, but best baked, grilled, or broiled. Medium oil content.
- **Pumpkinseed:** A great-tasting perch that can be fixed any style but is excellent dusted in cornmeal and panfried to light crispness. The meat is white, delicately flavored, and flaky.
- **Queen Angelfish:** Lean to medium in oil content, suitable for most forms of preparation. The experts say, however, that it is best panfried.

• **Queen Triggerfish:** Excellent, firm, white meat similar to frog legs in texture. It can be fixed any style, since the oil content is low. Triggerfish also makes good sashimi. Always remove the skin before cooking.

• **Rainbow Runner:** Excellent quality fish, medium in oil content. Can be fixed any style; makes a good sashimi. Gently dusted in flour, sautéed, and smothered in a cream sauce, rainbow runner is the star of a much-acclaimed dish.

• **Rainbow Smelt:** Medium to high in oil content, but like the other smelts can be fried as well as smoked. The best way to fix this fish is to smoke it over hickory chips. Do keep in mind that the flesh is rather soft and will spoil quickly if left unrefrigerated.

• **Rainbow Trout:** Excellent any style. The cream-colored flesh is delicately flavored and sweet-tasting. Medium to slightly oily, but the fish fries rather well.

• **Redbreast Sunfish:** Like all the other bream, this one is low in oil content and can be fixed any style. The best preparation, though, is coating it lightly with cornmeal and panfrying to a golden-brown crispness.

• **Red Drum:** The second most popular fish along the Louisiana-Mississippi-Texas coastline, the red drum is more commonly called the "redfish." It can be fixed any style—filleted and fried, grilled, smoked, or baked. The larger species, called "bull reds," are usually coarse and tough, but the smaller fish—up to about 10 pounds—are prized for the table.

• **Redear Perch:** Excellent any style, but usually prepared panfried. Lean, white, flaky meat.

• **Redeye Bass:** Good quality, similar in taste and texture to largemouth bass. Can be prepared any style, but most are filleted and fried or broiled with lemon butter.

• **Redfin Pickerel:** Like the other pikes, it is very bony, but the flavor is good and it's worth the trouble to clean the fish. Best way to eliminate the Y bones that run down the fillets is to crosshatch the meat and fry super-crisp, so that you can eat the bones and all. I do not recommend any preparation other than frying.

• **Red Grouper:** Excellent quality meat. Medium-low oil content. All groupers can be fixed any style, but the best method is usually steaking and broiling. The red grouper is also very tasty when smoked. The meat is firm and white, and it "fingers" well.

• **Red Hind:** Excellent table fish in the grouper family. Because of the small panfish size and the medium-low oil content, it can be prepared any style.

• **Red Snapper:** One of the most popular saltwater fish. Its medium-low oil content makes it excellent any style. Don't forget to fry the cheeks and the throat.

• **Rock Bass:** Medium oil content. Very good, tasty fish for panfrying and broiling in lemon butter. Can be fixed any style. Louisianians call these "goggle-eyes."

• **Rockfish:** Excellent quality meat. Firm, white, very flaky when cooked. Low-oil fish that's good fixed any style.

• **Rock Hind:** Another member of the grouper family, which means you can fix it any style. Very white meat, low in oil content.

• **Roosterfish:** While not common as a table fish, it is of excellent quality, has a medium oil content, and can be fixed any style.

• **Rubberlip Sea-Perch:** This is the best-tasting fish in the sea-perch family. Medium oil content; good fixed any style. The best method is to fillet and broil or grill with lemon butter or white wine.

• **Sablefish:** One of the best smoking fish you can get because of the high oil content. And that is all I'd recommend you do to this species—*smoke only*. Do not fry, bake, or broil.

• **Sacalait:** The Louisiana name for both the white and black crappie. It is excellent any style, but is usually rolled in cornmeal and panfried. Oil content is low.

• **Sailfish:** Very high oil content, so I suggest you smoke sailfish rather than fry or bake it. The only exception is pit-grilling—it comes out well over charcoal. The meat is very firm.

• **Sailor's-Choice:** Very tasty, medium-oily fish that can be prepared any style.

• **Salmon:** Excellent when fresh-smoked, grilled, broiled, or baked. It can also be poached in a courtbouillon for salads. I do not recommend you fry salmon, because of the high oil content.

• **Sand Sea Trout:** Also called "white trout" in Louisiana, this slightly oily fish is often discarded as trash because the meat has a tendency to be softer than its speckled cousin. But it is very tasty when prepared any style. It must be iced as soon as it is taken from the water to keep the meat from turning mushy.

• **Sauger:** Similar to walleye, so good any style. The smaller fish can be panfried, and the larger ones are excellent when broiled or grilled. Medium oil content.

• **Scamp:** A member of the grouper family, which means you can fix it any style. Very tasty white meat that can be fried in "fingers," steaked and grilled, filleted and baked, or poached in stock. Oil content is low.

• **Schoolmaster:** Excellent quality. A member of the snapper family, thus suitable for any style of preparation. Rarely gets over five pounds. Medium-lean.

• **Scup:** In the northeast states this fish is prized for smoking and jelling. But in the Gulf of Mexico area it is generally considered a trash fish and used only in the fishmeal industry. Very oily.

● **Sea Robin:** Rarely eaten, but quite tasty. Usually taken during shrimp trawling. The fish are medium oily but can be fixed any style. Should be filleted to remove the oil pads in the skin. Delicate flavor.

● **Sea Trout:** This is the famous "speckled trout" of Louisiana, which really isn't a trout at all, but a member of the croaker family. It is low in oil content, very flaky, white, and fine-textured. Fix any style, but remember to keep this fish well iced since it will spoil quickly once removed from the water.

● **Sheepshead:** One of the most underutilized species that swims. Most folks don't bother with these fish because they are difficult to clean, but the meat is white, extra flaky, tender, and delicately flavored. Oil content is medium and the sheepshead can be fixed any style, including poached in seasoned water and served as "mock crabmeat."

● **Shellcracker:** A common name for the redear bream. Very delicately flavored, white, flaky meat. Fix any style. Low oil content. Quality is excellent.

● **Shortbill Spearfish:** Excellent and highly prized. Best prepared smoked, but delicious, too, when grilled or baked. Some cooks like it steaked, cut into fingers, and deep fried in a batter. Unlike many other billfish, this one is only slightly oily.

● **Shortnose Gar:** Not good for anything but flaked for gar balls (boulettes). Very soft meat. Spoils quickly. Medium oily. Texture tough and stringy. **Do not eat the roe—it's toxic.**

● **Sierra:** A member of the Spanish mackerel family, this fish is very oily and lends itself only to smoking. Grilled steaks turn out only fair, and any other style is less than appetizing.

● **Silk Snapper:** Like the other snappers, very good quality flesh that can be prepared any style. Oil content is low. Often marketed as red snapper.

● **Silver Hake:** A soft-textured fish similar to white trout, this species should be chilled immediately upon removal from the water to keep the quality high. Oil content is low, so it can be fixed any style while fresh. Can be preserved well in the freezer.

● **Silver Sea Trout:** Another soft-flesh fish similar to white trout; spoils easily and can't be preserved well in the freezer. Usually small in size (rarely over a pound), they panfry well. The taste is good, although the texture is sometimes too flaky. Oil content is low.

● **Skate:** Underutilized species rather low in fat content. The "wings" are excellent and resemble scallops. They are very good poached, baked, or deep fried in a heavy batter. I do not recommend you broil or grill them.

● **Sleeper:** Fair quality as food fish. Most experts agree that this medium-oily fish should be broiled or baked instead of fried, primarily because of the flavor of the meat.

- **Smallmouth Bass:** Excellent! Can be prepared any style, but best rolled in cornmeal and panfried. Oil content is medium.
- **Smallmouth Buffalo:** One of the best buffalo species in the water. The meat is white, flaky, and delicious when cooked in stock, baked in foil, broiled in lemon-butter sauce, or poached in wine. But because the oil content is medium to high and because frying tends to dry the fish out and make it tough, I recommend you do not fry it.
- **Smallmouth Grunt:** Very good table fish, but small in size, so the best way to fix it is to panfry it. I do not recommend any other method of cooking since it will dry out the meat. Oil content is low.
- **Smalltooth Sawfish:** The small ones are excellent panfried—the meat is white, firm, and full-bodied. Larger ones can be filleted, steaked, or chunked, and grilled, broiled, baked, or smoked. Oil content is high in the larger fish, lower in the small ones.
- **Smooth Puffer:** Considered a delicacy if prepared properly, but can be toxic if not! Cut the fish in half, crosswise, so that you use only the tail section. Remove all the skin and clean the fish thoroughly. Low oil content makes this species excellent for frying. Don't prepare any other way.
- **Snook:** Excellent, medium-oily table fish that can be prepared any style. Fillet or steak the larger species; smaller ones can be baked or grilled whole.
- **Sockeye Salmon:** A superb fish, highly prized by most anglers. It has a high oil content, but the meat is a nice, pleasing color. Delicious when broiled, grilled, poached in stock, baked, or even panfried (another exception to the not-frying-oily-fish rule). But by far the best way to prepare sockeye is to smoke it.
- **Sole:** Excellent table quality. A member of the flatfish family, thus medium lean. Lends itself to virtually any style of preparation, but best broiled or stuffed with crabmeat.
- **Southern Flounder:** Excellent flatfish. Delicious any style. Low oil content.
- **Southern Hake:** Member of the cod family, medium low in oil content, and delicious any style.
- **Southern Stingray:** As is the case with most other rays, only the wings are utilized (as mock scallops). But I suggest you use a method other than frying—poaching, broiling, baking, or grilling. The flesh is fine-grained and medium low in oil content.
- **Spanish Grunt:** Good table quality, low oil content. Delicious any style.
- **Spanish Hogfish:** Excellent any style because its flesh is white, firm, and delectable. Medium low in oil content.

● **Spanish Mackerel:** A very oily fish that does not fry well, but it becomes one of the better fish you can put on the table when you smoke it. I also recommend you try Spanish mackerel pit-grilled. Other cooking methods are mediocre.

● **Speckled Hind:** A small grouper that is tasty when prepared any style. Medium low oil content.

● **Speckled Trout:** One of the most sought-after saltwater fish. Lends itself to any style of preparation. The meat is white, tender, and flaky.

● **Spot:** This fish has soft flesh that sometimes turns wormy, but it can be panfried if iced down immediately when removed from the water. Since its oil content is relatively low, it can also be cooked in courtbouillon or made into chowder. Flavor fair to good.

● **Spotfin Croaker:** Fair food fish, best filleted and panfried or ground into patties. Oil content is medium low.

● **Spotfin Surfperch:** Fair food fish, best filleted and panfried, although it can be broiled or baked. Medium oily.

● **Spotted Bass:** Also called Kentucky bass. Excellent any style. Low oil content.

● **Spotted Bullhead Catfish:** Small catfish, but edible. Firm, slightly oily meat that is best when panfried, but can also be cooked in courtbouillon.

● **Spotted Gar:** All gars have soft meat, so the best method is to grind the meat and make boulettes (balls). **Do not eat the roe—it's toxic.**

● **Spotted Sea Trout:** See "Speckled Trout." This is the same fish.

● **Spotted Sunfish:** Excellent food quality. Best way to prepare is to coat in cornmeal and panfry, but can be fixed any style. Low oil content.

● **Squirrel Hake:** A member of the cod family, medium low in oil, good fixed any style. Especially good filleted and panfried or broiled in lemon butter.

● **Stargazer:** Edible either panfried or poached, but only fair in flavor. Medium oily.

● **Starry Flounder:** Like all the other flounders, this fish is low in oil content, and excellent prepared any style.

● **Stonecat:** Fair food value, best when panfried to crispness. Can also be used in courtbouillon. Medium oily.

● **Stone Roller:** An excellent, lean little panfish. The meat is sweet-tasting and can be fixed any style, but the best way is to roll in cornmeal and fry.

● **Striped Bass:** A very dry fish with a low oil content. I suggest you pan-sauté the smaller species, but the larger ones will have to be basted or cooked in a stock. Fish over 20 pounds tend to be coarse and chewy regardless of how you prepare them.

● **Striped Marlin:** Reddish meat, but extra high in quality. In spite of the high oil content, it is excellent steaked, filleted, or chunked, and grilled, broiled, baked, poached, or smoked.

● **Striped Mullet:** Flesh is firm and white and called "Biloxi bacon" along the Mississippi Gulf Coast. The fish is best when hickory- or pecan-smoked, but delicious any style. Even the roe and testes are considered gourmet delicacies. Medium oily.

● **Striped Seaperch:** Fair food quality and suitable for preparation in any style. The oil content is medium, and the meat is semicoarse yet flaky.

● **Sturgeon:** Excellent table fish and a good source of protein. Very oily, best when smoked. In fact, I do not recommend you prepare this fish any way other than smoking. Its roe is the best source of caviar.

● **Summer Flounder:** Excellent, low in oil, and good prepared any style.

● **Swordspine Snook:** Very good table fish. White, flaky, and full-flavored meat that lends itself to any style of preparation. Best method is panfrying.

● **Tarpon:** Great game fish, but not worth eating in my opinion (see next section). Very tough, coarse, pungent meat. High oil content. Some experts say the roe can be a delicacy when panfried, but I don't eat tarpon at all.

● **Tarpon Snook:** Excellent when filleted and skinned. Can be panfried, broiled in butter, baked, or cooked in stock. Medium-low oil content.

● **Tautog:** Very good table fish when panfried, baked, or broiled. Also delicious when poached and drained. Medium-low oil content.

● **Tilefish:** Rarely caught and marketed, but very delicious when prepared any style. Firm, white, delicately flavored meat. Low oil content.

● **Tomtate:** Member of the grunt family. Contains very little oil and is excellent panfried. I wouldn't suggest you prepare it any other way.

● **Totuava:** Member of the weakfish family, with some of the characteristics of the speckled trout. Excellent any style; medium-low in oil content.

● **Triggerfish:** Very good quality meat; white, firm, and tender. Medium-low oil content. Good fixed any style.

● **Tripletail:** Called "Blackfish" along the Mississippi Gulf Coast. Very good, medium-oily food fish; can be fixed any style.

● **Turbot:** Good-tasting fish, but extremely high in oil content. I don't suggest you fry it. Open-grill or smoke the fillets or the whole fish. I recommend that you remove the skin to eliminate the pungency.

● **Wahoo:** Excellent and rather lean, in spite of the fact that it belongs to the mackerel family. Meat is white, tasty, and semifirm. It is best filleted or steaked, and broiled or open-grilled with spices. Basting with lemon-butter adds the right amount of oil.

● **Walleye:** Savory flesh with a medium-low oil content. Excellent fixed any style.

- **Walleye Pollock:** Member of the cod family, thus low in oil content. Excellent table fare served any style.
- **Walleye Surfperch:** Very good taste, but slightly oily. It can be fried, but it's better when baked, broiled, grilled, or poached.
- **Warmouth:** The "Louisiana Goggle-Eye," as it is called, is excellent any style, but is best when rolled in cornmeal and panfried.
- **Warsaw Grouper:** A very large fish with excellent flavor. Medium low in oil content, but good fixed any style. Steak the fillets for frying, cut chunks or cubes for chowder or courtbouillon, and try "finger-strips" for poaching, baking, or broiling. Too dry when smoked, though.
- **White Bass:** Excellent any style, but best when panfried. Low oil content.
- **Whitebone Porgy:** Very good smoked or grilled, but poor prepared in any other style. Very high oil content does not lend itself well to frying.
- **White Crappie:** Excellent any style. Meat is flaky, delicate, and pure white. Medium-low oil content.
- **White Grunt:** Excellent any style, but like the other firm-meat grunts it is best panfried. Low in oil.
- **White Margate:** Largest of the grunts and good prepared any style. Depending upon the recipe, I recommend you either fillet or steak it. Medium-low oil content.
- **White Marlin:** Despite the size, this medium-oily fish is succulent served in any style. It even fries nicely, but it is best, by far, when hickory-smoked.
- **White Perch:** The true northern fish (not the crappie which is referred to as white perch down South). It is excellent as table fare—in fact, the experts say there is no finer eating fish anywhere. Firm, white meat, good any style. Low oil content.
- **White Sea Bass:** A member of the corvina family, it can be prepared well in any style. But the meat does tend to spoil quickly when not iced immediately. Medium oily.
- **White Seaperch:** Good, tender, delicate meat. Excellent fixed any style. Medium-low oil content.
- **White Sturgeon:** A prized fish wherever it's found. Excellent any style except fried, especially good smoked. Oil content is medium high. The caviar is exquisite.
- **White Trout:** See "Sand Sea Trout."
- **Whiting:** Referred to most commonly as "channel mullet." Very tasty panfish. Good any style, but best panfried. Medium-low oil content.
- **Winter Flounder:** Like the summer flounder, excellent any style, but it is best when filleted and fried, stuffed with crabmeat and baked, or broiled in lemon butter. Medium-low oil content.

- **Yellow Bass:** Called the "barfish," it is good panfried. Meat is lean, light, flaky, white, and delicate. I don't suggest you prepare it any other way.
- **Yellow Bullhead:** Excellent catfish. Can be fixed any style. The meat is usually medium oily and cream colored, but it changes depending upon where the catfish is feeding. Ice right away or the flesh will turn mushy.
- **Yellowfin Grouper:** Excellent fixed any style. Like all the groupers, it is low in oil. Note: This fish is often toxic in the West Indies.
- **Yellowfin Sole:** Excellent any style, but best when filleted, panfried, and covered with a shrimp sauce. Medium-low oil content.
- **Yellowfin Tuna:** Best boiled, poached, or pit-grilled. Much too oily to fry or bake in a gravy. Superb when smoked!
- **Yellow Goatfish:** Fair eating, but will turn mushy unless chilled right away when taken from the water. Good fried or broiled. Low oil content.
- **Yellowmouth Grouper:** One grouper that doesn't fry all that well. Oil content is medium high. Very good when smoked or pit-grilled. I do not suggest baking or poaching.
- **Yellow Perch:** Excellent any style. One of the best panfrying fish you can find. Medium-low oil content.
- **Yellowtail Flounder:** Excellent any style. Medium-low oil content. Fries exceptionally well.
- **Yellowtail Rockfish:** Good any style. Medium-low oil content. Fillet and fry the panfish size for a gourmet taste treat, or roll in cornmeal and deep fry.
- **Yellowtail Snapper:** Superb any style. Lean, white, firm, tender, and delicate meat.

THE FISH I SUGGEST YOU DON'T BOTHER COOKING

- **Alligator Gar:** Actually, all the gars are rather poor in table quality because of the softness of their meat, but they are used by some folks in making those famous Louisiana "gar boulettes." The one thing you don't want to do is eat the roe (eggs); they are quite toxic!
- **Angel Shark:** Very high in uric acid, therefore producing a strong pungent taste and quite a displeasing odor. A good test to determine the edibility of shark meat (many species are delicious) is to smell the fillets up close for the odor of ammonia. If you detect any at all, toss the shark out.
- **Atlantic Bumper:** Very poor flesh quality and full of bones.
- **Atlantic Horse-Eye Jack:** Very oily, very bloody, and said to be quite toxic in some locales.
- **Atlantic Menhaden:** These are the "pogies" you always hear about, but do not confuse them with porgy fish. Porgy fish make very good eating, but the pogies—menhaden—are extremely oily trash fish which are primarily converted to fish meal, cat food, and fertilizer.

- **Atlantic Sharpnose Shark:** Very poor quality, and high in uric acid.
- **Atlantic Stingray:** Of all the rays, many of which are used as "mock scallops," this one is the poorest in texture. The meat tends to be tasteless and is quite coarse. Also, be extremely careful when handling any stingray—the spine in the tail, when stuck in the human hand, is extremely painful.
- **Bermuda Chub:** Some are eaten occasionally, but most are unsuitable for the table because of a brassy, biting off-taste.
- **Black Jack:** Suspected of being toxic in many areas.
- **Blueback Herring:** Very coarse meat and completely lacking in taste.
- **Blue Runner:** Poor meat quality, very bloody, and much too oily to be cooked satisfactorily.
- **Blue Shark:** Poor quality and high in uric acid.
- **Bonito:** Too bloody to appeal to American tastes. The meat is extremely red and federal regulations prevent it from even being canned and labeled as a tuna.
- **Bowfin:** This is Louisiana's notorious "choupique," which is anything but appealing. It is poor in quality, tough, stringy, and cottony.
- **Cutlass Fish:** Found in Texas and often valued in the Orient, but the quality and taste just aren't appealing to American seafood lovers.
- **Gaff-Topsail Pompano:** Not to be confused with *the* pompano. This fish is rough, chewy, and quite coarse. No matter how you prepare it, it remains inedible.
- **Greenland Shark:** Meat is toxic when fresh. Some who eat it in foreign countries air-dry the flesh to make it edible. But even dried it is tough-textured and lacking in flavor.
- **Green Sturgeon:** Dark meat and very bloody. It also has a disagreeable taste and odor.
- **Ladyfish:** Too bony to be used in any dish.
- **Leatherjacket:** Very dry meat and very bony. Flavor is poor.
- **Mooneye:** Too dry, full of bones, and very poor in flavor. The only way it can be prepared is smoking, but even that leaves a lot to be desired.
- **Moray Eel:** Some are highly toxic. I suggest you do not eat any!
- **Northern Hog Sucker:** Poor quality meat, extremely soft texture, and full of bones.
- **Pacific Hake:** Poor quality, soft to mushy meat, and easily spoiled.
- **Pacific Horse-Eye Jack:** Some species are toxic, and since there is no way to determine which are and which aren't, I suggest you avoid eating any of them.
- **Queen Parrot Fish:** Can be eaten, but the meat is unusually tough and stringy. Very poor quality.
- **Ratfish:** Very poor taste and too oily for any kind of preparation.

● **Round Whitefish:** Very soft and spoils easily. The texture is extremely dry and tasteless. Those that are prepared are usually fried, but they are no treat.

● **Sacramento Perch:** Stringy, poor flavor, and unsuitable for any dish.

● **Scup:** Poor taste and unsuitable for any dish.

● **Sea Catfish:** Called "hardheads" in Louisiana, these catfish are considered trash species. They are edible, but the quality of the meat is poor and the taste is unappealing.

● **Silver Surfperch:** Very unappealing because of the texture of the meat, which is tough and quite stringy.

● **Skipjack Herring:** Too bony, too oily, and too bloody for any recipe. Not even a good trash fish!

● **Southern Puffer:** This fish is almost always toxic and it should never be used for food.

● **Spiny Dogfish:** Oily, coarse, and usually only good for making fish meal, fertilizer, and cat food.

● **Spotted Jackfish:** Considered poor by most experts because of the high oil and blood content.

● **Tarpon:** Eaten in some parts of the world, but rarely used for human consumption in America because of the poor quality of the meat and possible toxicity. Those who have eaten tarpon report that the meat has a laxative effect on the human digestive tract.

● **White Sucker:** Very soft meat and very bony. Totally lacking in flavor.

As you can see from the preceding list, there are only a handful of fishes that are not suitable for human consumption. Which brings me to the point of this entire chapter on fish: *You can cook succulent Louisiana-style dishes no matter where you live*. Just use *our* recipes and *your* fish! It's the next best thing to being born a Cajun and living on Bayou Lafourche!

GOURMETS CALL IT CAVIAR

When properly prepared, fish eggs (called "roe") are considered a delicacy. While the most expensive fish eggs are called "black caviar" and are products of the sturgeon, don't pass over the roe of other delectable species—shad, salmon, speckled trout, dolphin, flounder, mullet, Spanish mackerel, and (in the north) bluefish.

The best way to prepare it is to wash the roe sacs extremely well, coat them in a light dusting of seasoned flour or seasoned cornmeal, and either deep fry or butter-broil them.

Keep in mind, however, that to be really tasty fish roe should be at a proper state of development. All the experts agree that the right size is no larger than the *head of a match*. Once the eggs grow past that point, they become too oily to cook.

Remember that the roe of gars and puffers should never be eaten. They are almost always toxic.

MISCELLANEOUS NOTES ABOUT FISH COOKERY

Before we get into fish recipes and their preparation, I believe it would be beneficial to touch on some of the basics of fish cookery, especially as it relates to specific species. Before anyone can prepare fish delicately enough to produce a notable dish, he or she has to have some degree of understanding of the seafood product. In other words, you have to know what it is you're cooking—and what you can expect from it.

For example, if you did not know that mackerel contain a high degree of oil, you wouldn't know that they do not fry well. So if, first, you take time out to learn everything you can about mackerel (or at least enough to get you through a dish comfortably), you won't have to apologize for a meal being less than you expected it to be. It's just a matter of understanding.

In this section, I hope to pass along to you some background information about fish cookery that all too often is taken for granted. We won't take it for granted, though. We're going to make it gospel! And if nothing else, you will learn *how* to handle the product and you will get answers to some of the most common questions about fish.

Food value: All fish are higher in protein than the best cut of beef. On the average, fish contain 40 percent more protein than beef. Incidentally, fish is also higher in protein than lamb or pork.

Calories: Fish are considerably lower in calories than beef. On the average, one pound of fish has about 30 percent of the calories of a pound of beef. The calorie count in fish is also considerably lower than in lamb and pork.

Mineral content: While fish and meat have similar mineral compositions, the concentrations of iron, phosphorus, and calcium are notably higher in fish. And if you prefer saltwater to freshwater fish, you get a significant source of iodine as well.

Digestibility: Because fish oils are *polyunsaturated* (which means they are rich in unsaturated chemical bonds), fish is easily assimilated by the body's digestive juices. And when you add that information to the fact that the fat content of all fish is extremely low (3 milligrams per 100 grams in fish as compared to 30 milligrams per 100 grams of beef), you have all the makings of a fine "light" meal.

Perishability: Like all seafoods, fish will spoil easily because of their chemical makeup. Fish with high oil contents like mackerel, tuna, bluefish, smelt, and flounders will usually spoil quicker than lean fish like bream, walleye, halibut, and speckled trout. In the storage process this same rule applies to rancidity: oily species will turn rancid and last for a shorter period of time in the freezer than will the leaner species. Just keep in mind that *all fish,* regardless of the species, should taste sweet and never "fishy." Any fish that takes on a fishy flavor was either handled improperly in the cleaning process or is about to turn rancid.

Habitat differences: The flavor and palatability of the same species of fish in different localities do differ considerably. You don't hear Louisianians boast much about bluefish caught in the Gulf of Mexico, while folks up north rave about the taste of locally caught species. The reason is that northern-caught bluefish are superior to the same fish landed in southern waters because of habitat differences.

Cooking lean fish/cooking oily fish: All methods of cookery do not apply to all species. Some fish lend themselves to virtually any style of preparation—speckled trout, red snapper, black bass, cobia, crappie, flounder, etc. It is the quality of the flesh (and its chemistry) that must be considered prior to cooking. I guess it's because when God made the fishes, he had favorites. . . . Some you can do anything to; they'll be succulent no matter what! But the remainder do have limitations if you want your culinary efforts to come out well. Because this cookbook is intended to have a national audience, I have already used considerable space listing the fishes of the entire United States and suggesting the methods you can use to prepare them either in original recipes or as substitutions for species which may not be indigenous to your locale. You should refer to the list before preparing a dish, so that you can make the right precooking decisions.

POACHING FISH

As I mentioned earlier, very few good Louisiana cooks will poach fish in plain water. Most use a seasoning stock of some type—buttered broth, commercial crab boil, milk, wine, beer, oyster water, or shrimp or fish broth. In fact, I wholeheartedly recommend that you never poach fish in plain water (nor do I recommend that you make soups, chowders, gumbos, or any other liquid-base dishes with plain water). *Use a good, flavored, seasoned stock.* It makes all the difference in the world when it comes to taste, simply because the flavors are concentrated. Several recipes I'll list later in this chapter will emphasize this point.

And, as with all other methods of cookery, *do not overpoach.* As soon as the fish begins to flake apart, it is done. In fact, poaching, because of the high temperatures of the liquid solutions, will usually cook seafoods quicker than other methods. I also suggest that since poached fish generally end up being cooked further in other dishes you cook *only* till the fish is opaque and no further.

STEWING FISH

In Louisiana, *stewing* fish means cooking them in a courtbouillon, a creole, a special sauce, or a traditional "Cajun stock" (which is a seafood broth or a milk chowder base). Before we go any further, though, let's clear up some questions of semantics.

Up north—and in other parts of the country, as well—a "courtbouillon" is nothing more than fish poached in salted water. That's not courtbouillon in Louisiana! *Courtbouillon* in the Bayou State means redfish or catfish or some other firm-meat species stewed in a rich red gravy loaded with lots of herbs and spices. It is just a few degrees short of a bouillabaisse. A *creole* is another rich, red gravy—it usually contains a thickening agent (e.g., flour) and is spiced with herbs, seasonings, and *cayenne pepper. Fish stew* in Louisiana is rarely made with water; instead a specially prepared fish stock, well seasoned and rather spicy, is used. I wanted to make that clear!

Consequently, if you want to prepare fish stew, I recommend you make your best soup/sauce/chowder/courtbouillon (whatever you call your stock base), select a nonoily species of fish, and simmer it down in a pot to delicate succulence. And don't skimp on the herbs and spices!

BOILING FISH

Boiling is another cooking term that must be clarified for Louisiana criteria. Ain't no good Louisiana seafood cook gonna *boil* his fish! Unless he boils it in seasoned water to produce cooked "flaked fish" to put in some other delectable dish. Because Louisianians just don't eat boiled fish plain!

Technically, most Louisiana boiling is really *poaching,* because a flavored stock is used. Tuna, sheepshead, puppy drum, croaker, and other firm-meat species are boiled or poached to yield cooked fish flakes for dishes such as tuna salad, fish patties, and so forth. Here's how to prepare them:

1. Fillet the fish so that you use only the side slabs, discarding all scales, bones, skin, and extra cuts. Set the fillets aside.

2. In a pot large enough to handle the fillets, add enough water to cover the fish; one small chopped onion; three cloves of garlic, chopped; one whole carrot, chopped; two tablespoons of lemon juice; one teaspoon of Tabasco sauce; and salt and pepper to taste.

3. Wrap the fillets tightly in cheesecloth, making sure that the bloodline in the fish has been trimmed away.

4. Bring the water to a boil, simmer in the seasonings for about 5 minutes, and place the fish in the water. Cook until the fillets flake easily (about 4 minutes). Use a medium-high fire.

5. Drain off the water, remove the fillets, and cool them down to room temperature. At this point you should be able to flake the fish as desired to make a variety of dishes, from sauces to stuffings to salads to sandwich spreads. One of the best boiled fish recipes can be found under the fish section in this book. It's called Mock Crabmeat. Look for it—it's super!

STEAMING FISH

While not a popular method of preparation in Louisiana because of the mild taste it yields, steaming is sometimes valuable when preparing fish to be used in other dishes where unseasoned flesh is needed in the cooked stage. I suggest you cook fish either in a commercial steaming kettle or in a colander over a pot of boiling water. Cook only until the fish turns transparent and flakes.

BAKING FISH

Baking is an excellent method to use when cooking large whole fish, fish that are stuffed, fish that are cooked with the skin on, or very thick fish that might dry out during a direct-heat cooking process.

Contrary to what you may have heard, fish can be baked both *covered* and *uncovered,* depending on the dish you are preparing. As a rule of thumb, I bake oily fish (king mackerel, tuna, large bluefish, Spanish mackerel, and so forth) uncovered on a drip-grill so that the excess oils "self-baste" and "drip out" in the cooking process, thereby leaving the fish less greasy when done. The lean fish I prepare I usually bake covered, tented, or wrapped in foil—because usually I have prepared a baste or sauce that I want the fish to absorb during the cooking process. The baste or sauce is the moistening ingredient and the flavoring agent. Baking temperature is 350 to 375 degrees, and you should always bake in a preheated oven. Of course you can achieve the same effect by using what most chefs refer to as *braising,* the technique of cooking lean fish in some type of stock (similar to *poaching,* the slow-boiling of fish in a flavored stock).

There are probably more recipes for baking fish than for any other method of preparation. The amount of creativity you can apply to your baked fish dishes is limited only by your imagination.

Here are some suggestions.

Fish baked in beer: Place your fish, either fillets or whole and cleaned, in a baking pan. Salt and pepper lightly and bake at 375 degrees. Baste until done (fillets will flake; whole fish will offer little resistance when pierced with a toothpick) with a mixture made of 1 10-ounce can of beer, ½ teaspoon of onion powder, ¼ teaspoon of garlic powder, and a dash of Worcestershire sauce.

Fish baked in lemon butter: Place your fish, either fillets or whole and cleaned, in a baking pan. Salt and pepper lightly and bake at 350 degrees until done. Baste as the fish cooks with a sauce made from 1 stick of melted butter, the juice of 1 lemon, a dash of thyme, and a dash of Tabasco sauce. Just before you serve, sprinkle with paprika and top with 3 or 4 pieces of thinly sliced lemon.

Fish baked in Italian dressing: Place your fish in a baking pan and baste with Kraft Zesty Italian Salad Dressing as it cooks.

Fish baked in Italian sauce: Prepare a tasty Italian gravy with tomato paste, oregano, basil, garlic, etc. (see recipe in chapter on sauces), and baste the fish with this sauce as it cooks.

Fish baked with shrimp sauce: Prepare shrimp sauce (see recipe in sauce chapter). Lay the fish out in the baking pan and completely douse it with sauce. Then bake covered until done. I also suggest you baste periodically during the cooking process.

Fish baked in canned soups: Bake your fish covered or uncovered (or completely wrapped in foil) in a can or two of cream of mushroom, cream of shrimp, or cream of onion soup. I suggest, however, that the soup be simmered with 1 small white onion, chopped (even the onion soup!); 2 tablespoons of minced celery; 2 tablespoons of finely chopped bell pepper; and a dash of Worcestershire sauce before basting. Then ladle the soup over the fish, basting as it cooks, until the fish is done.

Fish baked in Ragu sauce: This recipe uses another red-gravy coating similar to Italian, but much lighter. The fish flavor, rather than the sauce flavor, is dominant. I suggest you apply Ragu tomato sauce (with onions and mushrooms, of course!) with a basting brush and continue to baste as you cook. I also suggest you serve the fish with lemon slices and fresh-chopped parsley as a garnish.

Baked fish with shrimp butter: Place your fish in aluminum foil so that it can be completely covered. Then finely chop 1 pound of shrimp and sauté them gently until pink in 1 stick of butter. Remove the pan from the fire and add to it 2 tablespoons of chopped celery, 2 tablespoons of chopped bell pepper, and 4 tablespoons of chopped green onions, stirring the vegetables into the shrimp and butter. Also stir in 4 tablespoons of white wine. Then spoon the mixture all over the fish, wrap it tightly in the foil, and bake at 350 degrees until tender (about 45 minutes for a 4-pound fish).

Fish baked and topped with Hollandaise: Salt and pepper the fish, place it in a baking pan, and cook till tender at 350 degrees, basting lightly as it cooks with melted margarine or white wine. Then, when it's done, top with lemon slices and fresh Hollandaise sauce (see sauce chapter) and serve piping hot.

Fish baked with onions and mayonnaise: Salt and pepper your fish and place it in a Pyrex baking pan. Using your fingers, lightly rub in enough mayonnaise to coat the fish evenly. Then slice a large white onion very thinly and lay the slices over the fish. Wrap in foil or tent (drape inverted V-shaped foil over the fish) and bake at 375 degrees until tender. Drizzle freshly squeezed lemon juice over the fish as it is served.

Dry-baked fish in spices: Using either whole fish or fillets, sprinkle the fish with salt, white pepper, black pepper, red pepper, basil, oregano, thyme, and several finely crushed bay leaves. Then wrap the fish tightly in foil and bake slowly at 325 degrees. When ready to serve, unwrap the fish and brush on tartar sauce (see sauce chapter) while the fish is piping hot. Serve immediately.

Baked fish in honey-lemon sauce: Place the fish in a baking pan and prepare a sauce using ¼ cup of lemon juice, ½ cup of clover honey, ¼ cup of melted butter, the finely chopped rind of 2 lemons, 2 tablespoons of cornstarch, and 1½ cups of water. Mix everything together in a saucepan over low heat. Then brush into the fish until it is well coated. Sprinkle lightly with salt and cayenne pepper. Bake uncovered at 350 degrees until done. *But keep basting often as it cooks*. (If you want to emphasize the lemon flavor, you can omit the honey.)

Baked fish in Sicilian sauce: Salt and pepper the fish and place it in a baking pan. Then prepare this mix: ½ cup of pure olive oil, 3 cloves of fresh garlic, 2 tablespoons of fresh-chopped parsley, 1 teaspoon of oregano, 2 teaspoons of basil, ½ teaspoon of fennel seed, and 4 tablespoons of Romano cheese.

Put all the ingredients in a blender and whip them until smooth. Spoon over the fish and bake at 350 degrees until done, basting every 5 minutes or so.

Baked stuffed fish: When preparing whole fish, like redfish or flounder, you can make your favorite stuffing (or you can use a stuffing recipe found in the shrimp or crabmeat chapters of this book) and pack it inside the fish before baking. I would suggest, however, that to get a full complement of flavors you also baste the stuffed fish every 10 minutes or so as it bakes to keep the flesh moist and succulent. (Keep in mind that you may have to bake longer than usual when stuffing is placed inside a fish.) Stuffed fish can be cooked uncovered or tented. It's done when the meat flakes easily.

Baked fish in mushroom-wine sauce: One of the richest sauces you can ladle over fish is mushroom-wine sauce. Melt down 5 tablespoons of butter, stir in 2 tablespoons of flour, and cook till smooth over low heat. *Do not brown.* Then stir in ½ cup of heavy cream (or half-and-half) and heat until smooth. At this point, finely chop the mushrooms and sprinkle them evenly over the fish. I suggest you use enough mushrooms to completely cover the fish you are cooking. Then drizzle on lemon juice (to taste) and about 6 tablespoons of white wine per pound of fish. Place in the oven and begin baking uncovered. After about 10 minutes pour the butter sauce over the fish and mushrooms and cook until tender. Serve hot!

Baked breaded fish with bacon seasoning: Works best with fish fillets rather than whole fish, but it can be delicious either way. Lay out fillets in a buttered baking pan. In a saucepan, fry a couple strips of bacon until they are well done. Remove them from the pan and let them cool, then crumble them up. When they're finely crumbled, put them back in the pan you fried them in and add enough coarsely ground bread crumbs to absorb all the bacon drippings. Stir the crumbled bacon and the bread crumbs until they are mixed uniformly. Salt and pepper the fillets, and, using your hands, sprinkle the bread crumbs over the top of the fish. Then drizzle lemon juice to taste over the crumbs and bake in a 350-degree oven for 25 minutes until the fish flakes easily. (To add even more flavor, finely chop a white onion and some fresh parsley and sprinkle them over the top of the baked dish (while it's in the oven) about 5 minutes before serving.

BAKING SUGGESTIONS

1. As you can see, fish can be baked with just about any kind of spice, condiment, marinade, or sauce that suits your taste. Because the idea behind this book is to allow room for creativity, I've only made a few suggestions for baking fish. You're the cook—go ahead and discover your own favorites!

2. I do suggest you salt and pepper all the fish you bake, whether they are

filleted or whole, before you put them in the pan. In the baking process the sauces and toppings are nothing more than flavor enhancers. And since in most instances the fish will produce its own liquids as it cooks, thereby diluting the sauces and toppings, the only way to get a full-bodied seasoning in the fish itself is to salt and pepper the fish itself. Incidentally, I recommend you use light, but equal, applications of salt, red pepper, white pepper, and black pepper on each dish. Use all the peppers—not just black!

3. I recommend that when you bake in an open pan, as opposed to baking in aluminum foil, you lightly grease the pan before you bake. It will keep the fish from sticking to the bottom. You can use Pam, vegetable oil, or margarine; but whichever you use, you should apply it very lightly and rub it in with your fingers.

4. It's strictly a matter of taste, but I find that *all baked fish* will come out tasting richer if, first, you rub them with real, melted butter. It provides a good coating medium and adds superb flavor, even to the oily species. I suggest you butter before sprinkling with salt and pepper.

5. As I've said, the best temperature for baking fish is 350 to 375 degrees. I recommend 350 when baking uncovered, and 375 when tenting or wrapping in foil.

6. *Do not overbake*. Most baked fish dishes will cook in 25 to 35 minutes. You want them to bake only to the point of flakiness. With fillets, test with a fork: if the meat flakes easily, it is cooked. With whole fish, test with a clean broom straw or a toothpick: if you get no resistance when you pierce the fish and the straw or pick comes out easily upon withdrawal, your fish is cooked. Actually, fish baked in sauces will usually cook much faster than 25 minutes because of the high temperature of the liquids. Watch them even more closely!

FRYING FISH

As noted earlier, there are two ways to fry: *deep frying* and *panfrying* (sautéing).

Deep frying is done in a large quantity of oil and is designed to cook the entire surface of the fish all at once, so that the juices are sealed in quickly. Just remember that when you deep fry fish whole or filleted, they must be coated in a batter to lock in the moisture and assure crispness. I talk about batters elsewhere in this book. And remember to cook *hot* when you deep fry (400 degrees or higher), and to cook smaller fillets or small whole fish at higher temperatures than larger fillets or large whole fish.

Panfrying is a good method to use when preparing small whole fish, small fillets, fish "fingers," or fish steaks that you don't want coated with heavy batters. Sautéed seafoods should be lightly coated with just salt and pepper, perhaps dusted with bread crumbs, or, at most, with a light dusting of all-purpose flour or corn flour. Then, to produce the delicate flavors you expect from sautéing, they should be cooked in a hot skillet over a low flame, *slowly*. If properly prepared, the fish should come out very moist, crisp, and tender, but not burned. As a hint, I suggest you cook only dry fillets or whole panfish; excessive moisture in sautéed seafood will produce steam, the steam will cause the butter or oil to splatter, and the fish will not come out crisp.

Here are a few hints on frying.

1. Put heavy batters only on fish that will be deep fried. On pan-sautéed fish you should only dust lightly in seasoned flour, bread crumbs, or cornmeal.
2. If you're going to use a heavy batter and deep fry, season the batter—not the seafood. If you are going to panfry, season the fish—not the dusting coat.
3. Do not overcook. Deep-fried fish will be done when they float to the surface. They should be fried hot so that the batter coating is crisp and the fish itself is tender and moist. Panfried fish will be done when they turn golden brown and the fillets (or the flesh in whole panfried species) turn transparent and begin to flake apart. Overfrying dries out fish and makes them chewy.

Frying Suggestions:

Fry only those fish I have listed in the Table Fish Checklist as suitable for frying. If you fry most oily fish, you will find that they develop a rather greasy taste, certainly not appealing to the palate. The best fish for frying are those considered lean to medium in oil content.

Serve fried fish piping hot, whether it is deep fried or pan-sautéed. As fried fish cools, it absorbs moisture from the air and the crispness diminishes. While I have eaten cold fried fish right from the refrigerator (that's because I love seafood so much, I'll eat it any way I can get it!), it really isn't the best way to serve it for full flavor.

Now, here is where the gourmet side of fish frying comes in—*it's not how well you fry it, it's how you serve it once it's fried*. Sure, fish is delicious right out of the oil, with or without a little lemon squeezed over the top. But for that extra something special, try these hints:

1. Coat your favorite fish lightly in flour and pan-sauté it in real butter, finely chopped onion, and coarsely chopped bell pepper. Then cover it with a mushroom sauce, a heavy cream-and-cheese sauce, or a chopped shrimp sauce.
2. Lay out your deep-fried fish on a Pyrex dish and smother them in sautéed onions. Then place them in the oven at 450 degrees for 5 minutes until the flavor of the onions blends into the seasoned batter.
3. Pan-sauté or deep fry your favorite fish. Then, instead of serving it plain

with lemon juice, Tabasco, and tartar sauce, make a pan broth of fish or shrimp stock seasoned well with onion, lemon juice, Tabasco, and your favorite spices and cook some rice in the broth until it's tender (about 14 minutes). Then place the rice in a casserole dish, bury the fried fish in the rice, cover the casserole, and bake until piping hot. Or thicken the pan broth, onion, lemon juice, and Tabasco with heavy cream, cook until it becomes smooth, and submerge the fried fish in the sauce. Serve it over buttered rice, pasta, or mashed potatoes.

4. Toast and butter a piece of French bread sliced lengthwise. Then sprinkle equal portions of grated cheddar and mozzarella cheese on each slice of bread and melt the cheese lightly under the broiler element. Place your fried fillet of fish in the bubbly cheese, top it with several thin slices of white onion, and then spoon generous helpings of a creamed shrimp sauce (see chapter on sauces) over the onions. Serve open-face with a buttered vegetable, brabant potatoes, a crisp green salad, and a chilled glass of white wine.

SMOKING FISH

Smoking is one of the best techniques for cooking oily fish. There must be a hundred recipes for smoking fish, and every one of them produces a tasty meal. But keep in mind that for best results you should probably select an oily or semi-oily fish (lean fish have to be marinated and basted in oil when smoked). You should also select a *smoker-cooker* that provides a good, evenly distributed source of smoke. With the many commercial devices on the market today, that is no longer a problem if you buy a quality product.

As mentioned previously, two smoking methods are standard: *hot-smoking* and *cold-smoking*. *Hot-smoking* completely cooks the fish at temperatures that range between 165 and 185 degrees. It is a shorter cooking method, more "cooking" than "smoking," and it's the way most folks "smoke" at home. *Cold-smoking* is how the commercial enterprises prepare smoked fish. It is more "cured" than "cooked," through a drying process that rarely exceeds 115 degrees Fahrenheit. Of course, depending on your smoker unit, you can do either at home.

Unless you're using the quicker recipe described earlier, your fish must be salted in brine and dried on a rack before they can be smoked. The salt inhibits the growth of bacteria, and the removal of excess fluids eliminates the medium the bacteria need to grow. So "salting and drying" is the preservative step in the smoking process.

There are several recommendations as to the amount of salt that should go into the brine solution, but a good standard is *four cups of salt to each gallon of water*. This is the preparatory brine (the solution that helps draw the blood from the fish). Your fish should be soaked in this brine for approximately 15 minutes. Then prepare a "seasoning brine"—two cups of salt, one cup of brown sugar, one tablespoon of black peppercorns, one teaspoon of crushed cayenne pepper, four finely crushed bay leaves, and one sliced lemon. Add all these ingredients to a gallon of water, mix them together well, and soak the fish you will cook in this solution for at least 2 hours, but no longer than 4. Most folks use just the preparatory brine. If you want a good smoked fish dish, use both!

Drying the fish after soaking is just as important as brining. When you remove the fillets or the whole fish from each of the solutions, rinse them well in fresh, running water until most of the exterior solution is removed. Then pat them dry with paper towels and set them out to dry in a cool, breezy, but shady place for about 3 or 4 hours, or until a nice slick sheen has developed on the surface. Only when the fish has dried in this manner is it ready to smoke!

The smoking temperature must be watched. If the temperature gets too high during the first few hours (say, over 120 degrees), the fish will cook too fast and it will fall apart. Keep in mind that the smoke cooking method serves to firm up fish because the internal fluids vaporize. After about 2 hours at a low temperature, build up a *dense smoke* and raise the temperature to about 185 degrees and cook at that level for about *4 hours*. Total cooking time for hot-smoking (depending on the thickness of the fish) should run between 4 and 8 hours. The texture of the fish at this point should be firm but tender, and it should be fully flavored with smoke.

The smoking woods are most important. Be sure you use only those fuels that produce a rich, aromatic smoke: *never use pine or any wood containing pitch*. I recommend hickory (the preferred wood), oak, sweet bay, pecan, apple, and cherry, but you can also use white birch, beech, maple, or ash. And make certain that you soak the woods in water prior to burning—the richest smoke is produced this way. Just as a hint, you might want to do what many experts recommend to keep the heat and smoke concentrations consistent: add a few charcoal briquets to your fire. They yield a constant source of hot coals which, in turn, keep the wood smoking evenly. And as a hint, try using hardwood sawdust—it smolders and yields a thick smoke.

Fish can be smoked whole, chunked, steaked, or filleted. Small species such as mullet, croakers, bream, and trout should be left whole. Medium-size fish like catfish, Spanish mackerel, salmon, and carp should be smoked as fillets. And large fish, from king mackerel to marlin, should be steaked or chunked for smoking. I do recommend that fish with a fishy-tasting skin, like wahoo or grouper, be skinned before smoking.

BROILING FISH

Broiling is the method of cooking fish fillets or small whole fish under the broiler element of your oven. You use direct heat—generally 500 degrees—and you cook quickly. But, as is the case in baking, depending upon whether the fish is lean or oily you can broil either in a pan so that the juices become a basting ingredient or over a drip-grill so that the fish dries slightly as it cooks to render out the excess oils.

A couple of hints will help produce a better broiled fish dinner for you:

1. Always preheat your oven before broiling fish so that the dish will cook evenly.
2. To make certain that the bottom portion of the fish (the side away from the broiler element) cooks as evenly as the top, and to keep from having to turn the fish while it is cooking (which you want to avoid whenever possible because fish are tender and will usually break apart if handled too much), I recommend you preheat the broiling pan to the thermostat temperature of your oven before placing the fish in the pan.
3. Always broil lean fish at a greater distance from the element than oily fish. This is because the lack of natural oils in lean cuts will tend to dry out the fillets if the heat source is too close.
4. I also suggest that you baste lean fillets with Italian salad dressing, butter, or pure olive oil throughout the broiling process. This will seal in the natural moisture and keep the fillets from drying out.
5. Whenever possible, avoid broiling thick cuts of fish or whole fish. The direct overhead heat makes thicker cuts unpalatable because the outside portions become dry and leathery before the inside portions are fully cooked.

Refer to the section on baked fish and see all the methods I suggested for cooking them; you can apply the same techniques to the broiler. Remember, the only differences between baking and broiling are *the source of the heat* and *the cooking time*. All the toppings and sauces and marinades work with either process.

Special recipes at the end of this chapter will highlight specific dishes, but for the most part fish can be broiled with just salt, pepper, and butter; topped or basted with your Italian salad dressing (or any other marinade or dressing you like); or submerged in a specially created sauce. Just keep in mind that the heat is extremely high, so you will have to keep a close eye on the fish as it cooks. And do not overcook! As soon as the fillet or panfish turns transparent and begins to flake, the dish is done.

Note: No cover or lid should ever be used when broiling. The reason for the overhead heat source is to produce a browning effect. The dish must be cooked open to get that effect.

GRILLING FISH

Unlike broiling, grilling (or barbecuing, as some folks call it) is a good technique to use not only for the thinner, leaner cuts, but also for the thicker, oily fish that ordinarily you wouldn't put under the broiler element. That's because the heat source is *under the fish,* the cooking temperature is usually lower, and the drippings fall out of the meat to form "flavoring smoke."

Keep in mind that hickory chips or other types of aromatic hardwoods (hickory, pecan, cherry) can be added to the grill coals to supplement the flavoring. And because grilled fish tend to cook "tighter" than broiled (meaning they come out firmer and less flaky), it is possible to turn most grilled fish over when cooking without their breaking apart. Grilling is a good method to use for whole fish, very-firm-meat species (grouper, jewfish, channel bass), oily fish (the mackerels), and fish steaks and chunked fish. But I don't recommend you grill *extra-lean* or *highly flaky* fish (speckled trout or flounder) unless you are proficient with a spatula. The fillets of these species tend to break apart very easily. Of course, once you get the hang of it . . . do your thing!

Grilled fish can be prepared with the same condiments, toppings, sauces, and marinades as baked or broiled fish; the resulting product will have more of an outdoorsy, robust, and open-pit flavor. On the pit, fish have to be handled delicately. Here are some suggestions to follow when grilling.

1. Always place the grill far enough away from the coals to keep the fire from flaring up (be especially careful with oily species of fish) and burning the fillets. It helps, too, if you remember that thicker fillets must be placed further from the heat source than thinner fillets to ensure that the cooking process is even, so the outside won't cook and dry out before the inside is ready.

2. Avoid turning the fillets any more than you have to. I recommend that you fully cook one side of the fillet or whole panfish before turning it over. This will give you firmness in the fish and reduce the chances of the tender meat breaking up when you flip it over.

Baste constantly as fish grill, especially leaner fish, because the high temperatures and heat convection of grilling tend to dry out seafoods. Even with oily fish it is imperative that you baste to replace the natural "fishy fats" with more flavorful, seasoned oils. As fish cook, the natural oils leach out. So if you replace them with butter, margarine, seasoned marinades, olive oil, Italian salad dressing, or one of your favorite sauces, the flavors will change for the better. Once more, that good ol' Italian salad dressing makes a great grilling baste!

Hint: To get a smoked flavor in fish without cooking it over hickory, you can use the product called "Liquid Smoke," which is nothing more than actual hickory flavoring dissolved in water. It produces a good flavor in fish and can even be used for adding a smoked touch to oven-baked dishes.

As with all other forms of fish cookery, do not overgrill. When the fish has turned opaque (lost its transparency) and begins to flake apart, it is done.

MICROWAVING FISH

One of the latest forms of cooking fish which is quickly gaining popularity is microwaving. It's a technique that requires a tremendous amount of experimentation on the part of the cook before a consistently good product can be prepared. Because each microwave oven has its own peculiarities, I suggest you keep a notebook near the oven and jot down those times you find ideal for various species.

Regardless of the oven type or the cooking times, however, you must be aware of the basics discussed elsewhere in this book concerning cooking oily fish or lean fish. Use a trivet for oily fish so that the fats can drip out and not cause pungent tastes in the meat. And remember to baste lean fish in butter sauce so they don't dry out during microwaving.

One more hint: Because microwave ovens cook all foods extremely fast, seafood will cook superfast in a microwave. A 6-ounce trout fillet, for example, will cook in under a minute in some microwave ovens. So keep an eye on the cooking process, and remove the fillet when it turns transparent and begins to flake. There is nothing as unpalatable as overcooked microwaved fish!

YOUR SPECIAL RECIPES FOR FISH

Cooking fish can be as complicated as you care to make it. There are as many different recipes for each species as there are species swimming in the water.

What I've done in this book is taken the easiest—but tastiest—recipes for the most succulent methods and explained them in detail. So if you fix the dishes I list on the following pages (using, of course, your own imagination here and there!) you'll have a lot of good eating in store.

Poached Redfish with Hollandaise

This is one of the best recipes for redfish that I've ever eaten. The flavor is full-bodied, the texture is superb, and the dish will do wonders to impress dinner guests. You can also substitute other low to medium-oily fish for redfish.

First poach the redfish:

2 lbs. filleted redfish
2 cups water
½ cup white Chablis

4 tbsp. lemon juice
salt and pepper to taste
1 bay leaf

The recipe comes out best when you cut the fish into 3-inch pieces, so go ahead and trim the fillets. Then take a saucepan, put the water in it, bring it to a rapid boil, and add the wine, lemon juice, salt, pepper, and bay leaf. To get everything blended, let me suggest that you stir constantly as you add these ingredients. Okay; now simmer this stock over a low fire for about 20 minutes. Then, when the seasonings are cooked in, drop the fish in the pan, *but do it gently.* It will start cooking right away, so keep a close eye on the edges of the fillets, especially when they begin turning white. All you want to do is cook the pieces until they *flake;* it should take about 5 minutes. (Of course, if the pieces are really thick, turn them over in the pan *once.*) After the fish is cooked, remove the pieces from the pan, set them on a platter, and put them in a warm oven.

Now make an easy Hollandaise:

4 egg yolks
2 tbsp. lemon juice
½ cup melted butter

Put the egg yolks in a blender and whip until the texture is smooth. With the blender running on medium, add the lemon juice and whip until it is completely blended with the eggs. *Keep the blender running.* At this point, *gradually* pour in the butter, hot but not brown, and whip until the sauce is smooth. If it thickens too much, add a few drops of hot water. And that's your hollandaise!

Pour the sauce over the fish pieces and serve with smothered zucchini and scalloped potatoes. Ummmmmm!

Summertime Oven-Smoked Trout Salad

Of all the recipes I've concocted in my kitchen, this is one of my favorites, because it's easy to prepare yet tastes special. But most important, it's light, easy to digest as an evening meal, and ultralow on the calorie charts.

For each individual salad you prepare, use:

1 medium speckled trout fillet	¼ cup canned mushrooms
salt and pepper to taste	6 black olives, pitted
1 tbsp. Liquid Smoke	and chopped
2 tbsp. shredded mozzarella	¼ head lettuce
cheese	1 medium tomato

Dry the speckled trout fillets thoroughly and sprinkle them with salt and pepper. Then put them on a pizza pan. To get an oven-smoked flavor, which is what enhances the salad, dribble the Liquid Smoke (available in most grocery stores) over each fillet and *broil* the fillets for about 10 minutes on one side only. When they are cooked, set them aside to cool, then place them in the refrigerator. (This part can all be done in advance.)

When you're ready to prepare your salads, put the ingredients in a salad bowl, take the fillets out of the refrigerator, and flake one fillet over each bowl of ingredients. Then dress each salad with *1 teaspoon* of apple cider vinegar, *1 tablespoon* of pure olive oil, and *1 teaspoon* of lemon juice. Toss everything together well. The smoked flavor should be so dominant that you won't need salt and pepper, but you can add them if you prefer.

Hint: The salad is best served ice-cold, alongside either melba toast or tortilla chips. To add an extra touch of color, you can also sprinkle it lightly with cayenne pepper or paprika.

Flaked Fish François

4 cups water	dash of Tabasco sauce
1 small white onion, chopped	salt to taste
2 small cloves garlic, minced	1 lemon, thinly sliced
1 medium carrot, chopped	4 fish fillets about 8 oz. each
4 tbsp. chopped celery	2 10¾-oz. cans cream of
1 tbsp. minced parsley	mushroom soup

In a skillet, bring the water to a boil and add all the ingredients except the fish and the soup. Boil the seasonings, covered with a heavy lid, until the flavors mix well. I suggest you slow-boil the ingredients for at least 10 minutes to form a good stock.

Reduce the heat to simmer, so that the stock just bubbles. Add the fish fillets and cook them till they turn opaque and start to flake.

At this point remove them gently so they don't fall apart in the pan, and set them aside to cool. While your fish are cooling, cook some rice (whatever you'll need for your family) *in the fish-vegetable stock*. Then heat the undiluted soup to bubbling (add a little of the stock you made if you want a thinner consistency), flake the fish, and drop it into the soup. Stir well and ladle the fish over the rice. (Hint: If you want a richer-tasting rice, butter it while it is still hot.)

Serve with a tossed green salad and a glass of white wine.

Suggestions: The seasoned stock in this recipe can be used to poach fish for almost any dish you will make. It lends a full-bodied flavor and dresses up flaked-fish recipes. Fish cooked this way goes well in salads, stuffings, courtbouillons, fondues, and gumbos. And if you want to add an extra kick to the flavor, instead of using Tabasco sauce substitute Zatarain's liquid crab boil. Your southern friends will be glad to ship you some up north!

Paw-Paw Cormier's Courtbouillon

There must be a million recipes for fish courtbouillon. But I have never tasted a more delicious dish than the one prepared by Paw-Paw Cormier at Paw-Paw's Seafood House in Lake Charles. Since early 1971 folks from all over Louisiana have driven into the heart of Cajun Country just to eat one bowl of this magic concoction. And those who haven't have regretted it every day! I suggest you make your next catfish or redfish courtbouillon with Paw-Paw's recipe. It'll make your taste buds talk! Incidentally, Paw-Paw's is at 300 Hwy. 171 in Lake Charles, his phone number is (318) 439-5410, and I suggest you make plans to go there to eat real soon . . . and I don't care if you live in New Jersey!

Allow about ½ pound of dressed, cut-up fish (catfish and redfish are particularly good) for each adult. Sprinkle on salt, pepper—both black and cayenne—and paprika, dip the fish in flour, and fry it in hot vegetable oil until it turns crispy and golden brown all over. Then drain it on paper towels while you prepare your courtbouillon, as follows:

½ cup Crisco oil	2 tbsp. finely chopped parsley
1 clove garlic, minced	1 #303 can tomatoes
1 large onion, finely chopped	1 cup water
1 cup celery, chopped (with a	salt, red pepper, and black
few minced leaves)	pepper to taste
½ cup chopped bell pepper	
½ cup sliced green-onion bottoms	
(plus all the tops that go	
with them, also sliced)	

In a large skillet, heat the oil and sauté all the ingredients except the water in the order listed over medium heat until the grease comes to the surface. This should take about 15 minutes. Then place the fried fish in this tomato preparation *so that no piece touches any other piece.*

At this point lower the heat, add the water, and put a heavy lid on the pot. Cook the courtbouillon for 25 to 30 minutes, but do not stir, because this would break up the fish. If you must mix the ingredients to blend them, agitate the pot with the lid in place *gently* from side to side. But at all costs, *do not break up the fish.*

When you're ready to eat, spoon the chunked fish and the courtbouillon *gently* over hot buttered rice in a gumbo or soup bowl. Paw-Paw says that if you serve it with a fresh, cold, tossed, green salad, you've got everything you need to celebrate the delicacy of a true South Louisiana Acadian meal.

Amen!

Cajun Fish Stew

An excellent dish when prepared with any firm-bodied fish like croaker, drum, sheepshead, and so forth. Goes great with mashed potatoes, buttered rice, French bread, and—of course—white wine!

1 10-oz. pkg. frozen mixed vegetables
1 stick margarine
4 tbsp. chopped celery
2 tbsp. chopped bell pepper
1 small white onion, coarsely chopped
1 chicken bouillon cube
1 cup boiling water

1 10-oz. can cream of chicken soup
½ cup half-and-half
1 tsp. salt
½ tsp. white pepper
½ tsp. red pepper
2 lbs. chunked fish fillets
2 tbsp. white wine

Start off by gently steaming the vegetables until they are just tender. Do not overcook them! When they are ready, set them aside for a while.

In a saucepan, melt the margarine over medium heat and sauté the celery, pepper, and onion until they wilt. At this point dissolve the bouillon cube in the boiling water and stir the liquid into the seasonings. Then add the chicken soup, the cream, and the salt and peppers. Keep stirring until everything is blended.

Drop in the chunked fish, cover the pan with a heavy lid, and simmer on reduced heat until the fish begins to flake (about 12 to 15 minutes).

When you're ready to eat, *gently* stir in the wine and pour in the steamed vegetables. Cover once more, and sauté until everything is piping hot. Do not stir rapidly—just swish the vegetables around so you do not break up the fish.

This recipe should feed about six persons . . . unless you happen to be *really* hungry! It's one of the best fish stews you can make.

Oven-Crisp Croaker

Now for this recipe, I have specified *croaker*. But that's only because I believe that this is the best recipe for croaker there is! You can use any lean or medium-oily fish and it will come out great!

1 cup crushed cracker crumbs
½ cup Parmesan cheese
1 tsp. onion powder
½ tsp. garlic powder
½ cup Crisco oil

1 tsp. tarragon vinegar
2 tbsp. fresh lemon juice
2 cloves fresh garlic, minced
2 lbs. fish fillets

Start off by combining the cracker crumbs, the cheese, and the onion and garlic powder; you want them mixed really well. Set the mix aside. Then make a marinade with the oil, vinegar, lemon juice, and fresh garlic. I recommend you run the mixture through your blender or food processor.

Take the fish fillets and lay them out in a baking pan. Pour the marinade over them, cover with Saran Wrap, and place in the refrigerator for about an hour, basting about every 15 minutes. Then, when you're ready to cook, take the fish out of the marinade, roll each fillet liberally in the crumbs, and place on a buttered baking platter or pizza pan. *Be sure the fillets do not touch each other.*

Set the oven at 500 degrees, slide the platter onto the center oven rack, and cook for about 12 to 15 minutes or until the fish fillets flake when you test them with a fork. You can dribble a little of the marinade over the fish as it cooks if you prefer.

This is good stuff, y'all! And it's so easy.

Hint: I suggest you serve this with potato salad and green peas, or french fries and buttered carrots. And for some reason or other, a cold beer seems to go best with this dish.

Fish Amandine

At first, I was going to eliminate the recipe for Fish Amandine from this book—everybody makes an amandine, right? But like Paw-Paw's Courtbouillon, I found a *better* amandine. So what the heck!

6 lean-fish fillets (9 oz. each)	**1 cup flour**
¼ tsp. almond extract	**1 cup slivered almonds**
2 cups whole milk	**2 tbsp. lemon juice**
2 sticks margarine	**2 tbsp. finely chopped parsley**
¼ cup Crisco oil	**1 cup finely chopped Swiss**
salt and pepper to taste	**cheese**

What makes this amandine better than the run-of-the-mill amandines is the care given to the fillets before cooking. What you do is place the fillets in a baking pan, add 1/8 tsp. of almond extract to the milk, and pour it over the fish as a marinade. Then you cover the fish, place it in your refrigerator, and let the marinade work for about an hour.

When you're ready to cook, melt down the margarine over medium heat and stir the Crisco oil into it; you're really making a buttery-flavored oil, and it makes all the difference in the world in the final taste.

Go ahead and remove the fillets from the marinade and salt and pepper them.

Then roll them in flour and sauté them in the oil mixture until they are crisp and lightly browned. At this point put the fillets on several paper towels on a platter in a warm oven (set the heat at low).

Strain the oil-margarine mixture and set it aside. Wipe out the pan, then reheat 6 tablespoons of the mixture to *sizzling*. Toss in the slivered almonds, the lemon juice, and the second 1/8 teaspoon of almond extract. With the heat on medium high, rapidly agitate the pan to brown the almonds and blend the lemon juice and extract together.

When you serve the fillets, generously spoon the sauce and almonds over the top and sprinkle with parsley and Swiss cheese.

Louisiana Fish Salad

The secret to getting a good fish salad is preparing the flaked fish that goes into it with care. Poach your fillets in seasoned stock, either with seasoning vegetables such as bell pepper, celery, garlic, and onions or seasoning herbs and spices. You might also want to use seafood stocks: shrimp, oyster, crabmeat, and so forth. Any poaching medium beats plain water. And poach only until the fish is *just tender*.

Try this salad for a real taste treat.

2 cups flaked fish
2 cups raw, broken spinach
1 cup diced celery
½ cup sliced radishes
½ cup chopped cucumber
¼ cup sliced shallots
3 tbsp. black olives, coarsely
   chopped

2 tbsp. diced pimentos
4 hard-boiled eggs, coarsely
   chopped
your favorite salad dressing
   (Green Goddess is best)
croutons
Romano or Parmesan cheese (to
   taste)

Completely chill all the ingredients and toss them together in a large bowl. Then top with the salad dressing and serve with croutons and a dash of Romano or Parmesan cheese. Very light for summertime meals.

Hint: For a special taste treat, prepare this salad with hickory-smoked fish. It's superb!

Mock Crabmeat

If you have priced lump crabmeat lately, you'll know why this recipe is included here. You don't have to buy—or pick—crabmeat to make a great mock-crabmeat salad, super mock stuffed crabs, or crabmeat dip or patties. All you need to do is fillet a firm-bodied fish like drum, croaker, or sheepshead and follow these directions. Whenever you can use *sheepshead*, use it! It's by far the best crabmeat substitute.

Here's how it's done:

Take a sheepshead and fillet it out completely, removing the skin, scales, and bones (including every bit of the bloodline). Then wash the fillets thoroughly in cold, running water and set them aside.

Bring to a boil enough water to cover the fish and season the water the same as you would if you were going to boil crabs, shrimp, or crawfish. You can use the boiling recipe presented earlier in this book—it's ideal.

Wrap the fish in cheesecloth and drop it into the seasoned water. Let it cook *only long enough so that it turns opaque* and begins to flake. Remove the pot from the fire and let it soak for about 15 minutes to pick up the seasonings. Then take the fish from the water, set it in a colander to drain, and allow it to cool. All that remains is "flaking."

I *defy you* to tell the difference between mock crabmeat made with sheepshead and the real thing! In salads, dips, fondues, stuffings, dressings, and patties, you'll swear that it's the real McCoy. And that's a guarantee, m'frien'!

Fish Boulettes

In Cajun Louisiana, one of the most economical (and tastiest) dishes you can serve your family is Fish Boulettes. Actually, folks elsewhere around the world call them fish cakes or fish patties, but in Bayou Country we roll 'em into "balls" (which is what *boulette* means in French!).

Garfish is the chief species used for boulettes—which is nice, because that's about all garfish is good for! But just about any species of lean to medium-oily fish can be transformed into boulettes. And here's the best recipe I've found for the dish:

1 cup seasoned cornmeal (with salt, black pepper, cayenne)
1 cup all-purpose flour
1 cup seasoned bread crumbs
2 cups flaked fish
2 cups cooked, chopped potatoes
2 eggs, beaten well
¼ cup whole milk
1 tbsp. finely chopped parsley
½ tsp. Tabasco
dash thyme
1 tsp. salt
4 tbsp. real butter
¼ cup finely chopped celery
¼ cup finely chopped white onion
¼ cup finely chopped bell pepper
2 tbsp. minced shallots (tops and bottoms)

First, make the coating mix: Blend together the cornmeal, flour, and bread crumbs and set them aside. In a large bowl, use your hands and mix together well the flaked fish, potatoes, eggs, whole milk, parsley, Tabasco, thyme, and salt.

Take a skillet, melt the butter, and gently sauté the celery, onion, bell pepper, and shallots until they wilt. *Do not overcook the seasoning vegetables*—you want them semicrisp in the boulettes. Pour the buttery seasonings into the fish-potato mix and blend everything together again. Make certain you have uniform texture.

Now begin rolling your boulettes—again with your hands. Form little balls (about ping-pong-ball size) and set them on waxed paper on top of the counter. When they are all made, roll them liberally in the coating mix (cornmeal, flour, and crumbs).

When you're ready to eat, drop the balls in your deep fryer and cook them at 450 degrees until they turn golden brown. At this point, either serve them *as is* with potatoes au gratin and buttered green beans, or cover them with your favorite sauce.

Beats the heck out of codfish cakes, y'all!

Baked Fish Pinwheels

Fish fillets can be served open-face on French bread, stuffed inside buns, and baked in pastry puffs. But one of the easiest ways to make "pocket-style" pastry entrées without all the hassle of stuffing and folding is to make pinwheels. And this one is my favorite pinwheel recipe. Incidentally, it can be a nice informal supper *or* an elegant touch in gourmet dining. And you can use your favorite kind of fish, too.

1 cup coarsely chopped onions
1 cup finely chopped mushrooms
1 cup finely chopped bell pepper
1 cup finely chopped celery
1 tbsp. finely chopped garlic
1 tbsp. finely chopped parsley
1 cup finely shredded provolone cheese

1 cup finely chopped colby cheese
2 8-oz. cans refrigerator biscuits or crescent rolls
1 stick melted butter
3 cups flaked fish
1 egg, beaten well

Before you get started on the pinwheels, mix up the vegetable ingredients. In a bowl, using your hands, thoroughly blend the onions, mushrooms, bell pepper, celery, garlic, and parsley. The mixture must be uniform to get even taste distribution. Set it aside for a while. Then, in a separate bowl, combine the two cheeses. Like the vegetables, they must be uniformly mixed. Set them aside.

And now for the most tedious part. Set out the biscuits on a floured surface and flatten them with a rolling pin. You want to get them as thin as possible without tearing them. After they are rolled out, take a knife and shape them into approximately 6-by-9-inch rectangles. You may have to put 2 or 3 biscuits together to get that length, but just splice them with a fork. Prepare 3 strips this size. With a pastry brush liberally butter the dough along its entire length. Allow the dough to set for a while so that the butter is absorbed. Then brush a second application of butter into the dough.

Next separate the ingredients into thirds so that you have enough for 3 rolls. Begin layering the ingredients, *thinly!* First put down a layer of flaked fish (you can use smoked fish for an extra tang). Then spread the layer of vegetables. Finally add the layer of cheeses. When everything is layered, begin rolling the first piece of dough lengthwise, jelly-roll fashion, *buttering the flip side as you go.* When you have it all rolled up, pin it with a toothpick, brush it all over with the beaten egg, and set it on an *ungreased* baking pan. Do all 3 rolls the same way.

When you're ready to eat, bake the pinwheels at 350 degrees for about 25 to 30 minutes or until golden brown. Then serve them piping hot with your favorite buttered vegetable, a bowl of fresh cole slaw, or a crisp tossed salad.

Fish Meunière

This is another one of those recipes I was going to leave out of my book because everybody has a recipe for meunière! But, like the amandine, this one seems to be the best I've ever tasted, so I wanted you to have it. Hope it meets your expectations.

6 fish fillets (lean is best)
1 12-oz. can beer
salt to taste
black pepper to taste
½ cup whole milk
1 egg, well beaten
flour (about 1 cup)

½ stick butter
4 tbsp. freshly squeezed lemon
  juice
2 tbsp. Worcestershire sauce
1 thinly sliced lemon
dash Tabasco sauce

Start off by marinating the fillets in the beer in the refrigerator for at least 3 to 4 hours. Then drain off the beer and pat the fish dry. Salt and pepper lightly. Mix the milk and the egg together well and dip the fish fillets in the mixture until they are thoroughly coated. Then roll them in the flour, dip them in the egg-milk mixture again, and roll them a second time in the flour.

Melt the butter over medium heat. When it is just foaming and starting to sizzle, add the fillets and sauté them on each side until golden brown. This should take just about 4 minutes on each side if you have the temperature set properly. Remove them from the butter when they're golden and crisp, set them on paper towels, and place them on a platter in a warm oven.

Strain the butter, put the clarified portions back in the skillet, reheat to medium (being careful it doesn't burn!), and add the lemon juice and Worcestershire. Stir well for about 3 minutes, making certain that the ingredients are blended. Then serve the fish and spoon the meunière sauce over the top. Garnish with the lemon slices and dab with the Tabasco.

Hint: Meunière sauce is best when served with a creamed vegetable, herbed rice, avocado salad, and fresh-baked French bread. I also suggest a dry white wine as the beverage.

Smoked Tater-Fish

Very few vegetables seem to go as well with fish as potatoes. No doubt you've eaten mashed potatoes, french-fried potatoes, brabant potatoes, potatoes au gratin, and potatoes a hundred other ways with fried, baked, and broiled fish. But how about putting the fish *in* the potato? Especially smoked fish—it's some good! Try this:

4 extra-large baking potatoes
1 stick butter, melted
½ pt. heavy cream
2 tbsp. finely chopped celery
1 tbsp. finely chopped bell pepper
2 tbsp. finely chopped shallots

2 tsp. salt
½ tsp. fresh-ground black pepper
¼ tsp. cayenne pepper
½ cup finely chopped mushrooms
½ cup grated colby cheese
2 cups flaked smoked fish

Wash the potatoes, dry them thoroughly, and bake them until a fork penetrates the entire potato easily (I suggest a 375-degree oven for about an hour). Then, very carefully, slice them lengthwise in half and scoop out all but ¼ inch near the skin.

Get a large bowl and get ready to prepare the stuffing. Take the potato centers you've scooped out, pour the melted butter over it, and work the mixture into a uniform paste, almost as if you were preparing mashed potatoes. Then add the cream, celery, bell pepper, shallots, salt, both peppers, mushrooms, and cheese and blend them together well. At this point gradually fold in the smoked fish, stirring constantly. The dish comes out best if some fish is flaked extra finely and some is flaked in chunks. Then, using a spoon, fill the hollowed-out potato halves with the mixture, place them on a pizza tin, and heat them in the oven at 350 degrees until the outer crust is lightly browned (about 10 minutes).

Serve piping hot. Makes 8 halves—and goes well with a tossed green salad and cold ginger ale. Ideal for summer!

Poissenot's Gourmet Fish-Fri Batter

Lloyd Poissenot is one of the finest New Orleans wildlife photographers ever to pick up a camera. But Lloyd isn't only creative with a Nikon, he's also an artist of French cuisine, especially when it comes to delicate sauces and mixes. The recipe below is the one he likes for sealing in juices and flavor in filleted fish. The taste is quite distinctive!

6 fish fillets
1 large lemon, cut in half
1 tbsp. pure olive oil
¼ tsp. freshly ground black
  pepper

1 egg, beaten well
½ tsp. Coleman's dry mustard
Zatarain's Fish-Fri (lightly
  salted) or yellow cornmeal

Wash the fish fillets thoroughly in *cold water*, cut them into pieces about 3 inches long, and set them aside to dry. After all the water has evaporated, place the pieces in a medium-size mixing bowl and squeeze the lemon over the fish. Use your hands to roll the fish chunks around in the lemon juice. Then pour the olive oil over the fish, add the black pepper and the egg, and *work both well* into the fillets. Again, use your hands.

Finally, toss in the Coleman's mustard and really mix it into the other ingredients, tumbling the fish over and over until all the seasonings are equally blended. Then set the bowl in the refrigerator for about half an hour so the mixture can chill. When you're ready to fry, take the fillets out of the bowl one at a time and coat them liberally with Fish-Fri or cornmeal. Use your fingers and the heel of your hand to *push* the Fish-Fri into the fillets; *coat them well*. The secret to crispy fish is to drop the fillets in hot grease (over 400 degrees) as quickly as you can get them from the coating mix to the pan—if the coating becomes moist it will get gummy. Fry until golden brown.

Serving Hint: After the fillets are fried, lay them on a paper towel–lined platter and cover each layer with some thinly sliced white onion. This will enhance the flavor.

Seafood-Garnished Redfish Courtbouillon

Most traditional Louisiana courtbouillons are made with either redfish or catfish. But this recipe, from the kitchen of Lois de Latour, combines the subtle flavor of oysters and shrimp with the roux and tomatoes to give a full-bodied enhancement to the baked fish. Without a doubt it's one of the best-tasting courtbouillons I've ever cooked—and I've tried a few. Don't skip fixing this one!

1½ cups flour
½ cup Crisco oil
1 stick margarine (plus some melted)
3 bunches green onions, finely chopped
5 cloves garlic, finely chopped
1 cup celery, finely chopped
3 bay leaves
pinch of thyme
pinch of rosemary

salt to taste
1 16-oz. can tomato sauce
4 doz. oysters (save the liquor)
1 lemon, squeezed (remove the seeds)
½ cup parsley, finely chopped
4 lbs. redfish fillets, cut into serving pieces
1 lemon, sliced
3 lbs. shrimp, peeled

The first thing you do is make a nice, brown roux using the flour, the oil, *and* the stick of margarine. Then add all your ingredients except the shrimp, redfish, oysters, parsley, lemon juice, and tomatoes. You want to cook all these ingredients until they're soft.

Then add the tomatoes and the oyster water (maybe add a little tap water if you don't have enough oyster liquor), but remember that you want to keep your sauce *thick*. When you have the consistency you want, add the lemon juice and the parsley and cook the entire mixture, just bubbling, for about an hour on low heat. While the sauce is cooking lay out your fish in a deep-sided baking pan. Then sprinkle each piece with salt, top with a lemon slice, and brush with melted margarine. Put the pieces in the oven and turn up the controls to 350 degrees. And as soon as the fish begins to cook (it will turn white), add the shrimp and oysters to the sauce and pour the sauce over the fish evenly. When the fish flakes and the shrimp are uniformly pink, the dish is done. It should take just about an hour to cook to perfection.

Hint: Try serving this with wild rice and a tossed green salad.

Poached Speckled Trout Mariniere

Poaching is a delicate way of preparing fish; it brings out deep-bodied flavors often suppressed by the harshness of baking and broiling. In this recipe, which is truly a gourmet treat, the speckled trout is the main ingredient, but the preparation is so delectable that the dish would probably come out just as good using a fillet off a choupique! You gotta try this one with your favorite lean fish.

4 speckled trout fillets
¼ cup plus 1 tbsp. butter (not margarine)
1 tbsp. Worcestershire sauce
½ tsp. lemon juice
1 cup water or fish stock
½ cup green onions, chopped

3 tbsp. flour
1½ cup milk
salt and pepper to taste
5 tbsp. Chablis
2 egg yolks, beaten well
dash paprika

Now follow this recipe closely, and don't skip any of the steps. Start off with a skillet large enough to hold the fillets without their touching each other. This is how you'll poach the trout. The fish has to be cooked before the rest of the recipe is prepared.

To the fish in the skillet add: 1 tablespoon of butter, the tablespoon of Worcestershire, the ½ teaspoon of lemon juice, and enough water to *just cover* the fillets. Then turn up the heat and simmer the fish until the outer edges go white. Don't overcook! When one side is done, flip the fillets and cook the other side. As soon as the fish are poached, remove them from the poaching liquid and set them aside in a shallow baking pan.

Now take a saucepan, pour in the ¼ cup of butter, and sauté the green onions until tender. Next, add the flour and cook it 3 minutes, stirring constantly. As soon as the mixture is hot, blend in the milk and stir until the sauce is thick and smooth. Finally, add the salt and pepper and the wine and cook for 10 minutes. After you remove the sauce from the fire, add the egg yolks and stir them in rapidly. You have to be fast or they'll cook hard!

When you're ready to eat, pour the sauce over the fillets, sprinkle the top with paprika, and broil lightly till hot.

Pickled Louisiana Catfish

Everybody's eaten catfish—fried, broiled, baked, and in Cajun courtbouillon. But if you haven't tried putting catfish in pickling spice and serving it finger-style, you've got a real taste treat coming! This is gooooood!

salt and water for brine solution
5 lbs. catfish fillets
2 medium white onions, sliced
1 medium bell pepper, chopped
2 4½-oz. bags Zatarain's dry crab boil or 2 oz. liquid crab boil

3 cups white vinegar (5% acid)
4 whole cayenne peppers

Before you start working with the fish fillets, make a good brine solution that will float an egg easily. The best way to do this is to add salt, a tablespoon at a time, to a large bowl of water, and keep testing the water with the egg until the brine is concentrated enough.

After your salt solution is ready, cut the raw catfish fillets into 1-inch cubes. Then soak the cubes in the saltwater for at least 24 hours (covered, and in a refrigerator). Don't cut this step short; it's what makes the catfish tender. When the fish has "cured," take it out of the refrigerator and let it warm to room temperature. Then drain off the brine. Now you're ready to pickle. Set out 2 quart-size Mason jars, get your ingredients ready, and start packing the jars as follows:

In the bottom of each jar put a slice of onion, then a tablespoon of chopped bell pepper. Add a handful of fish fillets, and top it all off with a sprinkling of crab boil.

Repeat the process of filling the jars in this manner until the fish and ingredients are about a half-inch from the top. Then make a half-and-half mixture of vinegar and water, add the remaining bell pepper and onions, and fill both jars to the brim. Before you seal the jars, put 2 cayenne peppers on the top of each.

Hint: To bring out the full flavor of the fish and seasoning, let the jars stand in your refrigerator for at least 30 days.

Fillets a la Thermidor

Jerald Horst—when he isn't working as the assistant area fisheries agent for the Louisiana Cooperative Extension Service—spends most of his time in the kitchen experimenting with new recipes. As a culinary scientist, he is quite a success. The recipe below is probably the best one he has come up with for fish, and I guarantee you'll like it.

3 lbs. filleted fish	½ cup margarine
2¼ cups whole milk	½ cup flour
1½ tsp. salt	½ cup lemon juice
dash black pepper	1 tbsp. Worcestershire sauce
½ lb. sharp cheddar cheese	3 tbsp. paprika

Before you do anything, preheat your oven to 350 degrees. While it's heating, start preparing your fillets. You can use almost any kind of low-oil fish for this recipe—speckled trout, flounder, croaker, sheepshead, or drum. What you want to do is cut the fillets lengthwise into 2-inch strips, roll them, and pin them with toothpicks. Set them in a shallow baking pan so they aren't touching.

Now pour the milk over the fish, sprinkle each roll with salt and pepper, and bake about 15 minutes or until the fish flakes easily. But *don't overcook;* you want to keep the fillets moist. While the fish is baking, go ahead and grate the cheese coarsely and melt the margarine.

When the fillets are tender, remove the baking pan from the oven and switch the oven to "broil." Drain the milk, but save it—you'll use it later. In the saucepan with the melted margarine, slowly stir in the flour to make a sauce. Then add the milk you saved and cook over low heat until the flour thickens. Then, *stirring constantly,* add the cheese, the lemon juice, and the Worcestershire sauce. When they are all well mixed, pour the mixture over the baked fillets and generously sprinkle with paprika. Return the fillets to the oven, brown lightly under the broiler, and serve with boiled potatoes and green peas.

Joe Collin's Famous Barbecued Trout

They say cabdrivers know all the good places to eat. Well, this recipe may not confirm that, but it will confirm that some cabdrivers know *how* to eat *good*. Because my cabdriver friend, Joe Collins, cooks this trout dish all the time. And I guess that's why folks keep asking him for the recipe, just like I did! Rating? Spicy, delicious, and four stars!

6 speckled trout fillets (skin removed)	6 tbsp. lemon juice
	1 cup chili sauce
2 small white onions, finely chopped	6 tbsp. Worcestershire sauce
	½ tsp. Tabasco sauce
4 tbsp. melted butter	6 tbsp. brown sugar
1 cup tomato catsup	1 tsp. salt

Start off by laying the trout fillets in a buttered baking pan. Make your barbecue sauce by cooking the onions in the butter for about 3 minutes and adding the catsup, lemon juice, chili sauce, Worcestershire, Tabasco, brown sugar, and salt. All this goes in the skillet together and simmers slowly.

Then, when your sauce is "cured" (it takes about 5 minutes), pour it over the fish fillets and bake the trout for about 30 minutes or until the fish flakes easily with a fork. That's all there is to it!

Joe says you can improve the flavor if you baste the cooking fish occasionally. You can also save the sauce in your refrigerator.

Hint: This dish goes well with buttered rice (be sure to spoon the sauce over it!), candied carrots, and a crisp cole slaw. And to add the final touch, serve it with a good white wine.

Fish Balls and Pasta Italianne

After I married a young lady of Sicilian descent, one of the first recipes I whipped up in her honor involved fish, real homemade Italian gravy, and fresh pasta. If you want to try a dish that smacks of Palermo flavoring, follow the directions listed below—*exactly*—and fix your family a real treat. The only thing you'll be missing will be the mandolins . . . but you won't care!

Gravy:

4 tbsp. pure olive oil
1 medium white onion, finely chopped
4 cloves garlic, finely chopped
2 12-oz. cans tomato paste
6 cups water

4 bay leaves
2 tsp. McCormick Italian seasoning
1 tsp. basil
¼ cup Burgundy wine
salt and black pepper to taste

Fish Balls:

3 cups broiled, unseasoned flaked fish
1 egg, beaten well
½ tsp. oregano
1 tbsp. pure olive oil

½ tsp. basil
1 tsp. finely chopped parsley
½ tsp. tarragon
1 cup seasoned Italian bread crumbs

Also:

your choice of pasta
grated Romano cheese

Let me tell you up front that this is a two-part recipe: the gravy is made first, the fish balls second. It is recommended you follow this order so that the gravy *cooks* while you're working on the fish. To put the gravy together, heat up 4 tablespoons of olive oil in a 4-quart stainless-steel pot and fry the onion and garlic until they are tender. Then add the 2 cans of tomato paste and fry until the paste is dark red.

Next add the water, bay leaves, Italian seasonings, basil, and wine, and stir everything together so that you get a smooth consistency. You can salt and pepper the gravy at this point, too. To get the gravy cooking as it should, bring the mixture to a boil. As soon as it starts to bubble, reduce the heat to *low.* You want it to *just cook;* otherwise you'll build up a high acid trace from the tomatoes. So watch the action in the pot. When it's cooking properly, cover it tightly. While your gravy is simmering on the stove, work on preparing the fish balls.

Start by raking a fork over the flaked fish in a large bowl. Ideally, you want to eliminate any big lumps of meat—*a fine consistency is best*. When the fish is ready, add the egg, the oregano, the tablespoon of olive oil, the basil, the parsley, the tarragon, and the bread crumbs. To do it right, each ingredient should be added separately and mixed in well before the next ingredient is blended in. If, however, you put them all in simultaneously, just take time to fold everything together before you shape the balls. The mix should be *sticky*. While the size of the fish balls is a matter of preference, I prefer "drops" about 2 inches in diameter. Use your hands and roll them around until you get them the way you want them. Then drop them individually into deep oil and fry them lightly. *Don't overcook*. Remember, the fish has already been broiled!

When the fish balls are ready, remove them from the grease and drain them well on paper towels. While they're draining, boil your pasta. You can use spaghetti, ditali, cavatuni, or noodles—it makes no difference which.

Okay, now here's the trick to timing. About *5 minutes* before the pasta is ready to be strained, drop the fish balls into the gravy and turn up the heat. *Any more than 5 minutes will overcook the fish balls and they'll fall apart!*

To serve, dish up the pasta, spoon generous helpings of gravy over it, and gently drop several of the fish balls right on top! Then sprinkle a lot of grated Romano cheese over the whole works! Hey, cumba—that's Italian!

Hints: It would be a shame to serve this dish without garlic bread. Believe me, you'll want to sop up the gravy. It would also be a shame to serve it without Italian salad to go with it. Make sure you put a lot of anchovies in it! And finally, it would be a sin to serve this dish without serving a full-bodied Italian red wine. After all, it only takes a dime more to go the best!

AND ABOUT ITALIAN GRAVY

Don't worry about how long to cook it. The longer it cooks, the better it gets. Just remember to keep the fire on low so that it just simmers.

Grilled Fish in Scales

This is one of my all-time favorite recipes for heavy-bodied, large-scaled fish (channel bass, drum, sheepshead, etc.) cooked over the open grill. And it is quite easy to prepare. Here's how:

All you do is fillet the fish, removing 2 tenderloins but leaving the scales on. If you buy the fish from a seafood market, ask the seafood cutter to be sure to dress the fish in this manner, because once the scales are removed you can't fix this recipe. Place the fish in a shallow baking pan and pour two 16-ounce bottles of Kraft Zesty Italian Salad Dressing over the fillets (the scales should face down in the pan). Cover with aluminum foil and refrigerate for at least 8 hours.

When you're ready to cook, fire up the grill (either charcoal or gas), drain the fillets, and salt and pepper them lightly. Then rub *1 teaspoon* of Liquid Smoke into each fillet with your hands. *Incidentally, I suggest you save the basting liquid so that you can brush it on the fish as it cooks.*

Next, after the grill has been lighted for about 15 minutes, place the fish over the coals—about 8 inches from the heat source—*scale-side down*. Then cover the grill and let the fish cook. Every 5 minutes or so check the cooking process—it shouldn't take long (20 minutes at most). When the fish has turned opaque and begins to flake apart, it's done. Remove the fillets from the grill and serve them piping hot with brabant potatoes, dirty rice, or cole slaw and hush puppies.

This is a pretty dish, too. The scales turn a scorched brown and curl up at the edges. You can garnish the fish nicely with sprigs of parsley, cherry tomatoes, or broccoli spears. And the best way to serve it is with a spatula; the fish scoops away from the scales very easily.

Paul Prudhomme's Blackened Redfish

The last recipe in this section is, in my opinion, the very best recipe there is for fish. And it is the creation of my very good friend, Chef Paul Prudhomme. If there ever was a Cajun who could cook, m'frien', it's this man! I've had the opportunity over the past 20 years to talk with and cook with lots of culinary talent, but none I've met approach the creative genius of Chef Paul. So much of what I've learned to do in the kitchen is because of my relationship with Paul, and I truly consider him the unequalled master of food preparation.

Consequently, of all the dishes I prepare, this one, Paul's recipe for Blackened Redfish, is my absolute favorite. Thank you, m'frien', for a real masterpiece. Here's why I like it so much. . . .

6 9-oz. redfish fillets	**½ tsp. granulated garlic**
12 bay leaves, finely crushed	**3 tsp. salt**
2 tsp. paprika	**¼ tsp. black pepper**
¼ tsp. basil	**½ tsp. white pepper**
¼ tsp. oregano	**½ tsp. cayenne pepper**
¼ tsp. thyme	**2 sticks butter, melted**
½ tsp. granulated onion	

Start off by drying the redfish fillets and chilling them in the refrigerator. Redfish is, by far, the best species to use for this recipe, but when I can't get redfish I use other heavy-bodied firm fish (drum, sheepshead, bass). The one important thing to remember is the *size* of the fillet. It cannot weigh less than 8 ounces or more than 12 ounces; otherwise it doesn't cook properly.

When you're ready to cook, place a black-iron Dutch oven on the burner and turn the heat up to high. *You must use an iron oven; no other metal can take the heat.* In fact you really should prepare this recipe outside because it makes lots of smoke. You want to get the pot almost *white hot*, hot enough to see a "flame circle" in the center. Remember, there is nothing in the pot—no oil, no shortening, no nothing. Just bare metal.

Lay the fillets on a sheet of waxed paper. Mix the bay leaves, paprika, basil, oregano, thyme, onion, garlic, salt, black pepper, white pepper, and cayenne in a small bowl. Sprinkle the mix over the fillets. *Do it lightly, but distribute the mixture evenly.* Then dip the fillets in the melted butter so that they are completely coated. And *immediately* drop them into the hot Dutch oven. I suggest you do them one at a time.

I can tell you that the fish will sputter and jump and sizzle and smoke, but that's what it is supposed to do! And it's gonna do it quick, too. Because in just 30 to 40 *seconds,* the side down against the metal will be cooked and it will be time to flip the fillet over. The cooked side should be dark brown, almost charred. That's the way you want it. Cook the flip side another 30 to 40 seconds and remove the fillet from the black pot. Your *blackened redfish* is done!

The texture is unbelievable! Crispy brown on the outer crust, but light, tender, and ultramoist on the inside. It is one of the finest fish dishes you will ever eat. I recommend you serve it with cole slaw or potato salad, some hush puppies, and a tall, frosted glass of the coldest beer you can get your hands on. If your mouth doesn't *run water* after your first bite, you've swallowed your taste buds!

SELECTED RECIPES FOR MULLET

Of all the fish species found along the Louisiana coastline, the *mullet* has to be the one species most overlooked as table fare. Folks in Florida seem to relish the fish, judging from their catch statistics—in 1978 over 35 million pounds were taken from the water—but Louisianians appear to be spoiled; we much prefer to cook trout, redfish, flounder, and bass. It is probably a safe assumption to say that only a small percentage of families in Louisiana have ever tasted mullet. And that's a shame. Because prepared properly, the fish is delicious!

My old friend Jim Ledbetter, who is a Florida fishing guide transplanted from New Iberia, Louisiana, sent me a batch of mullet recipes he picked up from the Gulf South and Atlantic Fisheries Development Foundation. Jim says he tried them all and they are the best he's ever eaten. So I'm including them in this section of the book for you to try.

One more thing. Because you've probably heard nothing but unfavorable comment about mullets, like how they eat mud and garbage, let me give you some factual information on the species:

- Mullet feed on microscopic plant and animal matter, not garbage. They are not scavengers.
- Those caught in the surf and in waterways with sandy bottoms rank best in flavor.
- The best method of catching mullet is with a cast net. They rarely bite on rod and reel, but if large schools are present a small treble hook baited with tiny bread balls or bits of shrimp will provide some sport action.
- Mullet are extremely rich in minerals. Their iodine content is 900 times higher than the best grade of beef. Their flesh has a mild, nutty taste.
- Mullet can be fried or baked, but they are best when smoked, broiled, or grilled. And the roe is often considered a delicacy.

Next chance you get, try these recipes.

Cajun-Fried Mullet a la Ledbetter

When Jim Ledbetter sent me these recipes, he raved about this one. So I tried it one Friday afternoon. I think I was still eating Saturday morning—you talk about good!

1½ lbs. mullet, cut into fillets	2.75 oz. dry onion soup mix
1 tsp. salt	½ cup Crisco or peanut oil
¼ tsp. cayenne pepper	sliced lemon wedges
1 egg, beaten well	1 large white onion, thinly sliced
1 tbsp. water	
1 cup instant mashed potato flakes	

First, lay the fillets on waxed paper and sprinkle them with salt and cayenne pepper. Then combine the egg and the water in a small bowl and mix together well. Pour the potato flakes and the dry soup mix into a flat baking pan and blend them together.

When you're ready to cook, dip the fillets into the potato mixture and shake off the excess. Then dip the fish into the egg and back into the potatoes. This will give you a thick and crunchy crust when the mullet is fried. For best results, panfry. Pour about an eighth-inch of Crisco or good grade of peanut oil into a saucepan and get it hot *but not smoking*. Then drop in the coated fillets and cook them on both sides until they are golden brown and flake easily. Your heat should be medium high (about 380 degrees).

After the fish is fried, lay it out on paper towels and dribble with lemon juice. Just before you serve them, top the fillets with thinly sliced onions.

Serving Suggestion: Because of the mullet's exceptionally delicate flavor, light complementary foods go best with it. You might try serving fried mullet, hush puppies, and pineapple-sweetened cole slaw.

Mullet Casserole St. Jacques

This is an especially flavorful dish that makes an excellent buffet item. Preparation is quick and easy.

1½ cups cooked, flaked mullet	½ cup dry vermouth
1½ cups chopped fresh mushrooms	1 tbsp. finely chopped parsley
	dash white pepper
3 green onions, finely chopped	1 slice stale white bread
4 tbsp. melted butter, divided	2 tbsp. grated Parmesan cheese
1 10¾-oz. can cream of chicken soup	dash paprika

The first thing you need to do is either poach or bake the mullet. *But don't season it.* Cook it without salt or pepper, then flake it and set it aside to cool. As it's cooling, sauté your mushrooms and onions in 3 tablespoons of butter. Get them tender, but don't let them brown too much. When they're ready, set them aside, too.

Next, combine the soup and the vermouth in a 1½-quart saucepan, bring the mixture to a boil, stirring constantly, and then cut the heat down to simmer. Let the mixture cook for about 5 minutes, until the flavors blend; then remove the saucepan from the fire. At this point add the fish, cooked mushrooms and onions, parsley, and white pepper to the saucepan and mix them all together well. Then spray a small baking dish with Pam and pour the mix into it, leveling it evenly in the dish. As it's cooling put the stale bread and the Parmesan in a blender and combine them thoroughly.

Finally, sprinkle the bread-crumb mix and the paprika over the top of the casserole, dribble the remaining tablespoon of melted butter over the crumbs, and bake the dish at 350 degrees for about 15 minutes or until lightly browned.

Hint: This casserole goes well with broccoli au gratin, steamed rice, and a tossed green salad. The recipe serves six.

Mullet Teriyaki Kabobs

Cooking mullet this way will give you all the fixin's for a backyard get-together. While you can cook the kabobs in an oven, they come out much better fired up on an open grill. Try this: Fix some and don't tell your guests they're eating mullet. They'll rave!

2 lbs. mullet fillets
½ cup fresh lemon juice
¼ cup dry sherry
¼ cup soy sauce
2 tbsp. brown sugar
1 tsp. ground ginger
1 tsp. dry mustard

1 tsp. garlic salt
1½ cups cherry tomatoes
1 cup fresh mushrooms
1 large bell pepper, cut in 1-inch squares
1 medium onion, cut in thin wedges

The first thing to do is cut the mullet into 1-inch squares. Then prepare your marinade by mixing together the lemon juice, sherry, soy sauce, brown sugar, ginger, dry mustard, and garlic salt. The marinade must be blended well, so take care with it or you'll lose much of the flavor. When your sauce is ready, lay out the mullet chunks in a shallow baking pan and pour the sauce over the fish. Be sure all the pieces are coated. The best technique to use is to set the soaking fish in the refrigerator for about an hour.

Next, get out the skewers and take the fish out of the marinade, *saving the marinade* because you'll baste with it while your kabobs are grilling. To put the kabobs together, alternate the fish pieces, cherry tomatoes, mushrooms, green pepper, and onion wedges.

In the oven, lay the kabobs over a baking pan, baste with the marinade mix, and grill for about 8 minutes, about 4 inches from the heating element. Then turn the kabobs, baste again, and cook for another 5 minutes until the fish pieces flake easily. *On the grill,* cook and baste directly over the coals (about 2 inches above) until tender. Just keep them basted!

BEFORE PREPARING ANY FISH

Keep the fillets cold and dry them completely with paper towels. They'll stay juicier and excess water won't dilute the seasonings in the sauces you prepare.

CHAPTER SEVEN

Crabs

HOW TO USE A CRAB KNIFE

Among Louisiana's most prized seafoods, very few species rank higher than the *blue crab*. Its delicate meat is highly flavorful, firm-textured, tantalizingly versatile, and easy to cook with.

But unless you plan to serve crispy-fried or broiled *soft-shell* crabs, which are eaten whole, you will have to boil the *hard-shells* and pick out the crabmeat. And lots of folks seem to have problems picking crabs. Getting the meat out of the chambers isn't that easy for the novice, and it could become quite a task since it generally takes about 10 to 15 boiled crabs to yield a pound to a pound and a half of crabmeat.

So that's why I've included this section in the book. It's all about picking crabmeat, whether you pick it to eat at a crab boil or pick it to make crabmeat au gratin. Once you master the technique explained in the next few pages, I guarantee you won't go back to primitive methods ever again!

I'm talking about using the *crab knife*, the little short-bladed device commercial pickers have been using for years, but domestic users have caught onto only recently.

You can actually buy a commercial "crab knife," a short-bladed, heavy aluminum or cast knife that sells for about $4 to $6 at most hardware stores. Or you can use any small, heavy, sharp kitchen knife (such as a paring knife) and get practically the same results. The object is to cut through the crab's *chambers* to lay open the meat, so that extraction becomes a very simple matter. All it takes is a little practice—I'd say that if you follow the directions in this chapter and cut through a half-dozen crabs, you'll just about have the procedure down pat.

Dr. Mike Moody, a seafoods technology specialist with Louisiana State University's Cooperative Extension Service, suggested that I use the photographs he produced for his course on seafood processing to illustrate crab-knife how-to. So, with Mike's assistance, here goes:

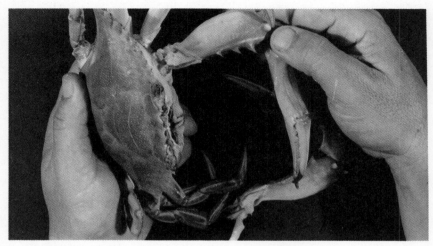

1. Firmly grasp the rear of the crab body with one hand and break off the claws, placing them aside for picking later. Meat should not be pulled out of the crab body when the claw is broken, or you will ruin the "lump" portion.

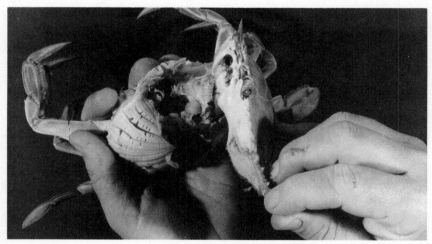

2. Grasping one of the large carapace (top-shell) spines, pull off the top shell and set it aside. Holding the crab as shown makes this procedure easy to follow.

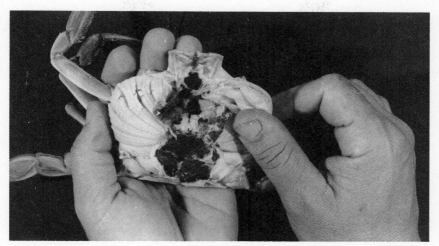

3. Using your thumb, brush the gills from both sides of the crab body. The gills, commonly referred to as the "dead man," are not edible and should be discarded.

4. Use the knife to clean the inside portions of the crab between the right and left cores. You should take out all the organs, fat, and eggs (if there are any). Holding the crab as shown will make this task a simple matter.

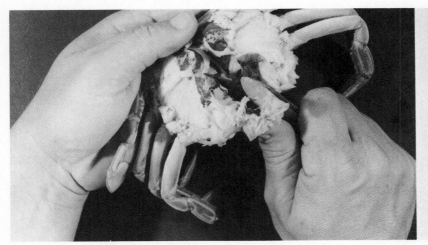

5. Cut off the mouth parts as illustrated. Be sure to cut close to the bottom shell and make the cut clean.

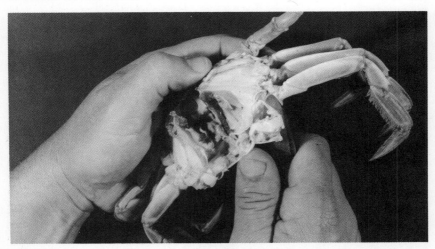

6. Rotate the crab upside down and remove the sockets where the claws were attached to the body. They should not be cut out, but pried upward and popped out.

7. Here's the critical part. Starting from the back of the crab body, with the point of the knife angled slightly *downward* and pointed toward the *center* of the body . . .

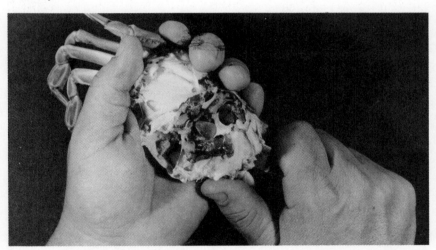

8. . . . make a cut *across the top* of the legs on one side of the crab and set the resulting piece aside. This cut must be made properly if the body chambers are to be opened. A common mistake is not making the cut low enough. Then rotate the crab 180 degrees in your hand and make the same cut on the other side of the crab. This step will probably take the greatest amount of practice, but after doing it a half-dozen times or so you'll have it mastered perfectly.

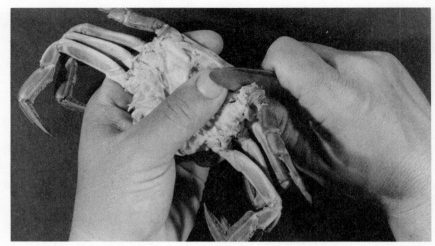

9. With your thumb firmly covering the open chambers, cut off the legs on the side you're holding down. Make certain you make the cut on the *inside edge* of the leg joints where they are attached to the crab body. Make the cut on the other side of the crab, too.

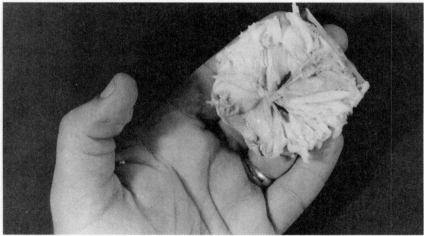

10. When it's fully cut out the crab body should look just like this, with the meat fully exposed and all the individual chambers opened.

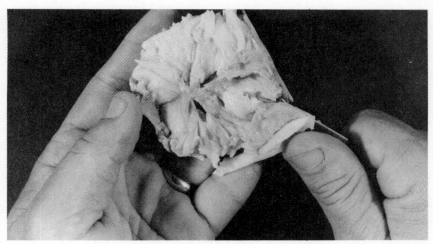

11. From this piece, carefully pry out the lump meat. If you made your cuts right, it should come out easily in one large piece. Use the knife to pick out the meat. Rotate the crab and remove the lump meat from the other side, too.

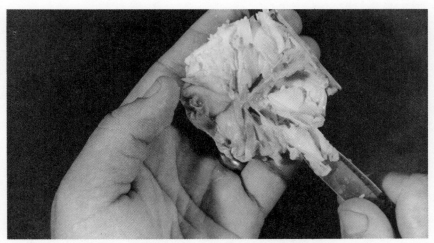

12. Now remove the meat from the opened chambers adjoining the back-fin chambers. If your cuts weren't just right, simply find the apex of each chamber and slide the knife through the chamber once to open it up. There should be five separate chambers on each side of the crab body.

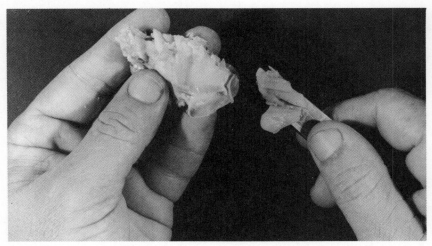

13. Pick up one of the two pieces set aside in step 8 and remove the loose piece of meat at the base end. This procedure reveals a shell covering as shown in the photograph. Simply make a downward cut through this covering and you will open up the chambers of meat.

14. Go ahead and extract the meat from the open chambers, using the point of the crab knife. When all the meat is picked clean, follow the same procedure with the other piece you set aside.

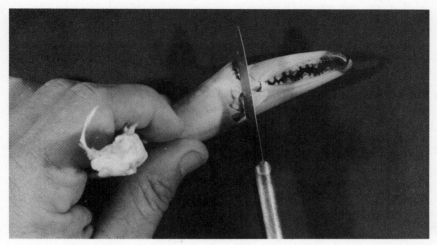

15. Remove the meat from the claws by laying each claw, with the arm pointed upward, on a hard, flat surface and sharply rapping it near the junction of the pinchers (there's a little "button" there) with the back edge or handle of the crab knife. This rap should crack the claw at the bottom. Be careful to *rap*, not *hammer* the junction. All you want to do is crack the claw—not smash it.

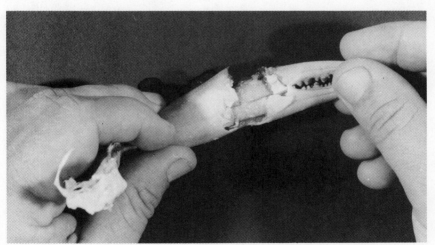

16. The claw meat is freed when the two halves are broken apart; it should come out looking just like this.

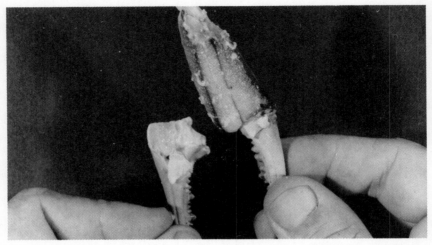

17. Carefully break off the stationary portion of the claw (the pincher that "wraps around" the other pincher) to make a *crab finger*. Be careful not to smash the meat when you snap the portions apart.

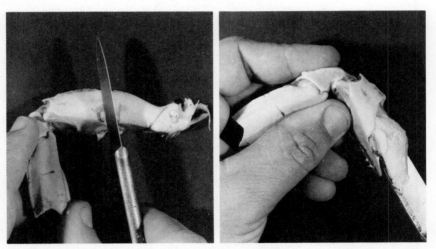

18. The meat from the arm of the claw can be extracted in a similar manner, except that after cracking it must be extracted using the point of the crab knife as shown in the photo. And that's all there is to it!

Let me make a couple of points here.

Before picking crabs, always wash your hands well, since you will be handling the meat. Once the meat has been picked, it should be chilled rapidly and stored under refrigeration (between 32 and 40 degrees) if not eaten immediately.

In order to prevent flavor loss, avoid washing or soaking the picked meat in water. You'll often hear that you should wash the meat but *don't do it*. It is not necessary.

Crabmeat can be frozen for long-term storage, but it may undergo some undesirable changes in texture and flavor if you don't package it properly. I recommend you freeze it as soon as possible after picking, use small containers that will permit fast freezing, and store at a temperature of zero degrees or lower.

CRAB DISHES

"Pie" Pendley's Fried Hard-Shell Crabs

This recipe, perfected by Marian "Pie" Pendley, is one you will want to try over and over again. It's fantastic for nibbling and picking! For watching a ball game on TV, for get-togethers with your friends, or for that something special to tempt your guests at parties, there's just nothing like it.

1 doz. crabs, live and uncleaned
6 cups whole milk
1 tbsp. freshly squeezed lemon
   juice
1 tbsp. paprika
¼ tsp. dry mustard

1 tbsp. soy sauce
2 cloves garlic, crushed
¼ tsp. cayenne pepper
salt to taste
2 cups unseasoned flour

The first thing you do is wash the crabs in clean water, then scald them in boiling water. Don't leave them in the hot water too long—just until they start to turn light pink. All you want to do is keep them from biting you! While the crabs are scalding, mix up your marinade by blending the milk, lemon juice, paprika, mustard, soy sauce, garlic, pepper, and salt in a large bowl. Set this aside for a while to cure.

While the marinade is curing, go ahead and clean your crabs. Remove the top shell, the gills, the mouth, the claws, the legs, and the fat. *Clean them well.* Then wash them under cold running water and set them aside to drain. When they're almost dry, cut them right down the middle so that you have a right and left half. At this point, drop the pieces into the marinade.

Marination is what makes this recipe so good, so cover the bowl, put it in the refrigerator, and let the crab halves soak for about 3 hours. (Keep in mind that the longer they soak, the better seasoned they will be.) Then, when you're ready to eat, drain off the marinade, roll the crab pieces thoroughly in the flour, and deep fry those rascals at about 375 degrees until they're golden brown.

Now you can roll up your sleeves, break out the cold beer, and go to it! You'll lick your fingers, for sure. No doubt about it, m'frien'!

Jerald's Crabmeat Croquettes

Just a few days after Jerald Horst sent me some of the recipes found elsewhere in this cookbook with his name stuck on them he called to tell me he'd come up with another super dish using crabmeat. So I jotted down the directions and the ingredients, and I tried it. Am I glad I did!

1 lb. cooked crabmeat	1 small white onion, finely
1 tsp. Worcestershire sauce	chopped
2 tsp. McCormick lemon pepper	½ cup whole milk
2 tbsp. real butter	2 eggs
3 tbsp. flour	1 cup bread crumbs (to make a
2 tsp. salt	coating mix)

First, get a bowl and put the crabmeat, the Worcestershire sauce, and the lemon pepper in it. Mix them all together really well. When you're sure you have a good blend, set the bowl aside for a while.

Put your butter in a saucepan and melt it. *As soon as it melts*, take it off the heat. Immediately mix in the flour, salt, chopped onion, and milk. Then put the pan back on the stove and cook over low heat. But keep stirring the mixture around, because you want everything folded well.

Okay, take the pan off the heat again and let the mixture cool. Now beat one of the eggs and add it to the crabmeat mix, working it in well. Add your cooled butter sauce and stir the whole works together. When you have it all mixed consistently, put it in the refrigerator for about 3 hours so it will stiffen up.

Then, when you're ready to eat, take the bowl out of the refrigerator, shape the mixture into little croquettes (or you can make patties if you prefer); beat the other egg; dip the patties into the egg, then into the bread crumbs; and deep fry them critters at 375 degrees until they're golden brown.

Hint: I suggest you serve the croquettes with creamed green peas, a mound of buttered mashed potatoes, and a frosty tomato salad.

Claire's Marinated Crab Salad

Sometimes you run into a recipe that you can't rave about enough because it's next to impossible to describe the blend of flavors, the succulence, the perfection. This salad creation by Claire Loverde is one of those recipes. You'll have to make it and taste it to find out how really delicious it is. And I promise you won't be at all disappointed.

2 doz. boiled crabs, picked
¼ cup vinegar
1 cup pure olive oil
1 8-oz. bottle Italian dressing
¼ cup minced parsley
2 cloves garlic, pressed
2 cups pitted green olives

½ cup pitted black olives
2 lemons, diced
1 stalk celery, sliced
1 bell pepper, thinly sliced
3 carrots, sliced
1 #303 can artichoke hearts, drained

First, boil or steam the crabs and pick out the meat, being careful to remove all the shell pieces. Also crack the claws, but leave the tips on. Then, in a large bowl (because you're going to have about 2 pounds of crabmeat), mix the vinegar, olive oil, and Italian dressing and blend them together. When they're well mixed, add the crabmeat and *fold it in gently*. Then take all the remaining ingredients and, one at a time, add them to the bowl. Mix them well, but mix them gently.

To bring out the full-bodied flavor of this dish, it is essential that the crabmeat mixture be covered with a tightly sealed Saran Wrap cover and that it be left to marinate in the refrigerator for at least 12 hours.

Note: Claire suggests that to distribute the flavoring throughout the dish you stir the marinade occasionally. This appetizer recipe makes about a gallon of crab salad and it will serve 12 to 15 people.

Cold Crabmeat Nacho

This recipe is not only nutritious, it's extremely popular at parties and get-togethers because it's easy and quick to prepare. While crabmeat is used in the original dish, you can also substitute chopped shrimp or crawfish for the crabmeat, and the basic mix is also excellent for stuffing avocados, tomatoes, celery stalks, and just about anything your taste dictates.

24 oz. Philadelphia cream cheese
2 tbsp. real mayonnaise
dash Tabasco
¼ cup minced green onions
¼ cup coarsely chopped celery
dash paprika

salt and pepper to taste
1 #303 can black olives, finely chopped
½ lb. flaked crabmeat
1 large bag Nacho Cheese Flavor Doritos

The best way to prepare this recipe is in a food processor, because it chops the ingredients finely enough and blends them together for you. But if a food processor is not handy, you can use a blender and a chef's knife. It will still come out great, no matter how you do it!

First, mix the cream cheese to a pasty consistency. It has to be soft and pliable. Then, in a large mixing bowl, whip together the cheese and the mayonnaise until the mixture is smooth. Toss in the Tabasco at this point and blend it in, too. Next, add the minced onions, the celery, the seasonings, the finely chopped black olives, and the crabmeat. Just put them all together—it's not necessary to add them one at a time. But it *is* necessary to blend them all *gently*. If you get rough, you'll smash the ingredients and you'll lose the crispness.

When you're ready to serve, lay out the *whole* bag of Doritos on a pizza pan and stuff each one, heaping on the crabmeat mixture and sprinkling the tops with paprika. To increase the flavor, put the stuffed chips in the refrigerator for an hour or two.

Note: This stuff goes fast, so you might want to double the recipe if you're gonna have a big party!

Avocados with Crabmeat Stuffin'

You've got to be a lover of both crabs and avocados to relish this recipe. If you are, there are few things that taste any better. Let me suggest that you rely on this dish for some satisfying summer meals. The secret to success is to serve it *cold*.

For every 2 avocados, use:

1 tbsp. tarragon vinegar	1 tsp. minced parsley
3 tbsp. olive oil	1 tbsp. minced bell pepper
½ cup coarsely chopped celery	½ lb. crabmeat
1 tbsp. chives	1 tbsp. lemon juice
1 tbsp. minced black olives	up to ¼ cup real mayonnaise

The first thing you want to do is put the avocados in the refrigerator; this recipe should be served cold to be delectable. Then collect the ingredients and prepare the stuffing.

Get a medium-size mixing bowl. Put in your vinegar and olive oil, then mix the two together well. Next, add the celery, chives, olives, parsley, and bell pepper. All these ingredients must be blended well with the oil and vinegar, so start whipping them around with a whisk.

Now here's where you get gentle. Take the crabmeat and, very carefully, *fold* it into the contents of the bowl. Be careful not to break apart the lump meat. Otherwise the stuffing will lose consistency. After everything is mixed well, toss in the lemon juice and gently mix it in. It's important not to skip any steps because short-cutting won't give you a good mingling of flavors. Finally, add just enough of the mayonnaise to blend everything together firmly. Then cover the stuffing and stash it away in the refrigerator until it is completely cold. When you're ready to serve, slice the avocados and fill each half with the crabmeat mixture. Serve with potato chips and tomato slices.

Cajun-Style Crabmeat Bundles

If you're fond of potpie-style dishes, if you like the flaky crusts of egg rolls, and if you want the seafood tastes of Louisiana to tempt your palate, this will probably end up being one of your favorite recipes. It's rich and full-bodied, but you shouldn't have trouble eating more than one. And you should have very little trouble making them, too. They're easy—and inexpensive.

½ stick real butter
¼ cup coarsely chopped celery
¼ cup finely chopped shallots
¼ cup coarsely chopped bell
  pepper
1 tbsp. finely chopped parsley
1 tsp. basil
1 lb. flaked crabmeat
2 8-oz. cans frozen Crescent
  Dinner Rolls (or other pastry
  dough)

½ cup small-curd cottage cheese
2 cups grated mild cheddar
  cheese
½ tsp. salt
½ tsp. cayenne pepper
¼ tsp. white pepper

In a skillet, melt the butter over low heat so it just sizzles (otherwise it will burn), and *gently sauté* the celery, shallots, bell pepper, parsley, and basil over low to medium heat. Let me explain here that you want to cook the vegetable seasonings just until they begin to soften—not too much! You want them crisp enough to retain some body when they go into the pastry. I suggest you stir-fry the vegetables for no more than 3 minutes. Then toss in the crabmeat, stirring constantly until all the vegetables and the crabmeat blend together uniformly. When it is well blended, *take the mixture off the heat.* Then let it stand uncovered until it reaches room temperature.

While the crabmeat mixture is cooling, begin preparing your pastry. Take the rolls out of the cans and work them together with your fingers, your hands, and a rolling pin. This is easily done by unrolling the crescents, splicing them together (long sides and short sides), and trimming the excess with a knife. *What you eventually want to end up with are dough strips that measure 4 inches by 6 inches.* These will form your bundles. Two cans of frozen dough should give you 4 bundles.

After the dough is ready, go back to your skillet and stir the cottage cheese and the cheddar cheese into the crabmeat mix. Be sure the mixture is cool enough so that the grated cheese does not melt. You want it to melt inside the pastry as it bakes—not before. Also season the mix with your salt and peppers at this point. Then begin spooning the filling into the center of the dough strips, but make certain you leave enough room to fold the dough over and seal up the edges. When all the strips are filled, fold and seal them (use a fork to mesh the 3 edges together). Filled bundles should be 3 by 4 inches when folded.

Then place the bundles on an ungreased cookie sheet so that they do not touch each other. You want them to cook evenly on all sides. Then put them in your preheated oven, set at 375 degrees, and bake the bundles for about 25 minutes or until they turn a golden, crispy brown.

Believe me, they come out better than potpies because of the texture of the dinner rolls. Serve them with a tossed green salad, perhaps some buttered broccoli, a good homemade tartar sauce, and onion rings. Incidentally, serve them piping hot for best flavor.

Hint: As in many recipes in this book, other forms of seafood can be substituted for crabmeat to make different taste treats. These bundles are good with crawfish tails, sautéed shrimp, and even flaked fish. Actually, you're limited only by your imagination; I've made these with bacon and oysters, diced chicken, Italian sausage, shredded pork—you name it! All the ingredients stay the same; only the meats change.

Crabmeat Mardi Gras

When you cook this New Orleans crabmeat dish, it's Mardi Gras any day of the year. Actually, it began as a Mardi Gras recipe because it could be prepared in advance of Carnival and stored in the refrigerator. After the family got back home from a day in the streets watching the parades, the dishes could be heated and everyone could sit down to a tasty and nutritious meal. Try it, even if it isn't Mardi Gras!

1 10-oz. pkg. egg noodles	¼ cup chopped shallots
½ stick margarine plus 1 pat	1 #303 can Petit Pois peas
1 cup flaked crabmeat	(green peas)
1 10¾-oz. can cream of	3 tbsp. grated Romano cheese
mushroom soup	salt and pepper to taste

Start off by boiling your egg noodles until they are *al dente* (cooked just firm). Then lightly coat them with 1 pat of margarine so that they don't stick together. (The best way to do this, incidentally, is with your hands; work the margarine into the warm noodles.) Then set them aside.

In a skillet, melt down the half-stick of margarine and bring it to the sizzling point—not too hot, but hot enough to bubble lightly. When it's ready, toss in the cup of crabmeat and stir-fry it, uncovered, for about 4 minutes. All you want to do is get it nice and hot. Then spoon in the cream of mushroom soup, stirring constantly until the soup is totally smooth and the crabmeat mixes in thoroughly. Your preferences are important here. If you want a thinner sauce, add a little milk; if you like the topping on your noodles thicker, use the soup undiluted. Then add the shallots, the green peas, and the cheese, cook uncovered for another 3 minutes over low heat, and season to taste. At this point remove the skillet from the heat, cover it, and set it aside to cool. Note: The residual heat in the sauce will make the shallots tender and blend the cheese flavors together nicely.

When you're ready to eat, just heat up the sauce (or spoon some over the noodles and heat them together in a microwave oven) and have at it! With some buttered French bread and a lettuce and tomato salad, this makes a great quick meal for working families. And it keeps well for days in the refrigerator, too.

Hint: If you have leftover shrimp, you can substitute it for the crabmeat and use a can of cream of shrimp soup instead of the mushroom soup. All the other ingredients remain the same, the cooking process is the same, and the serving suggestions are the same.

New Orleans–Broiled Soft-Shells

For a really elegant meal, instead of frying your soft-shell crabs you might want to "New Orleans–broil" them, which includes marinating them in a rich lemon-butter sauce in the refrigerator for several hours before broiling them quickly under the top element in your oven or on the open grill of your barbecue pit. Whichever way you do it, this cooking technique is nothing short of magnificent!

1 **cup melted butter**	1½ **tsp. salt**
2 **tbsp. McCormick lemon**	¼ **tsp. white pepper**
pepper	**dash Worcestershire sauce**
4 **tbsp. fresh lemon juice**	6 **soft-shell crabs, cleaned and**
1 **tbsp. pure olive oil**	**washed**
2 **strips bacon, fried crisp,**	1 **large onion, thinly sliced**
drained, and crumbled	

In a small saucepan, heat the butter over medium heat and mix in all the ingredients except the sliced onion and crabs. While the butter is still warm, thoroughly coat each crab (including the parts under the shell flaps) with the mixture. Then place the crabs in the bottom of your refrigerator—*covered*—for 3 hours or more.

When you're ready to cook, take the crabs and place them on an oven rack inside a baking pan. Set the oven to 500 degrees (broil), and cook the crabs until they turn succulently tender (about 10 minutes). During the broiling process the juices will drip from the crab. I suggest you baste the cooking crabs with the drippings periodically to keep the flavoring in the seafood. I also recommend that you broil the crabs on both sides, initially with the bottom of the crab facing the broiling element and finishing with the top shell facing the element. You should also pierce the crabs twice to keep the pressures from building up inside the individual chambers.

On an open grill: Simply prepare the crabs the same way you would for cooking in the oven, including marinating them for 3 hours. Then, when you're ready to cook them, place them on the grill as close as possible to the heat source (the coals) and cover the grill to keep the intensity of the heat constant. Remember that some grills cook faster than others, so keep a close eye on your crabs. When they turn crisp on the outside and the inside meat is totally white (opaque and bubbly), they're ready to eat. *Do not overcook.* Keep basting with the lemon-butter mixture as they cook. Serve the sliced onions over the crabs as garnish.

Hint: As is the case with fried soft-shells, a good shrimp sauce spooned over the top of each crab when it's served will further enhance the flavor. And for a unique experience, grill your soft-shells over a hickory-chip fire. The delicacy of the crabmeat and the sweetness of hickory make a good combination.

Frank's Bayou-Style Crabmeat Dressing

Whether you need a crabmeat dressing to stuff a flounder or a red snapper or a crabmeat stuffing to complement fried fish, shrimp, or oysters, I guarantee you this one will serve the purpose beautifully. In fact, I seriously recommend that you keep folks away from the stove while you're cooking this recipe—more than one person has been known to eat it right from the black pot!

1 stick butter
½ cup finely chopped shallots
½ cup finely chopped white onions
1 tsp. fresh minced garlic
¼ cup chopped celery
1 cup sliced fresh mushrooms (optional)
1 tbsp. finely chopped parsley
2 tbsp. chopped bell peppers

1½ lbs. flaked crabmeat (lump meat is best)
1 cup toasted bread crumbs
1 tsp. salt
¼ tsp. white pepper
¼ tsp. black pepper
¼ tsp. cayenne pepper
2 large bay leaves
dash thyme
2 raw eggs, well beaten

Start the dish off by melting your butter in a medium-size saucepan and sautéing the shallots, onions, garlic, celery, mushrooms, parsley, and bell peppers until they become tender. The best method is to cook them, stirring constantly, for about 7 to 10 minutes. Of course, since you're using real butter, remember to keep the heat on medium so that the butter doesn't burn. Then, a little at a time, begin stirring in the flaked crabmeat. You want to mix this ingredient with the vegetables until there is complete uniformity; otherwise the flavors won't blend properly. When all the crabmeat is mixed in, turn the heat up to medium high and fry for about 5 minutes, *stirring briskly all the time.*

At this point remove the dressing from the fire and begin adding the toasted bread crumbs. These should be sprinkled in a *little at a time* also, and stirred well between additions—otherwise the crabmeat will take on a bready consistency in certain spots. Take your time and mix it well. When the crumbs are in the mix, stir in the salt, peppers, bay leaves, and thyme. By this time the temperature of the dressing should have decreased considerably. So you can now add the beaten eggs and stir them in *briskly*. And the dressing is done!

All that remains is deciding how you intend to use the mixture. If you're going to use it as a stuffing, go ahead and stuff it *as is* into your flounder, red snapper, lobster, whatever. I do suggest you make one last *taste test* to see that the seasoning is to your liking. Add more salt, pepper, and dried spices if necessary.

If you plan to use it as a dressing to serve independently with an entrée, you should place the mixture in a casserole dish or individual ramekins, top with a light coating of bread crumbs and a dash of grated Romano cheese, and bake in a 350-degree oven for about 20 minutes or until the top is toasty brown.

To make hors d'oeuvres, you can add a few extra bread crumbs for stiffness, form the mixture into small boulettes (balls), roll in seasoned pancake flour or biscuit mix, and deep fry briefly.

One more creative use for this stuffing is in casseroles. Don't overlook the possibility of combining the basic stuffing you've just made with sliced eggplant, sliced mirliton, chunked squash, artichoke hearts, or zucchini strips. Bake these vegetables together with this mixture and you'll get a standing ovation from your guests!

Caution: Do not make the mixture too bready—the crabmeat should be dominant, or it will taste like a commercially prepared freezer product. And that would be a mortal sin!

Louisiana-Style Stuffed Crabs

The Bayou-Style Crabmeat Dressing above is all you have to prepare to make an outstanding stuffing for stuffed crabs. All you do is mix the dressing, save the top shells of the crabs you pick (or you can use ramekins), clean the shells well, and heap the dressing inside the shells. Then sprinkle some toasted bread crumbs over the shells, add a dash or two of Parmesan cheese, cap with a pat of butter, and bake in a 350-degree oven until the crumbs are golden brown.

Note: For a delicate change in flavor, instead of butter on top of the stuffed crab you might want to place about a half-teaspoon of real mayonnaise. And to get a stronger Italian flavor, try sprinkling a little rosemary over the top of the bread crumbs before you bake the crabs.

Pan-Fried Soft-Shell Crabs

This is one of those recipes that just about everybody knows how to fix, but just as a memory refresher and to explain a little bit of trickery, I'll go through it with you once. Of course, we'll do it Louisiana style!

6 medium-large soft-shell crabs	cayenne pepper
2 cups Wesson oil (or Mazola corn oil)	white pepper
	black pepper (or lemon pepper)
garlic powder	2 cups milk
thyme	2 raw eggs
salt	4 cups seasoned corn flour

Start by washing the crabs thoroughly under cold running water. Then, using a paring knife, lift the left and right top shell "end points" and remove the gills (the "dead man") which lie under the covers. Wash the gill area well. Then cut off the mouth portion of the crab and use the point of the paring knife to pry out the eyes and eye-stalks. Wash these two areas again. Turn the crab over on its back and remove the "flap." Just pry it up, push it between your thumb and the knife, and pull it loose. Repeat the washing process. Then set the crabs in a colander to drain for about half an hour. While they are draining, get your skillet ready and heat your cooking oil to about *375 degrees* (high to medium high on most stove tops). This is also a good time to whip up your coating mix.

Next, lay the cleaned crabs on a sheet of waxed paper, and sprinkle them lightly with garlic powder, thyme, salt, and all the peppers. When they have all been sprinkled, use your hands to rub the seasonings in. Set them aside again for a few minutes and make your *egg-wash:* just blend the milk and the raw eggs together. When you're ready to cook and the oil is at the right temperature, run the crabs through the egg-wash, dip them lightly in the coating mix, run them back through the egg-wash, once more lightly through the coating mix (shaking off all the excess), and place them in the hot grease. Three things to remember here: (1) The crabs must be dipped and coated one at a time. You cannot dip and coat them all at once—the coating mix will become gummy instead of crisp. (2) Place the crabs in the oil one at a time. Otherwise the oil temperature will drop too much and the grease will be absorbed by the crab. And (3) as soon as you place the crab in the oil, take a cooking fork or an ice pick and pierce a few holes in the soft-shell. This will keep pressures from building up inside the crab shells so they won't "explode" as they fry. It sure keeps the grease from splattering all over you.

Fry your soft-shells on both sides, using a spatula to turn them over. If you can manage it, *turn them only once*. It is not necessary to overcook them. A few minutes on each side until they turn *golden brown* is all that's needed—you want them crisp and juicy, not half-burned and rubber-dry.

Soft-shells should be served piping hot, open-face on buttered light toast, to get the best possible flavors, but like most other Louisianians I like the little rascals cold right out of the refrigerator the next day, too. *Hot is best, though.*

Hint: For a touch of elegance in a soft-shell crab meal, you might want to whip up one of my cheese or shrimp sauce recipes and ladle a generous helping over the top of your crispy fried crabs. I also suggest you treat soft-shell crabs with the respect they deserve by serving them with brabant potatoes, creamed and buttered broccoli or sautéed spinach, perhaps a few hush puppies, and a cold tomato-avocado salad. Of course you should have a good bottle of wine to go with it! Incidentally, soft-shell crabs may be deep fried, but I find that the best flavor and crispness is produced in the sautéing pan. It's up to you, though.

Chipped Crab and Noodles

Just about everyone you meet raves over crabmeat au gratin. The texture and flavor of fresh-picked crabmeat blended with cream and cheese is hard to beat. If you're an au gratin lover, try this derivation. It couples the crab, cream, cheese, and other spices and herbs with fresh-cooked pasta. Mama mia—what a way to fix crabs!

½ stick butter
1 small white onion, finely chopped
4 tbsp. finely chopped bell pepper
2 tbsp. finely chopped celery
1 tsp. finely chopped fresh parsley
1 cup fresh sliced mushrooms
2 cups heavy whipping cream
2 cups half-and-half
1 tsp. salt
½ tsp. cayenne pepper
1 tsp. lemon juice
¼ cup white wine
¼ cup Parmesan cheese
¼ cup finely grated cheddar cheese
1½ lbs. crabmeat (lump meat is best)
1 10-oz. pkg. egg noodles

In spite of the fact that this recipe appears complicated, it is about as easy as fixing Corn Flakes and milk—give or take a few ingredients. All you're gonna do is make a super cream sauce and stir in the crabmeat. It's really that simple. Here's how it's done:

In a large skillet with a cover, melt the butter over medium heat and sauté the onion, bell pepper, celery, parsley, and mushrooms. Just add them to the butter and keep stirring until they become tender. Then pour in the heavy cream. You'll notice that this recipe has no flour—that's because you are going to simmer the heavy cream until it thickens to the desired consistency, so you really don't need flour. This one step, cooking the cream, is important, though, and it must not be rushed.

When the cream is thick, gradually stir in *half* of the half-and-half and mix it in well. Then stir in the salt, pepper, lemon juice, and white wine. Cook these ingredients for at least 5 minutes (you want the alcohol to evaporate, leaving only the essence of the wine). Then taste the mixture for seasoning balance, and make whatever adjustments you desire. Now add the cheeses, the cheddar and the Parmesan. Stir them in until they have melted completely into the solution. The sauce should turn a nice golden color and be rich in cheese flavor. At this point, add more half-and-half if you want a thinner sauce. If it's to your liking the way it is, leave it alone.

And now you're ready to stir in the crabmeat. A little at a time, begin blending it into the sauce. Take pains to do in small amounts, because if you rush this step the consistency won't be uniform. Then, when all the crabmeat is added, cover the skillet, reduce the heat to simmer, and let the mixture cook about 12 minutes. While it's simmering, boil your noodles *al dente* (just to the point of being tender). Then drain them in a colander, stir in a pat of butter to keep them from sticking together, and serve piping hot, with the crabmeat sauce heaped generously over the top. It's crabmeat au gratin and pasta all in one dish—or as we say in Louisiana, the best of all the worlds!

Hint: A crisp tossed salad, bacon-smothered broccoli, a loaf of fresh-baked garlic bread, and the remainder of the bottle of wine you cooked with makes this dish a meal fit for royalty!

Baked Crab and Eggplant

One of the finest casserole-type baked eggplant dishes I've ever tasted came to life late one night while I was in the process of cleaning out the refrigerator! Now, I know that doesn't sound very professional, culinarily speaking, but it's the truth. I had an eggplant about to overripen, a small container of cheddar-mozzarella cheese mix left over from lasagna I'd made, the bottom of a can of Parmesan, and about a half-jar of Ragu tomato sauce that my daughter had used to make "instant" pizzas on sliced bread. And I refused to throw them out! So I whipped up this recipe, and I've been cooking it upon request ever since. Oh, yeah—the crabmeat was left over from a crab boil we'd had the night before.

2 medium eggplants, peeled and
   thinly sliced
salt and pepper to taste
margarine (for greasing pan)
1 cup Ragu tomato sauce with
   mushrooms
1 cup bread crumbs
1½ lbs. picked crabmeat (shells
   removed)

1 small white onion, finely
   chopped
1 cup grated cheddar cheese
1 cup grated mozzarella cheese
¼ cup Parmesan cheese
sliced mushrooms for topping

Start off by laying the sliced eggplants on a sheet of waxed paper; salt and pepper them well. It works best if you do both sides and pat the seasonings into the "plant" with your hands. Then lightly grease a Pyrex baking dish with margarine (just a few drops of liquid margarine will do, because you want to rub it into the glass well) and get ready to start building layers.

Using a basting brush, *lightly* coat both sides of the eggplant slices with Ragu sauce, placing them back on the waxed paper to soak while you're working. Then, when you get all of them coated, begin forming the casserole as follows: In the bottom of the dish, lay one layer of eggplant slices. On top of that, sprinkle on some bread crumbs (*not too heavily!*), then a light application of crabmeat, then a sprinkling of onion and cheddar-mozzarella cheese mix, then a dash of Parmesan. *Keep the layers thin.* Then add another layer of eggplant and repeat the mixture process. Then another layer of eggplant, another layer of mix, and so forth. Note: You don't want too much Ragu because you don't want a heavy tomato sauce—keep it light and the tomato flavoring will be exquisite! But if some of the eggplant slices seem to have absorbed the Ragu coating, you might want to brush on a tad more as you build the layers.

Finally, when all the layers are in the dish, take your hands and push down lightly to pack the mixture tight. Not too hard, though—just snug it up! Lightly sprinkle a little more mozzarella-cheddar mix over the top, dash on a little more Parmesan, and decorate the surface with the fresh mushroom slices. The only thing left is the baking. Cover the Pyrex dish with aluminum foil and place it in the oven. You want the casserole to cook about 35 to 40 minutes at about 375 degrees. When it's cooked, serve it up with a crisp Italian salad, a generous helping of garlic bread, and a bottle of imported Sicilian red wine. The only thing that could improve on the flavor is listening to Italian love songs by candlelight while you eat!

Hint: This recipe also makes delicious hors d'oeuvres, heated in a chafing dish and spooned out over crackers. And it's delectable cold, right out of the refrigerator, when you want a tasty TV snack. Try 'em all!

Crabmeat Neapolitan

If you enjoy good dips and toppings made with fresh seafoods, you're sure to like this crabmeat recipe. I don't know how true it is, but I've been told that a Cajun once whipped up this dish on Bayou Lafourche and that almost everybody within a 4-block radius gained 5 pounds just smelling the ingredients simmering! For that reason, I don't count calories anymore!

2 12-oz. pkgs. Philadelphia
  cream cheese
whole milk (as needed to blend)
1 stick butter
1 medium onion, finely chopped
2 stalks celery, coarsely chopped
2 tbsp. finely chopped bell
  pepper

4 tbsp. finely chopped
  mushrooms
1 tbsp. minced garlic
½ tsp. oregano
½ tsp. basil
salt and black pepper to taste
1 lb. flaked crabmeat

Using a large mixing bowl, mash the cream cheese in about half a cup of whole milk to form a curdlike consistency. Sauté all the vegetables and seasonings in the butter—but remember not to overheat the butter and cause it to burn. Next, pour the butter and seasonings over the cream cheese and milk a *little at a time*, mixing as you pour and working it all together in a paste. Then, with a fork, work the crabmeat into the paste. Don't hurry this step, though—the better you blend the mixture the better the dip will taste. And speaking of taste, *taste it* often as you mix to be sure you have included enough seasonings. If you need more milk as you mix, just add it about a quarter-cup at a time.

After everything is mixed well, set the dish (covered) in your refrigerator for about 3 hours to "cure." The flavors will blend and the dip will come out full-bodied. For added flavor enhancement, you might want to sauté the crabmeat lightly with the butter and vegetable seasonings. It makes a considerable difference in how potent the crab flavor becomes.

Serve Crabmeat Neapolitan a variety of ways: as a *dip* with tortilla chips, as a *spread* on Escort crackers, as a *topping* over baked noodles, and so forth. It's one of those recipes with uses limited only by your imagination!

Louisiana Crabmeat Salad

If you want to allow your taste buds to experience a little bit of heaven, whip up this salad! You can serve it as a dinner main dish, a party special, a midday lunch—any time you want to dine on the finest in flavors. Words don't describe this one, y'all!

1 tbsp. finely chopped white onion
1 tbsp. real butter
1 lb. lump crabmeat
1 cup shredded lettuce
½ cup sliced cucumber
½ cup coarsely chopped bell pepper
½ cup thinly sliced celery
½ cup coarsely chopped black olives
½ cup thinly sliced fresh mushrooms

¼ cup shredded purple cabbage
¼ cup shredded raw carrots
3 hard-boiled eggs, coarsely chopped
1 diced avocado
1½ tsp. salt
¼ tsp. black pepper
¼ tsp. cayenne pepper
½ cup sour cream
1 medium tomato, sliced in wedges
dash romano cheese

Gently sauté the finely chopped onion in the tablespoon of butter. Remember to keep the heat on medium so that the butter doesn't burn, but you want the onions to turn completely transparent before you add them to the salad. While your onion is cooking, put all the ingredients except the tomato wedges, sour cream, and Romano in a large stainless steel bowl (I recommend stainless because it retains cold temperature and keeps the salad ingredients crisp). Mix them together well so that you get a uniform blend.

When the onions are sautéed, stir the sour cream into the onions just enough to mix the onions and butter with the cream. When the mixture is smooth, begin folding it into the salad ingredients. *Thoroughly blend the dressing into the salad.* Above all, make sure there is uniformity in the crabmeat texture—you don't want isolated lumps!

When all this is done, place the tomato wedges on top of the mixture in a decorative pattern and lightly sprinkle the Romano over the top of the salad. Then place your creation—*covered*—in the refrigerator for at least an hour before serving so that the flavors can blend. When it's ready to eat, serve it up with breadsticks or Rye Krisp crackers. You'll agree it's the best seafood salad you've ever eaten!

Hint: This also goes well with any seafood main dish; and I suggest it as an appetizer, too, especially for Yankee folks who just moved in!

Crabmeat Deluxe

If you savor the richness of gourmet foods, if you like original concoctions that amaze your guests, and if you relish being creative when it comes to preparing special foods for your family, you'll have to fix Crabmeat Deluxe soon. I put this one together several years back for a supper party, and it disappeared immediately! Try it and see if you get the same response.

1 cup lightly steamed chopped broccoli
1 cup lightly steamed chopped spinach
1 cup lightly steamed chopped crookneck squash
1 cup lightly steamed diced eggplant
1 cup lightly steamed sliced carrots
1 cup lightly steamed chopped cauliflower
2 cups whole raw mushrooms
1 stick butter plus 1 pat
2 cups heavy cream

¼ tsp. garlic powder
dash thyme
¼ tsp. marjoram
¼ tsp. cayenne pepper
¼ tsp. white pepper
½ tsp. lemon juice
1½ tsp. salt
1 cup white Chablis
1 large white onion, thinly sliced
4 hard-boiled eggs, finely chopped
1 cup grated cheddar cheese
2 cups grated Swiss cheese
1½ lbs. crabmeat

Start off with a 4-quart casserole dish (preferably Pyrex), lightly greased with a pat of butter. Then layer the bottom of the dish by evenly distributing the broccoli, spinach, squash, eggplant, carrots, cauliflower, and mushrooms. Use your creativity and arrange them any way you wish. When you've done this, set the dish aside for a while.

Take a saucepan, melt the butter on medium-low heat, and sauté the 2 cups of heavy cream in the butter until the mixture is uniform. Stirring constantly, add the garlic powder, thyme, marjoram, cayenne, white pepper, lemon juice, salt, and wine, and simmer the mixture while you stir for about 10 minutes. While the sauce is cooking, lay the sliced onions evenly over the top of the vegetables, then sprinkle the eggs evenly over the onions. Finally, sprinkle the two cheeses evenly over the entire casserole.

At this point begin to ladle the cream sauce over the ingredients. To do this, I recommend you take your time and use a large kitchen spoon to dribble the sauce carefully so that every portion of the casserole gets a coating. In order for the dish to come out right, this step can't be rushed. Then put the crabmeat gently on top, *using your fingers to break up the flakes*. Now use a kitchen fork and gently push the crabmeat down into the sauce topping. Keep in mind that if the crabmeat stays out of the sauce, the flavors won't mingle and, since you will bake this dish, the heat from the oven will dry the meat out. When you're ready to cook the casserole, cover the dish with a layer of aluminum foil, and bake in a preheated 325-degree oven until the vegetables become tender, the sauce bubbles, and the cheeses melt thoroughly. Then serve it to your guests piping hot. Garnishing with potato chips lends a nice touch.

Hint: This is a great vegetable dish to go with almost any fried seafood entrée, as well as a dish to complement steak, pork, or chicken. You will also find it popular over a chafing dish for party snacks.

How to Marinate Hard Crabs

Not only can you fashion Crabs T-Bernard out of your leftovers, you can also make marinated crabs. And what a tasty treat they are!

All you do is clean the crabs as you would for the next recipe (remember, they're already boiled!), and whip up your marinade mix:

1 cup Kraft Zesty Italian Salad Dressing
1 cup thinly sliced celery
1 tbsp. Worcestershire sauce
2 tbsp. finely chopped bell pepper
¼ cup finely chopped green onions

2 tbsp. finely chopped parsley
3 tbsp. lemon juice
3 cloves garlic, minced
1 tsp. dry mustard
¼ cup white wine
2 bay leaves
1 tsp. Tabasco sauce

Mix all the ingredients together (you can run them through the mixing blade of the food processor) and pour the mixture over the crab parts. Then stash the critters (covered) in the refrigerator for at least 12 hours before you eat them. Super!

Crabs T-Bernard

If you have ever wondered what you can do to create a little gourmet magic with leftover boiled crabs, well, my old friend Tom Bernard can tell you! He's come up with a concoction that is guaranteed to please your palate. He also says that this recipe will feed six normal Americans or two seafood-lovin' Cajuns! So judge accordingly.

1 cup Crisco oil
1 cup all-purpose flour
24 oz. tomato sauce
1½ tsp. Worcestershire sauce
2 large onions, finely chopped
2 medium-size bell peppers,
   quartered
2 cloves garlic, finely chopped
1 tsp. finely chopped parsley
½ cup finely chopped shallots

2 bay leaves
½ tsp. Tabasco sauce
¼ tsp. white pepper
¼ tsp. black pepper
2 tsp. salt
4 cups water
1 doz. boiled crabs, well
   seasoned
1½ lbs. shrimp, boiled and
   peeled

You're gonna like the simplicity of this dish. All you do is put *everything* except the water, crabs, and shrimp in a 6-quart heavy aluminum Dutch oven—that's all the seasonings and all the vegetables—and cook them over *medium-high* heat for about 10 minutes. Now, you'll have to stir everything together to get the right blend, but there is no need to use any particular order in the additions: just toss them together and mix 'em up! Do stir the mix periodically, though, to keep it from sticking.

Next, pour in the water, bring the heat to *high,* and stir the liquid into the mixture *until it boils.* Then cover the pot, reduce the heat to simmer, and cook for about 2 hours (actually, the longer the better, but for a *minimum* of 2 hours). At this point the gravy should have the consistency of *stew,* and the vegetables should be extremely fragile. If that's the case, it's time to add the seafood. Clean the crabs (remove the top shell, insides, gills, mouth parts, and legs) and cut them into right and left halves. Then drop them into the red gravy. Stir them around well, making sure they are completely coated and submerged. Then pour in the shrimp, stirring them in as well. Go ahead and cover the pot once more, and simmer again for 30 minutes. If the gravy is too watery (and not enough like a stew), cook longer, until it thickens. If it is too thick, add water ¼ cup at a time.

When you're ready to eat, just ladle out generous helpings and spoon it over steamed rice in a shallow bowl. Naturally you've got to have French bread and a fork, but don't be reluctant to get in there with your fingers. You won't want to miss a single flake of this succulent crabmeat!

CHAPTER EIGHT

Crawfish

Frank's Infamous Crawdad Sauce

The next time you sauté your redfish or trout fillets in butter and get them nice and crispy . . . before you serve them set them aside for a moment and whip up this sauce. You've got to try it spooned over the top of the fillets! I promise, it is the closest to heaven you'll get in this life!

2 cups boiled, deveined crawfish
  tails
½ stick butter
1 tbsp. chopped white onion
2 tbsp. chopped shallots
1 large clove garlic, finely
  chopped

¼ tsp. cornstarch
1 tsp. salt
½ tsp. white pepper
1 cup whole milk
1 cup shredded cheddar cheese

Here's what you do:
   Run the crawfish tails through the slicing blade of your food processor and set them aside. In a large saucepan, melt the butter and fry the onion, shallots, and garlic until they are tender. Then toss in the crawfish tails and sauté them for about 5 minutes, stirring constantly.
   While everything is simmering away, liquefy the cornstarch in a little water and stir in the salt and pepper. Then, a little at a time, begin adding the milk to the crawfish mix. Make sure the fire is on low and stir as you add the milk so that it doesn't burn. Pour in the cornstarch and stir vigorously until the sauce begins to thicken. Turn up the heat again to *almost boiling,* cook for 2 minutes, then *reduce to simmer*. Cover and cook for another 5 minutes.
   If the sauce isn't thick enough for your liking, simply cook in some extra *liquefied* cornstarch, adding about a teaspoon at a time. Then, when you're

ready to serve up the fish fillets, place them on heated plates, liberally sprinkle them with the grated cheddar cheese, and ladle the hot sauce over the top of the cheese. Shoooo-eeee!

Note: You can use this sauce over almost any deep-fried or panfried seafood—soft-shell crabs, shrimp, fish, oysters, and so forth. It really enhances the flavors. And when crawfish aren't in season, you can easily whip up a similar sauce by substituting shrimp for the crawdads!

Tony's Stuffed-Fried Crawfish Tails and Bisque

Here's a recipe of Tony Chachere's you are sure to relish, especially if you are fond of crawfish, because it gives you two dishes for the price of one. The uniqueness of the recipe makes it memorable, so I recommend you fix this for the next elegant dinner you serve. But one word of warning is in order: Unless you plan on inviting the neighbors to eat, you'd better keep the windows closed while it's cooking!

2 lbs. boiled crawfish tails and fat	6 eggs, beaten
2 medium onions	2 cups unseasoned bread crumbs
2 medium bell peppers	salt and pepper to taste
4 ribs celery	1 2-oz. can paprika
4 cloves garlic	48 cleaned crawfish heads
2 tbsp. chopped green onion tops	1 cup flour seasoned with salt and pepper

Start off by coarsely chopping the boiled crawfish tails and the vegetable seasonings to a uniform texture—the tails *with* the onions, bell pepper, celery, and garlic. But remember to *chop them—don't grind them.* (The pieces should be about the size of Grape-Nuts.) Then mix everything together in a large bowl until the blend is uniform.

Stir in the raw eggs, the bread crumbs, the crawfish fat, and the salt and pepper. Again, mix everything really well at this point. Then add the can of paprika and mix again. If the stuffing seems too dry, you can add a few tablespoons of water, but don't add too much. You want the mix *just pliable.*

Next, take the cleaned heads (with the eyes, mouth, insides, and gills removed) and stuff them with the mix. Then roll them in seasoned flour. The ones you want to serve as hors d'oeuvres (I suggest no more than half) you should set aside in one dish, and the ones you'll put in the bisque should go in another. *Note: If you're planning a big party, you may have to double this recipe.*

Now whip up the bisque, as follows:

2 sticks margarine
4 tbsp. all-purpose flour
1 chopped onion
2 cloves garlic, minced
1 rib celery, chopped
1 bell pepper, chopped
¼ lemon, sliced
1 can tomato sauce
1 tsp. sugar

1 #303 can whole tomatoes
2 qt. warm water
1 tbsp. Worcestershire sauce
salt and pepper to taste
1 lb. peeled crawfish tails and
    fat
1 tbsp. chopped green onion tops
1 tbsp. chopped parsley

Make a roux with *1 stick* of the margarine and the all-purpose flour. I suggest you use an aluminum Dutch oven because a black pot will cause your crawfish to turn dark. When the roux is cooked, remove it from the pot and set it aside in a large bowl.

Now melt the other stick of margarine in the Dutch oven and sauté the onions, garlic, celery, bell peppers, lemon slices, tomato sauce, sugar, and whole tomatoes until tender. It should take about 15 to 20 minutes, and you should continue to stir the ingredients as they cook.

Then, in the bowl with the roux, stir in the water and the Worcestershire sauce. Keep stirring until the mix is well blended. Then *gradually* stir the roux mixture into the pot with the simmering vegetable seasonings, *and drop in the stuffed crawfish heads you prepared earlier.* You need to stir gently, so you won't knock the stuffing out of the heads! Bring the bisque to a boil, then reduce the heat, and slowly simmer for about 2 hours. When the cooking is finished, check the bisque and season with salt and pepper to taste.

Then drop in the peeled crawfish tails and the fat and cover the pot. Simmer for *another hour.* This is when the full-bodied bisque flavor emerges. When you're ready to serve (and you should serve bisque over bowls of steamed rice), drop the stuffed heads you set aside as hors d'oeuvres into deep fat and fry at *350 degrees* until they float. Spoon the bisque over the rice, garnish it with chopped onion tops and a sprinkling of parsley, and put both dishes on the table at the same time. To top off the meal, prepare a crisp fresh spinach salad (highlighted with sliced raw onions and vinaigrette dressing) . . . sit down . . . and enjoy true Acadiana!

Hint: Tony says you can use this same recipe to prepare both shrimp and lobster bisque when crawfish are not in season.

Cajun Crawfish Jambalaya

One of the oldest dishes in Louisiana—and probably one of the tastiest yet most economical, too—is *jambalaya*. There are a myriad recipes for this traditional concoction, from shrimp to sausage to chicken to duck to whatever, but if you'd like to whip up a crawfish jambalaya, well, have I got a recipe for you! No promises, but you'll probably rate it a "ten."

½ cup Crisco oil
6½ cups water
1 chicken bouillon cube
1 cup finely diced hot smoked sausage
1½ cups coarsely chopped white onion
¾ cup finely chopped shallots
1 cup finely chopped celery
¼ cup finely chopped bell pepper
2 tbsp. finely chopped garlic
1 #303 can whole tomatoes

3 tbsp. tomato sauce
1½ cups ground boiled crawfish tails
1½ cups whole boiled crawfish tails
2 tsp. salt
½ tsp. black pepper
1 tsp. cayenne pepper
2 bay leaves
3 cups uncooked long-grain rice
2 tsp. minced parsley

In a large cast-iron Dutch oven, pour the oil and half of the water, add the bouillon cube and the smoked sausage, and sauté everything for about 4 minutes over medium-high heat. Cook and stir until the bouillon cube melts and the sausage begins to shrivel up. Then, with the heat still on medium high, toss in the onions, shallots, celery, bell pepper, and garlic and quickly stir-fry everything until the vegetables wilt *slightly* (not too much—you just want them tender). At this point toss in the whole tomatoes (you can cut them up in chunks for best results) and the tomato sauce, and stir-fry them for a couple of minutes. Then, put in the crawfish tails, both the whole and ground pieces, along with the rest of the water, and stir everything together well. Incidentally, the heat should still be on medium high!

Now, as you're stirring, sprinkle in the salt, black pepper, and cayenne, and toss in the bay leaves. Cook them into the mixture for about 3 or 4 minutes. Then reduce the heat to *medium* and begin gradually adding the rice. You will have to take care to see that the rice and the mix are well blended; otherwise the flavoring won't be uniform.

Reduce the heat to simmer, put the cover on the pot (make sure it fits tight!), and let the mixture cook for about 18 minutes. *Do not remove the cover until the rice is cooked.* The water will all be absorbed, the flavor will have permeated the mixture, and the texture will be just right. Just before you serve the jambalaya, stir in the parsley as a garnish.

Eat it hot from the Dutch oven, cher!

Crawfish Milneburg

I have no earthly idea what the origin of this recipe is, but it must be extremely popular with a lot of New Orleanians because several of them have sent it to me in one form or another—plus or minus a few ingredients. It appears to be in the Newburg style, but after having cooked it several times to get the ingredients right, I found that the crawfish lend a lot more flavor than lobster. (Incidentally, Milneburg (pronounced Millin-berg by N'awlins folks) was an old amusement park out on Lake Pontchartrain, accessible only by a steam locomotive called the *Smokey Mary*.) I'm sure you'll like the recipe. And it's simple!

1 stick butter	1 tsp. cayenne pepper
½ cup finely chopped onions	2 slices American cheese
2 tbsp. sherry	4 cups peeled boiled crawfish
2 tbsp. flour	tails
1 pt. half-and-half	¼ cup finely chopped parsley
2 egg yolks, beaten well	6 large baked pastry shells
1 tsp. salt	

In a skillet, melt the butter over medium heat and sauté the onions and the sherry for about 4 minutes. Then toss in the flour and stir it around until the mixture is smooth. Next begin a steady stirring motion and gradually start pouring in the half-and-half. Remember to keep the heat at medium so that the cream doesn't stick. When the mixture is hot, take a few tablespoons and add it to the egg yolks to bring up the egg temperature and to keep the yolks from cooking when you add them to the rest of the sauce. That done, stir the yolks into the sauce and keep on stirring until the sauce is smooth and has turned a uniform golden color. Add the salt and pepper, too.

Continuing to stir, put in the cheese one slice at a time and melt it into the sauce. Your sauce should now be nice and creamy, with everything blended in. Reduce the heat to *medium low,* but continue to stir. Finally, dump in the crawfish tails and the parsley and stir them into the sauce (lots of stirring, huh?). Simmer the whole concoction for another 2 or 3 minutes. Then go ahead and spoon out generous amounts of the mix, filling the baked pastry shells to overflowing. Serve piping hot with buttered broccoli or carrots, dirty rice, and a tossed green salad with French dressing. The taste is ultrarich!

TRY BUTTER-SAUTÉED CRAWFISH TAILS . . .

in a salad. One of the lightest springtime lunches or suppers consists of peeled crawfish tails sautéed in butter liberally sprinkled over a lettuce and tomato salad. Hmmmm!

Frank's Perfect Crawfish Etouffée

Of all the dishes featuring crawfish, *etouffée* is my favorite. So naturally I've worked on perfecting this recipe harder than any of the others. And I think I've come close, y'all! I'm not gonna say any more—you try it out and let me know what you think. I confess that it's a cross-breeding of about 25 different methods . . . but it's good!

3 lbs. peeled crawfish tails	2 tsp. tomato paste
4 cups crawfish stock	2 tbsp. cornstarch (in water)
½ cup crawfish fat (from the heads)	½ tsp. paprika
2 sticks real butter	1 tbsp. salt
2 cups finely chopped onions	1 tsp. cayenne pepper
¼ cup finely chopped celery	½ tsp. white pepper
¼ cup finely chopped bell pepper	¼ tsp. black pepper
1 tbsp. minced garlic	dash thyme
2 tbsp. finely chopped green onions	dash basil
	dash Worcestershire sauce
	1 tbsp. finely chopped parsley

You start off by boiling about 15 to 20 pounds of crawfish in lightly salted water. Since you are going to use the water as a cooking stock, you want to make certain that the crawfish are washed thoroughly before you put them in the pot. Use only enough water to barely cover the critters. Your boiling time should be about *4 minutes* (timed from the point when the water begins to boil rapidly). When they are cooked, immediately remove the crawfish from the water with a strainer ladle and set them aside to cool. Then, using several thicknesses of cheesecloth, strain out *6 cups* of stock (you want to have extra stock just in case you need it) and set it aside. Peel the meat out of the crawfish tails, scoop the fat out of the heads, and devein the tails. Then divide the tails into two equal portions. Leave one portion whole, and grind up the other portion until the meat is finely ground.

In your heavy 12-inch *stainless-steel or aluminum* (not black iron) skillet melt the butter over medium heat and begin sautéeing the onions, celery, bell pepper, garlic, and green onions, cooking until they wilt. This should take about 7 minutes, and you should stir constantly. When the vegetables are ready, stir in the tomato paste and cook it about 2 or 3 minutes. Then pour in *4 cups* of the crawfish stock, stirring it well into the vegetable mixture. Also stir in the crawfish fat. When it is mixed well, cover the pot and let the liquid simmer over *low heat* for about 10 minutes. After the simmering process, remove the cover and gradually stir in the liquid cornstarch (dry starch dissolved in just enough water to make it fluid). Then cover the pot again and let the sauce simmer over low heat for another 5 minutes. *Remember: You still have 2 cups of stock, and you can use it later to adjust the consistency of the sauce.*

Next, add the ground crawfish tails, stir them into the gravy, and mix in the paprika, salt, cayenne, white pepper, black pepper, thyme, basil, and Worcestershire sauce. Blend everything together really well, and taste the dish *for each ingredient.* If anything needs adjusting (more salt, more pepper, etc.), do it now. Then cover the pot, bring the mixture to a *near boil,* and immediately take the pot off the fire. Leaving it covered, let the etouffée cool down to room temperature so that the flavors will be distributed evenly. After making this dish over and over again, I've found that this one step is probably the secret trickery that makes my etouffée succulent. Add more stock if desired.

Finally, after the mixture is cool—and when you're ready to eat—reheat it to serving temperature, put in the whole crawfish tails, stir in the parsley, cover the skillet, and simmer for 3 minutes. Then spoon the etouffée over steamed, buttered rice . . . and pretend your folks came from Nova Scotia!

Hint: Because of the flavoring process, this etouffée will increase in richness the longer it sits. For some reason, it seems to taste better the next day. And it will freeze well. Also note that the sauce should have the consistency of heavy cream—not thick, but not watery either!

Mudbugs and Macaroni

Most seafoods go well with pastas, and crawfish are no exception, particularly when the little mudbugs are simmered in red gravy and spread over macaroni. This recipe is a good one to make when you have crawfish left over from a "boil" (a Southern-style crawfish party). Simply peel the meat from the tails, remove the back veins, and add 'em to your sauce. Try it!

1 stick margarine
2 tbsp. finely chopped bell pepper
4 tbsp. minced celery
1 large onion, finely chopped
4 cloves garlic, finely chopped
1 6-oz. can Contadina Tomato Paste
1 #303 can peeled whole tomatoes
1 tsp. flour

1 tsp. salt
½ tsp. cayenne pepper
¼ tsp. black pepper
dash oregano
2 cups water
½ cup red wine
16 oz. elbow macaroni
6 cups peeled boiled crawfish tails
1 tsp. minced parsley

This recipe may seem a bit complicated at first, but it really isn't. You just have a few steps to follow, and they sound more time-consuming than they really are. So with that in mind:

Get out both a 12-inch aluminum skillet and a 4-quart stainless Dutch oven and put them on the stove. In the skillet, melt the margarine over medium heat and begin sautéeing the vegetables—the bell pepper, celery, onion, and garlic. It should take you about 5 minutes to cook the seasonings just right.

In a small bowl, mix together the tomato paste and the whole tomatoes (you should chop up the whole tomatoes—in fact, it's best to run them through the blender or processor). Then add them to the skillet and cook them into the vegetables. Note that the margarine and seasonings will be absorbed by the tomatoes and the result will be a nice paste. At this point you should also stir in the flour. *Keep stirring* so the mix doesn't burn. While you're stirring, sprinkle in the salt, cayenne, black pepper, and oregano. Put in the 2 cups of water and the ½-cup of wine and stir over *medium-low heat* until the paste blends into a smooth gravy. Cover the skillet, reduce the heat to low, and let the sauce cook for about 30 minutes. One little hint: I suggest you occasionally check your gravy to see that it's the consistency you desire; if you want it thinner, add a little more water.

You can now go ahead and boil your macaroni in the Dutch oven. Add the pasta to about 3 quarts of water and boil it only until it is *al dente* (just cooked).

Then drain it and set it aside. (I like to put it in a Pyrex baking dish and stick it in the oven on "warm.") When the gravy has simmered down, add the crawfish tails and stir them in well. Then cover the skillet again and simmer the sauce for 15 minutes more. Finally—*5 minutes* before you serve the dish—toss in the parsley, swoosh it around a time or two, and cook it for *2 minutes*.

All that's left is the eatin'! Spoon some of the macaroni into a big soup bowl, ladle a generous helping of the crawfish tails and sauce over the top, douse the sauce heavily with some grated Romano or Parmesan . . . and enjoy!

Note: If you use unseasoned crawfish, prepare the recipe as I have indicated. But if you use crawfish left over from a crawfish boil (already seasoned with salt and pepper and lemon and such), reduce the seasoning amounts to taste. In other words, I'd suggest you taste at each stage as you go and do not add the salt, cayenne, and black pepper until minutes before you serve the dish. Previously boiled crawfish will release seasonings into the gravy, so adding more might make the dish too potent. Use caution, y'all.

FRIED CRAWFISH ARE GOOD!

You can take parboiled crawfish, peel out the tails, remove the vein, dip in milk and egg (and coat with seasoned flour), and deep fry them for extraspecial treats. But remember not to overcook them. Fry for only *2 minutes* or so. It's easy!

Crawfish Sauce Piquante

Among Louisiana's favorite seafood dishes are shrimp creole and crawfish etouffée. But if you want to prepare a traditional Louisiana stew-type dish that has "bite"—because this recipe is *peppery*—you have to fix Crawfish Sauce Piquante (which means "hot sauce"). Over steamed rice, it'll bring tears—of joy—to your eyes!

1 stick real butter
1 large white onion, finely
  chopped
¼ cup coarsely chopped shallots
2 cloves garlic, finely chopped
1 tbsp. basil
½ tsp. thyme
2 6-oz. cans Contadina tomato
  paste
1 tbsp. finely chopped bell
  pepper

2 qts. water
1 bay leaf
salt to taste
1 tbsp. cayenne pepper
1 tsp. white pepper
4 tbsp. crawfish fat
3 lbs. boiled crawfish tails
  (half ground, half whole)
4 tbsp. finely chopped parsley

In a medium-size Dutch oven (or a 4½-quart saucepan), melt the butter over low heat, *but don't let it burn*. Then stir in the onions, shallots, garlic, basil, and thyme and let everything simmer for about 20 minutes over low heat. It will be necessary to stir the vegetables occasionally, but constant stirring is not essential since the temperature is reduced.

When the vegetables are wilted, add the tomato paste and bell pepper and stir them into the mixture. Again, keeping the temperature on low, simmer for about 15 minutes, stirring occasionally. Then pour in the 2 quarts of water, add the bay leaf, and stir in the salt and peppers (both cayenne and white). Put the lid on the pot and simmer the sauce on *medium high* for about 15 minutes (keep it from boiling, though). I suggest you taste the sauce every now and then, too, to make certain the seasonings are right. (It should be peppery, remember.) Go ahead and add the crawfish fat, stir it into the mix, and continue to simmer for another 15 minutes.

Stop here to taste the mixture again to check on the seasoning and to adjust the thickness of the sauce. If you prefer a thicker gravy, cook the mix with the cover off for about 15 minutes; if you want it thinner, add more water about a quarter cup at a time. When it's just the way you want it, stir in the crawfish meat and the parsley, put the lid back on the pot, and simmer the piquante for another 10 minutes.

Serve hot over steamed, buttered rice with French bread.

Looo-Zee-Annah Crawfish Pie

There are probably more recipes floating around for crawfish pie than there are politicians campaigning in Baton Rouge! And I don't think I've ever eaten any I didn't like! But this one—I do have to admit that I may be prejudiced—seems to be head and shoulders ahead of all the others. I mean, this one has *body*. This one has *intensity*. This one is *gooood*.

1 frozen, unbaked double pie shell	3 tbsp. shredded carrots
2 lbs. crawfish tails with fat	¼ cup parsley
1 stick butter	2 tbsp. paprika
2 medium white onions, finely chopped	½ tsp. cayenne pepper
¼ cup finely chopped shallots	½ tsp. white pepper
½ cup finely chopped celery	1 tsp. salt
½ cup finely chopped bell pepper	2 hard-boiled eggs, chopped
3 cloves garlic, finely chopped	2 tbsp. heavy cream
	1 egg yolk, beaten

Start by thawing the pie crust until it becomes pliable and easy to work with. Then place it in your refrigerator until you have your filling prepared. Here's how that's done:

For the best possible texture in this dish, you should separate the crawfish tails into two portions, leave one portion whole, and run the other portion through the grinder or food processor until the tail meat is finely chopped. Only by preparing the tails this way will you get uniform crawfish flavor throughout the pie. (Oh—grind the fat into the tails, too.)

Then get out a large skillet—the 12-inch size works best—and melt the butter over medium heat. At this point sauté the onions, shallots, celery, bell pepper, garlic, and carrots, and continue to cook them until they turn *just tender*. *Do not overcook* the ingredients or they will lose texture in the pie. Just 4 minutes should do nicely.

When the vegetables are wilted, remove the skillet from the fire and begin adding the remaining ingredients as follows, stirring all the while: Put in the parsley, then the paprika, then the two kinds of pepper, then the salt, then the chopped eggs, and then the heavy cream. Between each addition, be sure you thoroughly mix the ingredients together for uniformity. And now the coup de grace: *You pour this mix into the bowl containing the whole and ground-up crawfish tails*. With a fork you begin working the seasonings evenly into the crawfish. When it's mixed just right, you're ready for your pie crust. Oh—better preheat your oven to 375 degrees, too.

Take the crust (you should have a bottom and a top) and begin spooning the filling into it. As you add the mix, take the spoon and pack the filling tightly across the bottom of the pie. Note: You want the filling to be rounded at the top, rather than level with the edge of the crust. When the pie is filled, place the top crust over the filling, crimp the edges with a fork, and make a 1-inch slit in each quarter of the top crust (4 slits in all).

Finally, reduce the oven temperature to 350 degrees, liberally brush the top crust with the egg yolk, and bake in the oven for about 40 minutes (or until the crust is golden brown and flakes easily). With a crisp tossed salad and a cold beer, this is one *Looo-zee-annah* dish you just won't be able to beat. Incidentally, crawfish pie should be served piping hot.

Acadian Crawdad Cakes

Whether or not you live in the South, you're probably aware that *rice* is one of the favorite foods of Louisianians. We serve it under red beans in New Orleans, mixed into Cajun etouffée throughout Bayou Country, and smothered with smoked sausage and chicken jambalaya in almost every kitchen of every home south of Alexandria. But this is one of the unique Louisiana recipes for rice. You won't be sorry if you take the time to fix it!

½ stick real butter
2 cups ground boiled crawfish
  tails
2 cups cooked long-grain rice
½ cup chopped bell pepper
2 slices bacon, fried crisp and
  crumbled

1 tbsp. finely chopped parsley
½ cup finely chopped shallots
¼ tsp. basil
dash thyme
1 tsp. salt
dash Tabasco sauce
3 eggs, well beaten

In a large skillet or griddle, melt the butter over low heat. While it's melting, begin shaping your patties as follows:

In a deep bowl, mix the crawfish tails, the rice, the bell pepper, the crumbled bacon, the parsley, the shallots, the basil, the thyme, the salt, and the Tabasco together well. Take care to see that all the ingredients are uniformly mixed—the best way to do that is to *use your hands*. Then pour the eggs over the mixture and blend them into the rice and seasonings. In order to have your patties stay together, it is necessary that you let the mix "set" in the refrigerator for about 30 minutes, *covered*.

When you're ready to cook, heat the griddle or skillet again to about medium. Then, keeping your hands moist with a few drops of water, shape the rice-crawfish mixture into small squares, approximately 3 inches by 3 inches (and ½-inch thick), and plop 'em on the griddle! They will sizzle nicely and turn light brown in a few minutes. Then flip them over and fry the other side until it turns light brown.

For the best flavor, you should serve them sizzling hot as a side-dish substitute for potatoes, pasta, or hush puppies. They go great with broiled trout, stuffed crabs, fried soft-shells, or sautéed shrimp.

Hint: To make an entrée, increase the proportions of ground crawfish so that the seafood is the dominant ingredient, fry as I've described above, place the cakes on a trimmed slice of toast, cover with a slice of American cheese, and brown under the broiler until the cheese melts! Serve hot.

WANT TO BE CREATIVE WITH DEVILED EGGS?

Just as bacon is a natural companion to oysters, for some reason crawfish just seem to go exceptionally well with eggs. So to give extra dimension to your deviled egg canapes, try grinding up some crawfish tails and adding them to the stuffing before you pack it back into the whites.

And for a super breakfast, cher, grind up a handful of crawfish tails and stir them into your bell-pepper omelettes. And don't forget to top them with a dash or two of Tabasco sauce! Huummm!

Cajun Crawfish Casserole

This is a nice dish to prepare for guests when you must fix an economical meal. It is also great for quick family dining and party snacks. All you need is a 1½-quart casserole dish and a couple of cups of cooked, peeled crawdads. Of course, you should also work up a good appetite, because this is good stuff, m'frien'!

2 cups coarsely chopped crawfish tails
4 hard-boiled eggs, coarsely chopped
½ cup finely chopped celery
½ cup coarsely chopped bell pepper
1 cup toasted bread crumbs
½ stick butter, melted
1 cup boiled and drained yellow squash

¼ cup half-and-half
4 tbsp. finely chopped shallots
1 tbsp. finely chopped garlic
1 tsp. salt
½ tsp. white pepper
¼ tsp. red pepper
1 cup coarsely crumbled cracker crumbs
¼ cup finely chopped parsley

You talk about simplicity! Nothing could be easier than this dish. All you do is take a large bowl and dump in everything except the cracker crumbs and parsley. And *mix it all together well.*

Then butter the insides of a 1½-quart casserole and spoon the mix into it, sprinkle the cracker crumbs over the top, and garnish the surface with the parsley. Then bake the dish for about 20 to 25 minutes in a 400-degree oven, and serve it hot with your favorite fried seafood or baked poultry. Good!

Hints: For a little added flair, you can top the cracker crumbs with thinly sliced mushrooms lightly sautéed in butter. Or spice up the whole dish by adding a teaspoon or two of liquid crab boil or Tabasco sauce. Or you can dress up the top of the casserole for parties by topping it with sliced black and green olives, or potato chips—or whatever! Go ahead, be daring!

ABOUT WINES FOR COOKING

Remember, I do not suggest that you use so-called "cooking sherry." It does not lend the kind of flavor you look for in wine cooking and most of it is poor quality. The best idea is to use the same wine to *cook with* that you'd *drink* with the meal. If it isn't good enough to drink, it isn't good enough to cook with!

Crawdads in a Bundle

This recipe was an offshoot from a crawfish boil that took place one Sunday afternoon. We had boiled a 48-pound sack of the little critters and had eaten all but about 3 pounds. Well, I wasn't gonna throw 'em away! So I peeled the tails, experimented a little, and came up with a whole new dish that I've cooked many times since that party. You try it—it makes a nice entrée as well as a good snack food for friends. And it's easy as the dickens to fix.

1 pkg. French bread rolls or sourdough rolls
½ stick butter
1 cup coarsely chopped celery
¼ cup finely chopped shallots
2 cloves finely chopped garlic
1 tsp. salt
½ tsp. white pepper
¼ tsp. cayenne pepper
4 cups boiled, peeled crawfish tails

6 hard-boiled eggs, coarsely diced
½ cup coarsely chopped black olives
½ cup mayonnaise
1 tsp. dry mustard
½ cup grated mozzarella cheese
½ cup grated mild cheddar cheese

Start off by laying the rolls on the counter top and carefully slicing off the top third of each roll. Then remove the insides of the bottom portions so that the rolls are hollow. Save the top from each bun.

In a 10-inch saucepan, melt the butter on *low* heat and gently stir in the celery, shallots, garlic, salt, and peppers. *Do not cook them. Just heat them* and coat them with the butter. While they are heating, pour half of the crawfish tails onto a chopping board and mince them.

At this point, remove the saucepan from the stove and stir in the minced crawfish *and* the whole tails and stir them around well. Then, one at a time, add and stir in the chopped eggs, the black olives, the mayonnaise, and the mustard. Take care to see that these ingredients are well mixed, because they will become a filling for the buns and you want an equal blend. Set the saucepan off to the side and let the mixture cool for about 15 minutes. When the mix has lost enough heat to keep the cheeses from melting, go ahead and stir in the mozzarella and the cheddar. Do this gently, a little at a time, because you also want the cheeses to be evenly distributed throughout the mixture. Then, using a wooden spoon, fill each of the hollowed rolls with the mix, put the tops back on the rolls, wrap each roll in aluminum foil, and stick them in a 400-degree oven. (For a little extra richness you can baste the outside of each roll with melted butter before wrapping.)

Bake your bundles for about half an hour and serve 'em up piping hot with a soup and a salad. You can also serve them open-face for parties, if you prefer, by leaving the tops off the rolls and stuffing them *full!*

Boiled Crawfish a la Terry Gagliano

Just about every New Orleanian will tell you that if you want to feast on some of the finest-tasting boiled crawfish you ever ate, you've got to sample the ones that come out of the pots at Gem's Supermarket on Franklin Avenue. In a back room of the grocery, Terry Gagliano has an array of boilers, burners, and picking boxes, and for the last 30 years he has been using them to cook seafoods that just seem to have no equal, at least in his customers' opinions. And I'd have to agree! You try his recipe and see what you think.

For every 43-lb. sack of crawfish, use:

2 cups cayenne pepper
½ cup crushed red pepper
3 heads garlic
½ cup Zatarain's liquid crab
  boil

8 lemons, quartered
2 yellow onions, halved
1 whole stalk celery, coarsely
  chopped
3 26-oz. boxes of salt

The first thing you do is empty your crawfish into a No. 3 washtub and cover them completely with cold water. Makes no difference where your crawfish come from, farm pond or swamp, the only thing you must do is *wash* them. *You do not have to "purge" crawfish in salt;* that's an old wives' tale, it isn't necessary, and it doesn't work. All it does is kill the little freshwater critters! But it *is necessary* to wash them several times. I recommend you do at least 4 or 5 washings, dumping the old water after each filling of the tub. In short, you should wash until the water comes out clean. Then drain off the last rinse completely and get your boiler ready.

In a large pot (60-quart size is recommended if you plan to boil the whole sack at once), put in enough water to completely cover the crawfish when they are added, and bring it to a rapid boil. Then toss in all the ingredients and boil them for about 10 minutes to let the flavors mix. If you want to add "lagniappe" (that little something extra) to your boiled seafoods, toss that in now, too—corn on the cob, small Irish potatoes, smoked sausage, etc. You want to cook the lagniappe ingredients until they are just about done, because it won't take long to cook the crawfish (and if you don't precook the extras, the entire boil won't all be ready at the same time).

When your extras are just about ready to eat, add your crawfish and cover the pot. The water will stop boiling immediately, so here's how you figure cooking time. Just keep a close eye on the pot. When the water comes back to a boil, time your crawfish for just about *2 minutes* and shut off the fire. Then "soak" them for at least 25 minutes in the hot water, allowing them to pick up the seasonings. I do suggest you test the seasoning about every 5 minutes or so to keep the crawfish from getting too spicy for your taste.

And that's all there is to it!

Crawfish Soup Italiana

Most Louisiana crawfish recipes—because of the origin of the critters—tend to be Cajun. But this is one I concocted for my father-in-law, Charles Bruscato, and his Sicilian tastes. He raves over it and tells all his friends how to cook it—and then *they* rave. Must be a good dish, huh? Anyway, I thought you might like to try it. Be sure you have a good Italian wine to go with it!

12 lbs. live crawfish	2 tsp. basil
2 qt. crawfish stock (from boiling crawfish)	1 tsp. white pepper
	salt to taste
1½ sticks butter	1 tsp. Italian seasoning
½ cup finely chopped shallots	2 pt. half-and-half
4 cloves garlic, minced	¼ cup creamed corn
2 tbsp. bell pepper	4 tbsp. white wine
1 6-oz. can BinB mushrooms (bits and pieces)	1 tbsp. grated Romano cheese

Start off by boiling the crawfish in just enough water to cover them (the water should be lightly salted). According to the experts, you should boil crawfish for cooking dishes for 4 minutes *maximum* (less if they're small). After they are cooked, remove them from the water, but save 2 quarts of the stock for the soup base. Then, when the crawfish have cooled, pick the tail meat, remove the vein, and finely chop the meat. (Note: 10 pounds of live crawfish will yield about 1½ pounds of meat.) Set the meat aside.

At this point, melt the butter in a 10-inch skillet and sauté the shallots, garlic, bell pepper, and mushrooms until they wilt. It won't take long—about 4 or 5 minutes should be just right, because they'll continue cooking in the soup. Then sprinkle in the seasonings—basil, white pepper, salt to taste (about 1 teaspoon), and Italian seasoning—and stir them into the vegetable-butter mixture. Simmer for about a minute.

In a 4½-quart saucepan bring the 2 quarts of crawfish stock to a boil, then reduce the heat to *medium*. Pour in the half-and-half and stir well. Then add the vegetable-butter mix, cover the pot, and simmer gently for about 5 minutes. While the base cooks, stir the ingredients around occasionally to keep the cream from sticking on the bottom of the pot. When everything is blended well, add the chopped crawfish, the corn, and the white wine, and stir again. Cover and simmer once more for 5 minutes.

When you're ready to serve, spoon the dish into soup bowls and sprinkle lightly with the Romano. Serve piping hot with saltine crackers or sesame breadsticks and chilled wine.

CHAPTER NINE

Alligators

Jean Picou's Alligator Sauce Piquante

I spent quite a few evenings in the kitchen experimenting with this creation, probably because it tastes so good I wanted to fix it more than once! But this is also one of those recipes you can enhance, as you will note in the hints below. And aesthetically, this gator is appetizing!

2 lbs. cubed alligator meat	2 8-oz. cans tomato sauce
1 cup white wine for marinade	2 tbsp. Worcestershire sauce
2 cups coarsely chopped onions	¼ tsp. oregano
5 tbsp. Crisco oil	1 bay leaf
4 tbsp. finely chopped bell pepper	¼ tsp. basil
½ cup finely chopped celery	1 6-oz. can sliced mushrooms
1 #303 can Rotel (spiced) tomatoes	salt and cayenne pepper to taste
	4 tbsp. finely chopped shallots
	¼ cup finely chopped parsley

First, cube the gator meat and soak it in the wine for about an hour. I suggest you use the same wine for the marinade that you plan to serve with dinner. The flavors harmonize that way. After marinating, drain the meat in a colander.

In a large Dutch oven, fry the onions in the oil until they are *dark* brown (caramelized). Stir them constantly so they don't burn. Then add the bell pepper and celery and fry them until they become tender. *Keep stirring.* Next, add the Rotel tomatoes and the tomato sauce and stir them in well. Then toss in the Worcestershire, oregano, bay leaf, and basil and simmer the mixture for 10 minutes, stirring occasionally. Finally, add the mushrooms and the drained alligator meat to the sauce, cover the pot, and cook on low heat for 40 to 45 minutes. Season with salt and pepper, then add the shallots and parsley and cook them—*uncovered*—for another 10 minutes.

Hint: Depending upon your taste, you can enhance the flavor by adding a few tablespoons of lemon juice or wine or both. And if you want real sauce piquante, add extra cayenne.

Easy Grilled Gator

You really don't need an expensive hickory-chipped open pit to grill gator meat and give it a smoked flavor. Any dime-store, picnic-type barbecue grill can be used to produce flavor using this recipe. Just follow the directions and you can't go wrong! See if you don't think this is easy.

4 ½-inch-thick gator-tail steaks	1 tbsp. olive oil
1 16-oz. bottle Kraft Zesty	4 tbsp. Liquid Smoke
Italian Salad Dressing	2 tbsp. Tabasco sauce
salt to taste	1 lemon

Get a bowl large enough to hold the 4 steaks so that you can cover them with the salad dressing. Then pour the dressing into the bowl. Allow the alligator meat to sit in the marinade in the refrigerator for 3 hours. When you're ready to grill the meat, take it out of the refrigerator, pour off the salad dressing, dry the steaks well with a paper towel, and sprinkle them lightly with salt.

Then make a *basting solution* by blending together the olive oil, Liquid Smoke, and Tabasco. With a barbecue brush, spread the baste over the steaks and put the meat on your grill.

Now here's the secret: *Make sure you cook slowly.* Only on low heat will the smoke flavor penetrate the meat, and only on low heat will the steaks stay juicy. As the gator cooks, continue to brush on more basting liquid (make more if you have to). Turn the steaks gently so the meat doesn't fall apart. When the alligator begins to flake, it's done. Just before you remove it from the grill, slice a lemon and spread a light coat of juice over each steak. Then serve piping hot.

Hint: Grilled gator goes well with hush puppies, snap-bean salad, and toasted French bread. And for some reason or other, a frosty, cold glass of lemonade just seems to be perfect as a beverage. And if you have any leftovers, grilled gator can be flaked and sprinkled over a lettuce and tomato salad for a light evening meal.

Fried Alligator a la Dixie

Just for the record, I'm partial to Dixie Beer because it's brewed in New Orleans, but if you are a Coors, Old Milwaukee, Budweiser, or Miller fan, feel free to switch brands. The gator won't care one bit!

1 12-oz. can beer	1 tsp. black pepper
½ cup flour	1 lb. thinly sliced fresh alligator
1 tsp. Season-All	meat
1 tsp. salt	cornmeal for dredging

Make a batter using the can of beer, the flour, and the seasonings, and coat the alligator with it. Then dredge the meat in cornmeal and deep fry at 375 degrees for about 12 minutes (or until the gator begins to float). You want the batter a golden brown, *but don't overfry* or the meat will dry out and the texture will become unsavory. Keep it moist!

Microwaved Alligator

Just for you microwave folks, I'm throwing in this recipe. But frankly, my dear, I'd rather have mine fried or stewed!

2 ½-inch alligator chops
1 tsp. McCormick lemon pepper
1 medium onion, thinly sliced

Season the chops with the lemon pepper and let them sit for a while. Then put them in a 1½-quart baking dish and cook them in the microwave oven (on the high setting) for about 4 or 5 minutes, *uncovered*.

Then arrange the onion slices so that they cover the chops. Cover the baking dish with plastic wrap. Put the gator back in the microwave and cook (on the low setting) for about 10 minutes or until the meat flakes easily with a fork. Allow the meat to stand 5 minutes before serving.

Cajun Smothered Gator

Now this is one of my favorite ways to prepare alligator as a main dish, especially if I have to feed several people buffet style. But while the ingredients are basic, something you'd likely find in practically any Southern stew, the alligator imparts a special delicate flavor you really should try the first chance you get. It's tasty!

¼ cup Crisco oil
2 onions, finely chopped
1 bell pepper, finely chopped
½ cup finely chopped celery
1 bay leaf
¼ tsp. basil

2 lbs. alligator meat, cut in chunks
4 tbsp. minced parsley
¼ cup shallots, finely chopped
salt and black pepper to taste

In a skillet, heat the oil so that you can fry the onions to a golden brown. Then add the bell pepper, celery, bay leaf, and basil and continue to sauté until the vegetables are tender.

Next, add the alligator piece by piece, and turn the fire down so that the meat just simmers for about 40 minutes. Be sure to keep the skillet covered so that the meat stays juicy. Keep in mind that old bull gators may take longer to cook, so it is a good idea to keep watch on the skillet. You may have to shorten or extend the simmering time. Just get the meat tender (it will flake easily when it's ready) and your dish will come out right.

When you're ready to serve, take the cover off the skillet, add the parsley and shallots, and season with salt and pepper. I suggest you allow these ingredients about 5 minutes to simmer in before you spoon the gator onto the china. I recommend, too, that you continue stirring the meat once you remove the cover.

Hint: Smothered alligator goes well with buttered rice, diced carrots, broccoli au gratin, and a tossed salad. And if you want to add a little lagniappe, I recommend that when you toss in the parsley and shallots you also stir in about 2 tablespoons of a good white wine. But this is optional, even for gourmets!

CHAPTER TEN

Oysters

Cajun Oyster Soup Royale

An old gentleman from Eunice, Louisiana, told me I just had to put this recipe in my cookbook because, as he phrased it, "Folks shouldn't pass on to their reward until they get to try this soup at least once!" Well, I fixed it in my kitchen one rainy Saturday afternoon, and I want you to know it's so smooth it's like savoring liquid sunshine! You'll see.

2 sticks butter (not margarine)	**2 bay leaves**
½ cup Crisco oil	**1 cup tap water**
2 tbsp. flour	**dash cream sherry**
1 cup finely chopped green onions	**pinch of thyme**
¼ cup finely chopped parsley	**salt and pepper to taste**
3 cloves fresh garlic, finely chopped	**1 cup half-and-half**
2 tbsp. coarsely chopped bell pepper	**6 doz. fresh-shucked unwashed oysters (save the liquor)**

In a black iron Dutch oven or a heavy aluminum pot, melt the butter in the Crisco oil and heat just to the bubbling point. Then sprinkle the 2 tablespoons of flour evenly into the oil and slowly simmer it until the flour turns a deep tan color (*do not brown*). When it's just right, toss in all the remaining ingredients except the oysters and the half-and-half, but go ahead and add the liquor from the oysters (about a cup or so). You want the mixture to simmer until the vegetables turn semisoft. (Be sure you keep stirring or you won't get a uniform blend.) Then you can add the half-and-half slowly, stir the ingredients into it, and reduce the heat to *low*. Now let this cook for about 20 minutes, with the lid on.

Some folks add the oysters to the soup base while the stock is cooking, but I recommend that you don't put your oysters into this recipe until about 15 minutes before you are ready to serve the dish. Then drop them in *one at a time* (so that you don't reduce the heat) and cook them on low for about 12 minutes.

Hint: If you want a thicker soup, I suggest you add instant mashed potatoes (one teaspoonful at a time).

Oysters alla Delicata

Virtually everyone has cooked oysters in bacon, because the two flavors combined just seem to complement each other nicely. But this particular oyster-bacon dish can be put on the table with almost anything from potatoes to rice to stuffing. It's easy to make, too!

½ tsp. salt	dash thyme
2 tbsp. parsley	¼ tsp. paprika
¼ tsp. black pepper	24 large oysters
dash marjoram	12 slices lean bacon

Before you begin working with the oysters and the bacon blend together the salt, parsley, pepper, marjoram, thyme, and paprika in a small bowl. Then set out the oysters to drain. For the best of flavors use fresh-shucked oysters whenever possible, but you can also make the recipe using oysters in a jar. Whichever you use, *drain them*. When you're ready to prepare the dish, place the oysters on a dry surface and lightly sprinkle them with the seasoning mixture. Sprinkle both sides.

Now slice the bacon into half-slices and wrap each oyster in one piece, holding them together with toothpicks. When you're ready to cook, put the oysters on a rack in the oven, but make sure they aren't touching each other. The best method is to place a large baking pan under the bacon wraps to catch drippings. You want to bake the oysters at 450 degrees until the bacon is crisp, which will generally be less than 30 minutes.

Hint: You can make a gravy out of the bacon drippings. It goes well on potatoes, rice, and even grits.

Oysters Rudolph

Every year in New Orleans the Louisiana Cooperative Extension Service holds a big 4-H cookery contest for kids, because in Bayou Country, even the *young Louisianians* like to cook good foods. This recipe, the contrivance of 4-H winner Mary Bourgeois, is among the finest for oysters I've ever eaten. And I want to share it with you!

10 slices bacon, chopped	2 bay leaves
2 tbsp. flour	24 oysters
5 green onions, chopped	10 drops Tabasco sauce
1 tsp. minced garlic	2 tsp. Worcestershire sauce
1 #303 can turtle soup	dash salt and pepper
1 tbsp. parsley	¼ cup sherry
1 2-oz. jar chopped pimentos	½ cup oyster liquor (optional)

First off, get a large skillet and fry up the bacon really crisp. Then remove it from the pan, leaving the drippings. After the bacon fat has cooled for about 5 minutes, add the flour to the pan, mix it in well, and put the pan back on the fire (medium low is best). Sauté the flour until it browns and then toss in the onions and garlic and cook them well.

Next you add the turtle soup. As soon as you do, take the pan off the fire again; you're going to have to start mixing the ingredients right away because you want everything to blend together. Throw in the parsley, the bacon, the pimentos (but first drain the liquid off!), the bay leaves, the oysters, the Tabasco, and the Worcestershire, and mix it all well. Season with salt and pepper to taste.

Now put the mixture back on the fire and simmer it over medium-low heat for no more than 10 minutes. This is what disperses the flavors. Finally, pour in the sherry and simmer the whole dish another 15 minutes or until the oysters curl up really tight. You'll have to keep stirring all the time the dish is cooking, but it smells so dang good you won't mind at all.

Hint: Thin to the consistency you want by adding oyster liquor 5 minutes before serving.

Cajun Oyster Pie

There must be a million recipes in print in Louisiana for oyster pie—the dish is that popular. But after having tasted variations of the dish from Ouachita to Barataria, I've found none that seems to have the full-bodied flavor and robust appeal that this recipe has. Give it a try and surprise your guests.

2 frozen, unbaked 9-inch pie
  shells
3 tbsp. butter (not margarine)
3 tbsp. Crisco oil
1 medium onion, finely chopped
1 tbsp. finely chopped shallot
  tops
½ cup finely chopped celery
2 tbsp. finely chopped bell
  pepper

2 tbsp. all-purpose flour
4 doz. oysters (save the liquor)
2 tsp. Worcestershire sauce
½ tsp. lemon juice
dash Tabasco sauce
1 tbsp. finely chopped parsley
  (optional)
salt to taste

First, thaw out the frozen pie shells and preheat your oven to 350 degrees. In a saucepan, blend the butter and the oil and heat to "just bubbling." Fry the onions, shallot tops, celery, bell pepper, and flour until the vegetables are wilted and the flour begins to brown slightly.

While your basic ingredients are sautéing, slice half of the oysters (cutting each oyster into about 3 pieces) and drain them (but save the liquor). Then add both the whole oysters and the cut pieces to the sauté pan and stir-fry for about *5 minutes* or until the whole oysters begin to curl up at the edges. Add the Worcestershire sauce, the lemon juice, and the Tabasco, and stir them into the mixture. The mix should begin to thicken about now, but don't let it get too pasty. If it does, add some of the liquor you saved to keep a "stuffing" consistency. Continue stirring.

When it is all cooked together and smooth in texture, taste the filling. You'll notice that you haven't added salt up to this point because, if the oysters are naturally salty, you may not need any. But now is the time to taste, especially for salt. If you'd like more, add it. If not, leave it out. It will be good without it.

Fill your pie shells with the filling (it should be slightly rounded over the top), then completely cap the mix with the second pie crust. Using a steak knife, make about 8 or 10 slits in the upper crust. Using a fork, seal the edges tightly. (Notice that the directions for adding the parsley have been omitted. That's because I consider the parsley an optional ingredient in oyster pie. If you want to add it, put it in when you stir in the Worcestershire and the Tabasco. But you can leave it out and the dish will still be super.)

At this point turn up the oven from 350 to 400 degrees, put the pie on the baking rack, and cook for about 20 minutes or so (until the crust is golden brown). Deeeelicious!

Oysters Velveteen

If you like oysters baked in their own half shells, you'll flip over this recipe straight from Cajun Country. Not only is the flavor magnificent; the preparation is simple and the presentation is suitable for both family get-togethers and elegant dinner parties. Just remember to save the shells!

3 doz. oysters (save the liquor)	1 tsp. dry barbecue spice
3 doz. oyster half shells	½ tsp. salt (optional)
1 cup melted butter (not margarine)	1 cup milk
	1 cup half-and-half
4 cups saltine cracker crumbs	¼ tsp. Worcestershire sauce
½ tsp. rosemary	1 cup grated sharp cheddar cheese
½ tsp. cayenne pepper	
2 tbsp. fresh parsley	

First strain the oyster liquor, remove the shell bits, and wash the half shells well inside and out. I also suggest you pick through the oysters themselves to make sure no shell fragments are mixed in with the meats. Set the half shells in the sink drainboard to dry.

In a large mixing bowl, combine the cracker crumbs (it is best if you make your own from saltine crackers), the butter, the rosemary, the cayenne, the parsley, and the barbecue spice. Thorough mixing is best achieved if you use a whisk. When the blend is uniform, begin adding oyster liquor and mixing it in until the cracker crumbs are *moist* (not wet!). Taste the mix at this point. If it needs salt, add it. *If the cracker crumbs are sufficiently salty to suit your taste, go ahead and leave it out.* (Also eat one of the raw oysters to see if they are salty. If they are, watch your additional salt.)

Next, pour the milk, the half-and-half, the Worcestershire sauce, and a little of the oyster liquor into a saucepan and heat the mixture on *low*. Stir well and let it simmer for about 15 minutes. Then take your half shells from the drainboard and lay them out on the counter top in front of you. With a spoon, begin to place a small amount of cracker-crumb mix into each shell, being sure to use exactly *half* of what you have mixed. In other words, spread the mix evenly on the half shells, reserving half of the mix for the top layer. When all the shells have mix in them, place the oysters on top of the mix. Then *very lightly* sprinkle the remaining cracker mix *on top* of the oysters.

When you're ready to cook the oysters, place them on a rack in a preheated 400-degree oven (if you've overstuffed them, put a baking pan under them to catch the drippings) or out on your barbecue grill fired up on high. Then spoon some of the milk sauce into each shell. It doesn't take much; you should have enough to fill all 36 shells. Bake in the oven or grill open-face until the mixture is bubbly and sizzling, and the oysters have curled. Then remove them from the rack or grill, sprinkle a pinch of the cheddar over the top of each oyster, and serve piping hot. It should serve six normal people—or two hungry Cajuns!

Hint: This is one dish with which you'll want to serve a chilled white wine as an accompaniment. I suggest a Chablis or a Rhine, and a California vintage is more than adequate. You might also want to wrap green beans in bacon, bake them until the bacon is crisp, and serve them with the oysters. Hush puppies also go well with these oysters. Of course, my favorite way to eat them is to double the recipe, eat the oysters by themselves, and ice down a couple of six-packs of beer to wash them down. That's bayou style, y'all!

NONSTICK SPRAYS VS. VEGETABLE OILS

Use corn oil and your fingers if you want to save money and avoid buying the nonstick sprays. They aren't really necessary if you do what many of the old-time Louisiana cooks do to prevent sticking. Simply pour a drop of vegetable or corn oil into the pan while it's cold and rub the oil thoroughly across the surface. Then place the pan on the fire and heat it up. Your food will not stick if you *don't overheat.*

KEEP ALL YOUR SEAFOOD COLD!

Cold seafood fried in hot oil will result in sealed, crisp outer skins and delicate, moist insides. You will also not lose flavor and texture if you keep your seafoods cold. Just allow enough time for the oil to reheat to proper temperature between batches!

Frank's Perfect Fried Oysters

Too many people complain that oysters are difficult to fry, and for the life of me I can't understand why! My oysters turn out fully coated, crispy, yet moist every time—and yours can too. Just follow this recipe. You'll see what I mean.

36 oysters	salt to taste
2 qt. water	cayenne pepper to taste
1 cup Zatarain's Fish-Fry; or	black pepper to taste
corn flour	Crisco oil for frying
1 cup cornmeal	

Shuck your oysters and drain them in a colander. Then bring about 2 quarts of water to a boil in a saucepan and pour the boiling liquid over the top of the oysters while they are still in the colander. The coatings sometimes fall off oysters because of the slippery surface on the raw oysters. The hot water strips away much of this slipperiness without affecting the texture and flavor.

When the oysters are drained well, place them in a bowl in your refrigerator and get them ice cold. *Oysters should never be fried when they are at room temperature;* the outside membranes do not seal in the juices. It's the cold oyster suddenly being submerged in the hot grease that seals in juices. When you're ready to fry, take the oysters from the refrigerator, pour off any residual drippings, and get your coating mix ready by combining the corn flour, cornmeal, salt, and pepper. If your oysters are naturally salty, be careful about adding salt. *The oysters must go from the bowl to the mix to the grease as quickly as possible.* If you allow time for the flour to get wet, the coating will get tough and the oysters will not be crisp.

Have your deep fryer ready (or a skillet, if you prefer, filled with enough oil to cover the oysters). The temperature should be 400 degrees. Then place whatever number of oysters you'll fry in a "batch" in the flour at the same time, rolling them around well to coat them thoroughly. When they're coated, drop them into the oil *immediately and quickly*. The minute they float to the surface, they're done!

Do not overload the fryer. It will reduce the temperature of the oil and the oysters will absorb the grease. And *do not add the oysters in a batch*. Add them quickly, but drop them into the oil one at a time. When they are cooked, drain them immediately on a platter coated with paper towels. So fry hot, fry cold oysters, fry quickly, *and fry only till they float*. They'll come out greaseless and crispy every time.

Ol' Harold Hill's Oyster Bread Dressing

When it comes to oyster dressings my old friend Tony Chachere has me convinced that none beats Harold Hill's Oyster Bread Dressing. Tony suggested I try the 130-year-old concoction for myself, and said that if I liked it I could use the recipe in my book. So do I have to tell you I liked it, cher? It's a "ten"!

2 loaves stale French bread	Tony's Creole Seasoning to taste
4 cups finely chopped chicken giblets	1 sprig fresh thyme
	2 whole fresh bay leaves
2 sticks margarine	1 cup green onion tops
2 cups chopped onions	1 cup chopped parsley
2 cups chopped bell pepper	1 qt. freshly opened oysters
2 cups chopped celery	4 eggs

Tony told me that Harold Hill's secret in this particular recipe is "allowing time between each ingredient to cook and blend." Stir well after each ingredient goes in and allow about 5 minutes after each addition for the blending to work. So with that in mind, start off by drying the bread in your oven at about 200 degrees and cutting it into cubes. Then, in a small pot, cover the giblets with water and boil them until tender. After they're cooked, remove them from the water, but keep a supply of the giblet stock for moistening the dressing.

Next, get out your black Dutch oven, heat it up on the stove, and melt *1 stick* of the margarine. Then sauté the onions, bell peppers, and celery until they're tender. When they are cooked, toss in the chopped giblets, brown them well, and add the bread cubes. At this point season the bread mix with Tony's Creole Seasoning and stir everything together well, adding small amounts of the giblet water to keep the moisture right. (Note: You don't want too much water—just enough to make the mix moist.)

When all the ingredients are blended together, toss in the other stick of margarine, the thyme, and the bay leaves and simmer everything together for about 15 minutes, stirring constantly. Then put in the onion tops, the parsley, and the cleaned and drained oysters. *Do not cut up your oysters; they go in whole.* And they continue to cook in the dressing until they curl up at the edges. As soon as the oysters curl, remove the pot from the fire, beat the eggs with a whisk, and stir them into the Dutch oven as quickly as you can. (Adding and stirring them too slowly will prevent them from cooking uniformly.)

Finally, spoon the dressing into a greased or buttered baking dish and bake at 350 degrees for about half an hour until the dressing "sets." Then serve—and watch your guests rave!

Creamed Oysters Barataria

For a number of years I experimented, trying to find the perfect blends of ingredients and seasonings to produce the best oyster stew ever. And I dumped out more misses than I care to admit. But then, one day, it happened! Everything just seemed to fall into place—the oysters were cooked just right, the cream picked up all the subtle flavors, the bacon was in the right proportion—everything meshed. You try my creation. I'd like to know how you rate it.

3 doz. fresh-shucked oysters
2 cups strained oyster liquor
2 tbsp. margarine
½ lb. sliced fresh mushrooms
½ stick unsalted butter
1 medium white onion, finely chopped
2 tbsp. minced shallots
1 bay leaf
3 cups half-and-half

3 slices bacon, fried crisp and drained
1 cup whole milk
1¼ tsp. salt
½ tsp. white pepper
1 tsp. finely chopped fresh parsley
1 cup grated sharp cheddar cheese

In a saucepan, heat the oysters in their own liquor until the edges curl up (I suggest you keep the fire set on medium low). Then separate the oysters and the liquor and save them both in bowls. Using the same saucepan, melt the margarine and quickly *stir-fry* the mushrooms. *You don't want them to brown*—just get them hot and lightly coated with the margarine. When they're ready, place them in the bowl with the oysters.

Using the same saucepan, melt the butter over medium heat and sauté the onions, shallots, and bay leaf (leave the bay leaf in the butter for only about 3 minutes, then remove it), simmering until the vegetables have wilted. Then pour in the half-and-half, reduce the heat to medium low, and cook until the mixture thickens. At this point you also want to add the crumbled bacon bits to the cream. When the cream and seasoning mixture has simmered for about 5 minutes, gradually stir in the milk and add the salt and pepper. Simmer gently for a few minutes more, then stir in the oyster liquor. Bring the heat up to medium and cook for about 5 minutes *(make sure it doesn't boil!)*. Then stir in the oysters, mushrooms, and parsley, *and again reduce the heat to medium low*. Cook for 3 more minutes. About a minute before you're ready to eat, *swirl* in the cheese. Serve the dish piping hot in deep bowls.

Hint: Sesame crackers and a crisp cucumber salad accompany this dish well. And some Riesling wine adds a nice touch.

N'awlins Smoked Barbecued Oysters

Recipes in this book come from numerous sources. Some are my own creations, some were solicited right from bayou families on the marsh, others were dropped in my post-office box by cooks, cabdrivers, construction workers, attorneys, doctors, and housewives. And still others, like this one, were called in by listeners on my radio shows. This particular oyster recipe seems to be a favorite whenever I teach a cooking class. I thought you'd like to have it!

1 1-lb. bag hickory chips	½ cup freshly squeezed lemon
1 lb. margarine or butter	juice
½ clove garlic, very finely	4 doz. oysters on the half shell
minced	saltines for sopping the drippings
cayenne pepper to taste	

Whether you use the regular charcoal barbecue grill or the new Charm-Glo gas-operated model, you will need to use the hickory chips if this recipe is to have all the zest it is supposed to have. You must also use a grill that has a cover, because you will partly "smoke" the oysters. So, to get up a good head of smoke, I suggest that the day before you cook you soak your hickory chips in water and let them float at least overnight.

When you're ready to cook, combine your butter or margarine (and I must tell you that Parkay Liquid Margarine works well) with the garlic, cayenne, and lemon juice and let the mixture simmer for about 10 minutes in a saucepan. Then fire up the grill, get it good and hot, and add the chips.

While all this is happening, open your oysters, leave them on the deepest half of the half shell, and place them on the grill over the coals. Immediately spoon about 2 *tablespoons* of the butter-lemon-garlic sauce over the oysters in the shell. Go ahead and douse 'em; make sure you've got garlic in each spoonful, too! Then cover the grill and let the li'l rascals smoke for a while. Make sure your grill is really smoking—if it's not, increase the amount of hickory.

Then, when the edges of the oysters start to curl up and the butter sauce is sizzling inside the shells (it takes about 10 minutes on a hot grill), eat the critters right off the gratings, on saltine crackers. Don't wait around till they cool off—put 'em down right as they come off the fire!

Just one note here: *Don't overcook them!* If you cook them too long, the oysters will dry out. You want them nice and juicy. You can crumble some crackers into the half shell after you've eaten the oysters, and get the juice, too! This is one dish you'll have to fight over, so I recommend you stand near the barbecue grill as they're cooking. If you don't like these, you probably swallowed your taste buds some time back!

Hint: I heartily recommend you serve these oysters with a six-pack of your favorite iced-down beer.

Acadian Mushroom-Baked Oysters

For a rich, succulent oyster dish, you may want to prepare this casserole concoction the first chance you get. It is ideal for Friday-night entertaining, but it is a taste treat regardless of the occasion. You'll like it, I'm sure—and it's simple to toss together.

½ cup coarse saltine cracker crumbs
½ cup unseasoned bread crumbs
¼ cup melted butter (not margarine)
3 doz. fresh-shucked oysters
1 10¾-oz. can cream of mushroom soup

1 10-oz. can BinB mushrooms (bits and pieces)
¼ cup Romano cheese
1 tbsp. chopped parsley
¼ tsp. black pepper

Start off by breaking the saltine crackers into coarse crumbs, blending them with the bread crumbs, and setting the mixture off to the side for a while. Then gently heat the butter in a saucepan, chop up the oysters (coarse chopping will do nicely), and lightly sauté them in the pan. When they're just about cooked, add the mushroom soup and the mushroom bits and pieces and stir everything around until the mixture is smooth. Reduce the heat to simmer.

Butter the bottom and sides of a Pyrex baking dish (or spray it with Pam if you prefer), and begin building "baking layers"—a thin layer of crumbs on the bottom, followed by a layer of the cooked oyster mixture, followed by another layer of crumbs, followed by another layer of the mixture, topped off by a thin layer of crumbs. Be sure to get the layers evenly distributed at about the same thickness so that the baking process will be uniform. Before placing the casserole in the oven (which you should set at about 350 degrees), lightly sprinkle the Romano cheese, parsley, and black pepper over the top. The dish will be cooked when the casserole is bubbling hot and the top layer of crumbs is lightly browned. It should be baked uncovered.

Suggestion: This dish goes great with barbecued chicken, baked turkey, roasted duck, fried fish fillets, or deep-fried oysters. It should be complemented by a tossed green salad, and possibly green beans baked in bacon strips.

Oysters and Eggplants

You've no doubt eaten eggplant stuffed with shrimp or eggplant stuffed with ground meat. But have you tasted eggplant stuffed with oysters? If not, first chance you get, fix this dish for your family. And get ready for the praise to come your way! It is truly unique. It has all the full-bodied flavor of a Deep Southern dish, and you won't ever want the aroma to leave your kitchen. Try it and see what I mean.

4 medium eggplants	1 tbsp. minced garlic
2 qt. unsalted water	¾ cup heavy cream
3 doz. medium-size oysters (save the liquor)	¼ cup finely chopped parsley
	1 tsp. Italian seasoning
½ cup unsalted butter	salt and black pepper to taste
1¼ cups chopped white onions	1½ cups buttered bread crumbs
2 tbsp. bell pepper	¼ cup fresh Parmesan cheese

Start by boiling the eggplants in unsalted water until a fork will pierce the centers easily. Then set the "plants" aside to cool. Take a moment to drain the liquor off the oysters (but save it!) and cut them into thirds (i.e., 3 pieces from each oyster). Set them aside too. Then, in a 6-quart Dutch oven, melt the butter over medium heat (be careful you *do not burn it*) and sauté the onions, bell pepper, and garlic until they become tender. Stir occasionally to get uniformity in the cooking process. While the vegetables are simmering, peel the eggplants and dice the pulp into small pieces. Place the chopped oysters in a pie tin and lightly broil them in the oven until they lose their transparency (about 3 minutes).

When the eggplant and the oysters are ready, add them to the Dutch oven and simmer them in the vegetable mixture. Note: It is important that you constantly stir the contents of the pot. You want the eggplant and the oysters to break down into stuffing consistency—not mushy, but well meshed. Your heat should remain on medium while this is happening.

When everything has simmered together, reduce the fire to low and put the lid on the pot. Heat covered for about 5 minutes, then stir in the cream, the parsley, the Italian seasoning, the salt and pepper, and the buttered bread crumbs. Again, mix all the ingredients thoroughly: you want total uniformity. When the mixing is done, *remove the Dutch oven from the heat*. At this point adjust the consistency by adding extra oyster stock (liquor) to the bread crumbs if necessary. You want the dish to be moist, but not *wet*. When you have it right, sprinkle on half of the Parmesan cheese and fold it into the mixture. Then lightly rub some butter into a glass baking dish (or into individual ramekins if you're preparing this for a party) and spoon out the mixture. Lightly sprinkle some bread crumbs over the top of the mix, add the remaining Parmesan cheese, and bake in a 350-degree oven for about 40 minutes.

When you're ready to serve, I suggest you put this dish on the table with creamed green peas, brabant potatoes, and cucumber salad, along with your favorite Rhine wine. It also makes a nice complement to hickory-smoked steak and brussels sprouts.

Estelle's Oyster Fritters

For more years than she cares to remember, Estelle Chretien supervised the culinary arts in public school kitchens . . . and the kiddies never ate so good. Her talents are almost unbelievable; she could take basic ingredients the schools bought in bulk and turn them into lunchtime meals that should have been served by candlelight. Now Estelle is retired, but she's still cooking. And every now and then she shows up at her old alma maters and brings the teachers a special treat, like these oyster fritters.

3 doz. oysters, cut in half	**2 eggs, slightly beaten**
2½ cups oyster water	**⅓ cup finely chopped onions**
3 cups flour	**⅔ cup finely chopped green**
2 tbsp. baking powder	**onions**
2 tsp. salt	**¼ cup finely chopped parsley**
½ tsp. white pepper	

Start off by draining the oysters and saving the water. For best results, you should use fresh-shucked oysters whenever possible.

In a mixing bowl, sift together the flour, baking powder, salt, and pepper, and stir in the eggs. Just mix everything around lightly. Then add the oyster water and mix the ingredients really well to form the fritter base. When the consistency is uniform, toss in the onions, green onions, and parsley, and again mix everything well. Then add the oysters and mix them in.

When you're ready to cook, set the deep fryer or the Dutch oven to *hot* (about 375 to 400 degrees), drop tablespoon helpings of the mixture into the oil, and fry until each fritter is golden brown on both sides. You may have to flip them or turn them over, but make sure they are cooked all the way through. This particular recipe will make 36 fritters. They can be served as hors d'oeuvres, TV snacks, or entrées. I promise, you're gonna love them!

ABOUT SELECTING AND SERVING WINES

There is a lot of ritual connected with choosing the right wine to go with a meal. For too long those of us who were not wine experts or connoisseurs avoided drinking a particular wine with a meal because we were made to *feel uncomfortable* about making the selection. Don't fall victim to this syndrome. While white wines are generally recommended for seafoods, if you prefer red wine, then *have* red wine. Drink what *you* like and suit your palate.

Dupry's Petit Pois Oyster au Gratin

I never knew Mr. Dupry's first name—as kids, all we ever called him was "Mr. Dupry." He lived a couple of houses down from me in New Orleans, on Tonti Street. The one thing we all remember about Mr. Dupry is his oyster petit pois au gratin: I can still taste it! Every time he got oysters from the French Market, he'd invite the neighborhood kids in to taste this dish. We all loved it. And, except for a few liberties I've taken with his creation, this is how it went.

4 doz. oysters, shucked and drained	1 cup sour cream
½ pound thinly sliced fresh mushrooms	½ cup whole milk
	1 tsp. white pepper
2 sticks butter	1½ tsp. salt
1 rib celery, coarsely chopped	2 tbsp. lemon juice
½ cup coarsely chopped onions	2 #303 cans Petit Pois peas
	4 slices American cheese

Drain the oysters well and slice the mushrooms. Then melt the butter over medium-low heat in a saucepan large enough to hold both the oysters and mushrooms and simmer them together uncovered until the oysters curl up and the mushrooms are tender (it should take you about 12 to 15 minutes). Be sure to keep stirring constantly. When the oysters and mushrooms are sautéed, remove them from the pan and set them aside. Then turn up the heat to *medium high* and sauté the celery and onions in the butter until they wilt (about 5 minutes). At this point add the sour cream and the milk, reduce the heat to *medium,* and simmer gently for about 5 minutes more.

When the mixture is well blended, put the oysters and mushrooms back in the pan. Add the pepper and salt, the lemon juice, and the peas. Turn the heat down to low and gently simmer for about 5 minutes, stirring occasionally. Note: If you want the mixture to be thick, simmer it longer. Ideally it should have a creamy consistency.

The last step is to pour the entire mixture into a buttered Corning Ware or Pyrex casserole dish and top with the American cheese slices. Then bake in a 325-degree oven about 10 minutes or until the cheese melts and begins to brown slightly. The best way to serve this au gratin is to spoon generous helpings into heated bowls and eat it with crisp French bread. But the last time I fixed this dish I ladled it on top of a handful of ruffled potato chips. It gave the oysters and peas a hint of crispness. I assume Nacho Cheese Flavor Doritos would also lend a nice touch. God bless you, Mr. Dupry!

Mary Clare's Good Ol' Oyster Dressing

Whether you're stuffing a Thanksgiving turkey, filling the cavities of Cornish game hens, making a side dish to go with baked red snapper, or putting together the fixings for a weekend party, nothing goes with those entrées as well as my wife's oyster dressing! Of course, I've got to admit that I'm a little prejudiced, but she really fixes the best dressing I've ever had!

½ cup melted butter
½ cup finely chopped smoked
   sausage
2 medium white onions, finely
   chopped
½ cup finely chopped celery
1 tbsp. finely chopped parsley
½ cup finely chopped bell pepper
1 tsp. finely chopped garlic
¼ cup thinly sliced shallot
   tops

5 doz. chopped oysters (plus
   liquor)
⅛ tsp. poultry seasoning
⅛ tsp. sweet basil
1 tsp. black pepper
pinch thyme
pinch cloves
1½ tsp. salt
3 cups Progresso unseasoned
   bread crumbs

In a large black iron Dutch oven, melt the butter over medium heat and sauté the smoked sausage, onions, celery, parsley, bell pepper, garlic, and shallot tops until all of them are tender. The one thing you want to remember is to keep the butter just hot enough so that it doesn't burn. Keep stirring the ingredients together to cook them uniformly.

Next, gradually stir in the chopped oysters. Notice I said *gradually stir in.* The reason for this is that you do not want to reduce the heat—lowering the heat will cause excessive water to be released from the oysters and you'll have to add too many bread crumbs to the finished dish. Cook the oysters gently for about *4 minutes,* stirring all the while. When the ingredients are well mixed, stir in the poultry seasoning, basil, pepper, thyme, cloves, and salt. About the salt: check the oysters to see if they are naturally salty before adding the prescribed amount. You may have to reduce the salt if nature has provided her own. At this point, therefore, *begin tasting the dressing,* and make whatever adjustments are necessary.

Now cover the pot and lower the heat to simmer. Let it simmer, still covered, for 5 minutes to allow time for the flavors to blend thoroughly. This is one of the secrets to making a really good oyster dressing. After the simmering process is over, begin stirring in the bread crumbs a little at a time. Note that you do not have to add all 3 cups. If you want your dressing moist, stop adding crumbs when you get to the texture you desire. If you want a drier stuffing, add all 3 cups—even more if your taste and needs dictate. Go ahead and take some liberties with the recipe: you can add flair and creative touches to suit your taste. For instance, for added richness in flavor you may want to quickly stir in a raw egg before you remove the dressing from the heat. Or you might want to sauté about a half-pound of fresh mushrooms and fold them into the stuffing. Or you can make the dish spicier by tossing in some cayenne. You be the judge.

When the stuffing is ready in your estimation, go ahead and take the pot off the fire and cover it for a few minutes to let it "set up." This is where the body comes in; it's how the final blending brings out the full flavor. And you can make adjustments at this point by moistening the dish with the *oyster liquor*—that's why you saved it.

All that you still have to decide is how you plan to use the dressing. It can be stuffed into birds (from chicken to doves to ducks) and baked, or used as a side-dish stuffing for seafood (flounder or broiled trout), or set out as a topping for canapes at a fall party. It's great stuff no matter how you serve it. But I do suggest you serve it *hot*. By the way, if you serve this recipe as a stuffing, I recommend you go one step further and spread the dressing out in a casserole, lightly sprinkle with more bread crumbs, top with butter, and bake about 20 minutes in a 350-degree oven.

AND WHEN COOKING WITH BUTTER

Keep in mind that *unsalted butter* lends itself better to recipes than salted, lightly salted, or whipped butter. It does not burn as rapidly (so you can use a higher temperature), and it does not impart as harsh a flavor as the salted variety.

You will also find that unless you are serving dishes such as lobster or rock shrimp, it is not necessary to *clarify* butter. The milk solids in the butter you cook with will add extra flavor, especially in seafood dishes.

Chipped Oysters Lafitte

One of the most attractive dishes you can serve to guests is one that comes enclosed in pattie shells—either the small or large size. But when you care enough to fill the patties with an oyster concoction, well, you're definitely from the South, m'frien', and I'll eat at your house anytime! Try these.

6 doz. oysters (save the liquor)	½ tsp. thyme
1 stick butter	½ tsp. celery seed
½ cup finely chopped green onions	2 bay leaves
1 10-oz. can mushroom bits and pieces	¼ tsp. rosemary
	¼ tsp. basil
½ cup finely chopped parsley	½ tsp. black pepper
4 cloves garlic, minced	½ tsp. cayenne pepper
4 tbsp. flour	½ tsp. white pepper
2 cups whole milk	1½ tsp. salt
	12 2-inch bakery pattie shells

Start off by cutting the oysters into small pieces (3 or 4 pieces each) and draining them in a colander. Be sure to save the oyster liquor; it's going to be your thickening—or thinning—agent in this dish!

In a large saucepan (the 10-inch size should do nicely), melt the butter on medium heat, and gently sauté the green onions, the mushrooms, the parsley, the garlic, and the chopped oysters. *You can toss them all into the pan at once.* Just keep stirring constantly and watch the heat so that none of the ingredients burn. Cook the mixture exactly 5 minutes. Then, with the heat still on medium, sprinkle in the flour to thicken the mixture, and stir it in well. Note: *Do not add all the flour at once*—it will lump up if you do. If the mixture gets too pasty, add some oyster liquor (see why you saved it?). It should be the consistency of pancake batter.

When everything is well mixed, begin stirring in the milk. Continue stirring until the blend is smooth. Then add the remaining seasonings—thyme, celery seed, bay leaves, rosemary, basil, peppers, and salt. Again with the heat on medium, go ahead and simmer the dish for another 5 minutes, stirring continuously. At this point *adjust the moisture* in the stuffing. If the mixture is too thin, continue simmering until some of the liquid evaporates. If it is too stiff, add some more of the oyster liquor. You want it to be slightly moist, but you also want it to hold together. Then, just before you're ready to serve, stuff the mixture into the pattie shells, place them on a baking tin, and heat in a 350-degree oven for 10 to 12 minutes. Serve piping hot!

Really Fast Oyster Soup Crabbie

Dwain Crabtree, who lives in Gretna, Louisiana, got so excited about this recipe he told me I had to include it in my cookbook. "I don't know if it's original or not, Frank," he told me. "I do know that I've been making it a long time and teasing lots of folks' taste buds. I want your readers to have a treat, too!" By the way, Wayne does admit that after you take the first bite . . . this recipe will serve only *one* person!

2 doz. fresh-shucked oysters (save the liquor)	salt and white pepper to taste oyster crackers (as desired)
2 pt. half-and-half	4 finely chopped green onions
½ lb. butter	

You start off by shucking the oysters and saving every single drop of the oyster liquor. You'll have to strain it, of course, to remove the small bits of shell fragments, because this isn't a crunchy soup. Incidentally, the best oysters to get for this recipe are medium-sized (they're the most succulent).

Take a large skillet (about a 10-inch size), heat the oyster liquor to bubbling, add the oysters, and cook them until the edges curl up. This should take about 4 minutes. Then reduce the heat and gradually stir in the half-and-half. When the cream is well blended with the oyster liquor, put in the half-pound of butter. Turn up the heat when you put in the butter and stir it around continuously as it melts. *Note: You want to heat the butter sauce almost to the point of boiling, but do not let it boil!* When it reaches the correct heat, take the skillet off the fire and salt and pepper the dish to taste (I recommend white pepper).

Just before you serve the soup crumble up a few oyster crackers (you can buy these in almost any supermarket) and sprinkle them and the green onions over the top. Then spoon out generous helpings. It's fast, it's simple to fix, and it's unbelievably tasty.

INVEST IN A FOOD PROCESSOR

If you spend a great deal of time in the kitchen preparing elegant meals, or if you like to cook a variety of dishes each week, one of the best investments you can make is in a *food processor*. In spite of what you may have heard, you cannot use a blender to get the texture you want from onions, garlic, celery, and parsley. The blender will not *chop* these ingredients; it purees them. It also doesn't chop oysters and shrimp and other seafoods. So buy a good processor, preferably one with an *instant on-off* (touch) control. You'll save a lot of time.

CHAPTER ELEVEN

Shrimp

Shrimp Dressing Casserole

This recipe, specially formulated for working housewives and put together by a St. Tammany Parish schoolteacher, is great for those evenings when you're hurried and in no mood to cook! A complete dinner in a dish, it's quick but full-bodied, easy but nourishing, and it tastes like you slaved over it all day long.

1 lb. raw shrimp	1 10¾-oz. can cream of
1 cup uncooked rice	mushroom soup
¼ bell pepper, coarsely chopped	1 10¾-oz. can cream of
1 stalk celery, finely chopped	onion soup
2 cloves garlic, finely chopped	dash cayenne pepper
¼ cup minced green onion tops	salt to taste
4 tbsp. minced parsley	

Peel your shrimp, wash them under cold running water, and let them drain in a colander. Cut them into pieces; if you cut each segment of the shrimp, the size should be just right.

Take a 2-quart casserole dish and add *all* the ingredients to it, mixing everything together well. Try to get a good blend so that the flavors are evenly distributed. All that's left is to cover the dish tightly, put it on the center rack in your oven, and bake it at 350 degrees for about an hour, or until the rice is tender.

Hint: For the sake of simplicity, I suggest you serve the casserole with a lettuce and tomato salad—and a frosty glass of iced tea.

Italian Shrimp Zucchini

It's been a longtime practice in Louisiana to cook squashes and squash-type vegetables in combination with shrimp. There's shrimp with mirlitons, shrimp with bell peppers, shrimp with eggplant, and shrimp with cuccuzzi, but it's tough to beat Italian Shrimp Zucchini! This is good with *anything*.

2 tbsp. pure olive oil
¼ cup chopped white onion
1 tbsp. tomato paste
1 tbsp. lemon juice
4 tbsp. water
¼ tsp. oregano

½ tsp. sweet basil
4 medium-size zucchini, sliced
    ¼-inch thick
2 cups chunked medium-size
    shrimp
4 tbsp. grated Romano cheese

You're going to need a skillet with a tight-fitting cover for this dish, because you're going to have to smother everything. So get the skillet on the fire and preheat it at the medium setting. Then pour in the olive oil. As soon as it gets hot, sauté the onions until they turn translucent. Then add the tomato paste and fry until it's well mixed into the olive oil and the onion.

Now add the lemon juice, water, oregano, and basil and simmer them for about *3 minutes*. Then gently toss in the zucchini and reduce the heat to *medium low*. Cover the skillet at this point and simmer for about 5 minutes. Next, put in the shrimp. Some liquid should have already been rendered from the zucchini, but if the base is too dry you can add a bit more water. *Not too much, though;* as the shrimp cook you'll get liquids from them, too, and the texture should be just right.

Stir the shrimp, zucchini, and the seasonings together well until they are uniformly blended, but *do this gently* so that you don't break up the zucchini. Then cover the skillet again, set the fire on low, and simmer the dish for about 10 minutes. When you're ready to serve, sprinkle the Romano cheese all over the zucchini and the shrimp. Mama mia! That's Italian!

Shrimp and Veal Rolls

Put this recipe at the top of your "specialty" list. It's one you'll want to serve not only to your family but to VIPs as well. While it might take a little extra effort to prepare, believe me, it's worth every minute! D-E-L-I-C-I-O-U-S!

1 stick margarine
2 cups peeled and raw diced shrimp
4 prime veal cutlets, thinly sliced
salt and pepper to taste
¼ cup grated Parmesan cheese
2 tbsp. finely chopped fresh parsley

2 tbsp. coarsely chopped black olives
1 medium white onion, coarsely chopped
1 10¾-oz. can cream of mushroom soup

In a large skillet, melt the stick of margarine and sauté the diced shrimp *lightly*. All you want to do is turn them pink—*don't cook them*. While the shrimp are sautéing, lightly salt and pepper the cutlets and set them on several strips of waxed paper. As soon as the shrimp are pink, pour them (and the margarine) into a mixing bowl and add the cheese, parsley, olives, and onions. With a spoon, turn everything over and over until it's blended well, then spoon the mixture onto the cutlets. Try to keep the shrimp layer the same thickness throughout.

Now roll the veal *tightly* and pierce each cutlet with several toothpicks to keep it together. When all four have been rolled, place them in a baking pan. Then open the can of mushroom soup and generously spoon over each cutlet. (If you have extra shrimp mix, dribble that over the soup.) Finally, place the rolls in the oven and bake them (basting occasionally) at about 325 degrees for about 45 minutes or until the veal is tender.

Hint: You should do this meal up right! I'd prepare stuffed mushrooms as appetizers, follow it with a subtle onion soup, then serve the veal rolls with buttered Irish potatoes, green beans, and a fresh spinach salad. I'd also select a nice Rhine wine to go with the meal. And I'd top it all off with fresh strawberries and cheesecake.

Mardi Gras Shrimp and Chicken Gumbo

On Mardi Gras day New Orleanians traditionally spend sunup to sundown roaming the streets. So one of the dishes that's most often cooked on Mardi Gras—because it provides a hearty hot meal after a day in the cold—is shrimp and chicken gumbo.

1 cup flour	**½ cup finely chopped parsley**
1 cup Crisco oil	**2 bay leaves**
1 large white onion, coarsely chopped	**4 qt. water**
	salt and black pepper to taste
3 cloves garlic, pressed	**½ tsp. cayenne pepper**
½ cup finely chopped green onion tops	**8 chicken breasts, deboned and chunked**
½ cup coarsely chopped celery	**2 lbs. medium shrimp, peeled**

In a Dutch oven large enough to hold all the ingredients, start off by browning the flour in the oil. You want to get it a nice dark brown, *but don't let it burn*. When it's ready, toss in the onions, garlic, onion tops, celery, parsley, and bay leaves, and cook them in the roux for about 4 minutes. Then add about a quart of the water and stir everything together well.

Next add your salt and peppers *and another quart of water*. At this point reduce your heat to the medium setting and continue to stir the mixture until you get a uniform consistency. *Now* put in the chunked chicken pieces—they should be cut into squares about 2 inches by 2 inches and the fat and skin should be *left on* the meat. Stir the chicken into the gravy, add the remaining 2 quarts of water, put the lid on the pot, and reduce the heat further to low. Let the chicken and the gravy simmer until the chicken starts to become tender (it will show signs of breaking up). Finally, about 35 minutes before you're ready to eat, add your shrimp. It doesn't take long for them to cook, and adding them too early will make them gritty and mushy. I suggest that after you add the shrimp you readjust the salt and pepper and continue to stir the gumbo until it's ready to serve. The consistency will come out better this way. *Never, never let your gumbo boil.*

Hint: The best way to serve this dish is over lots of rice in a heaping soup bowl, along with buttered saltines. And if you want to spice up the flavor, dash on a little Tabasco sauce and a sprinkling of crushed sassafras leaves.

Louisiana Shrimp-Pie Singles

Here's a nifty recipe that's easy to make. It's also one you might get the kids to help you with, because they'll have fun shaping the dough into little cups. Oh, if you don't have shrimp, don't worry . . . you can substitute lump crabmeat or crawfish, or whatever your heart desires. They're all good!

4 frozen single pie shells	**1 cup shredded Swiss cheese**
1 tbsp. margarine	**½ cup real mayonnaise**
1 cup chopped medium-size	**4 tbsp. coarsely chopped celery**
shrimp	**¼ tsp. salt**
¼ cup coarsely chopped shallots	**5 tbsp. half-and-half**
½ cup fresh mushroom stems	**¼ tsp. dill**
and pieces	**2 eggs, well beaten**

The first thing to do is defrost the frozen pie shells. You can roll out your own pastry if you want to, but the recipe is a lot easier using frozen pie crusts. After they are thawed, cut out 12 circles 4 inches in diameter and fit them into muffin tins.

After your pie shells are ready, take a sauté pan and heat it on the stove. Then drop the margarine and the chopped shrimp into the pan and stir them around *rapidly* over medium heat until the shrimp turn slightly pink. *Use no oil and no water.* When the shrimp are ready, remove the pan from the stove and stir in the shallots and the mushrooms. *You just want to get them hot, not to cook them.* Spoon the mix into your pies, topping them off with the shredded cheese.

When all the pie shells are filled with shrimp and mushrooms, put the mayonnaise, celery, salt, cream, dill, and eggs in a bowl and *beat them* to a uniform consistency. Pour the sauce over the cheese (actually down *through* the cheese!) so that it fills most of the inside of the pie shells. Then place all the "singles" in the oven and bake them at about 400 degrees until they're golden brown (which should take about 20 minutes or less).

Hint: These little "potpies" are super if you serve them with a raw vegetable tray—carrot sticks, celery sticks, chipped cauliflower, and radishes.

Barbecued Shrimp a la Bourbon

New Orleans has several dozen recipes floating around for barbecued shrimp, and virtually every one of them comes out great. But this one is truly "barbecued"—and it's fit for a king. The secret ingredient is the bourbon!

2 lbs. jumbo shrimp
2 cups prepared barbecue sauce
6 tbsp. freshly squeezed lemon
    juice
2 tsp. dill weed

2 tbsp. Worcestershire sauce
1 16-oz. bottle Kraft Zesty
    Italian Salad Dressing
3 tbsp. bourbon whiskey

The first thing you do is dehead the shrimp and wash them well. But leave the shells on! It's the shells that keep the juices locked inside the shrimp tails.

Next, get a glass baking pan large enough to hold the 2 pounds of shrimp and put them in the pan *in your refrigerator*. I recommend that you chill the shrimp about 30 minutes before proceeding with the recipe. While the shrimp are cooling, make your marinade by blending the barbecue sauce, lemon juice, dill weed, Worcestershire sauce, salad dressing, and bourbon *over low heat* on the stove top. It comes out best if you simmer these ingredients for about 10 minutes, uncovered. What happens is that the alcohol in the bourbon and the vinegar in the salad dressing cook out, leaving only the flavoring effect. And that's what makes the barbecue so tasty!

After your marinade is cooked, set it aside and let it get just warm enough so it doesn't crack your baking pan. (If you use a metal pan, you don't have to allow the marinade to cool.) Then pour the sauce over the shrimp, stir everything together well, and put it all back in the refrigerator for *4 hours minimum*. Keep in mind that the longer the shrimp marinate the better they will taste. When you're ready to cook, remove them from the marinade *one at a time* and toss them onto a fine-mesh wire on an outdoor grill. You want to cook them hot and fast (about 5 minutes), and you'll have to keep turning them. But don't overcook. As soon as the shell starts to separate from the tail, take the shrimp off the grill. (Oh, and heat up the marinade, too. It makes a great dip if you lace it with Tabasco sauce.)

Just peel, and eat!

Easy Sautéed Shrimp

Whenever you need a batch of shrimp sautéed quickly and you want a nice, tasty sauce to go with it but don't have time to spend preparing something exotic, try fixing this. I guarantee there's no way you can ruin the texture or the taste. And it will please almost any palate!

1 16-oz. bottle Kraft Zesty
   Italian Salad Dressing
1 stick butter
½ cup beer

salt and pepper to taste
dash Tabasco sauce
1 lb. shrimp, peeled

All you need to fix this recipe is a large skillet, a stove, and your ingredients. It's super-simple, and it's a great way to teach youngsters how to cook gourmet treats. Start by putting the skillet on the fire (which you set at medium) and preheating. Then pour in the bottle of salad dressing and simmer it just below the *bubbling point* until you can no longer smell the vinegar aroma. It should take about 15 minutes. Stir occasionally.

Then add the stick of butter and the beer and stir everything together. When the butter melts, reduce the fire to *low* and continue cooking until you can no longer smell the aroma of beer. At that point season with salt, pepper, and Tabasco, drop in your shrimp, and sauté them until they turn pink and tender. On low heat this should take about 4 to 6 minutes. When they're cooked, remove them from the sauce and use them in any dish you desire. The beer will enhance the flavor, whether you eat them as snacks, put them in salads, or fix them in a creative main dish.

Hint: You can do one of two things with the sautéing liquid—save the mix in a Mason jar in your refrigerator and have it ready the next time you need it, or put it back on the stove, set the fire on medium low, and stir in a couple of teaspoons of arrowroot. This will give you a sauce of any consistency you want to serve over rice or potatoes. What you get is a delicate flavor, seasoned but not overly spicy. You can also use the liquid to sauté shrimp, crabmeat, fish, crawfish tails, etc.

Note: This dish can also be prepared in a baking pan in the oven. Just set the temperature at 400 degrees for about 15 to 20 minutes, depending upon shrimp size.

Shrimp Dip a la Frank

As simple as it may sound, learning to make a truly delicious shrimp dip took much more trial-and-error time in the kitchen than some of the more exotic recipes in this book. I think I must have experimented with several dozen concoctions before coming up with this one, but *this one* I wrote down. Because it's a hand or two above the average—as you will soon see.

1 10¾-oz. can Campbell's Cream of Shrimp soup
¼ cup sun-dried shrimp (optional)
½ stick margarine
1 lb. small raw shrimp, peeled
1 tbsp. finely chopped green onions

4 tbsp. finely chopped celery
1 8-oz. pkg. Philadelphia cream cheese
1 tsp. Tabasco sauce
dash Worcestershire sauce
salt to taste
whole milk (if needed)

In a small saucepan, heat the soup to bubbling and add the sun-dried shrimp. Then reduce the fire to simmer, cover the pan, and let it stand for a while—about 15 minutes, or until the shrimp are moist. While the dried shrimp are simmering, melt the margarine in a small skillet and sauté the fresh shrimp until they are a *deep pink*. (If you choose not to use dried shrimp, heat the soup, melt the butter, and simmer the fresh shrimp until they turn pink.) Then, using the cutting blade on your food processor, *finely* chop the onions and celery. Add the sautéed shrimp *and the margarine*, and coarsely chop the shrimp. Be careful you don't chop it too long—just a few seconds will do. Finally, spoon out the dried shrimp from the soup and chop *them* in the processor. After soaking in the soup for 15 minutes they should cut fast, so keep an eye on them! By processing *in this order* you should get the right consistency. Just don't overcut.

Now switch to the mixing blade (plastic tines) and slowly blend in the Philadelphia cream cheese, adding the Tabasco, Worcestershire, and salt at the same time. Keep the machine on and fold everything together, gradually adding as much of the hot soup as you need to get the consistency you want.

Hint: I suggest you make your dip just a tad on the liquid side because it tends to thicken as it sits in the refrigerator. To thin the consistency, add milk. And this dip should be served cold.

Shrimp Pasta Bruscato

Any cook will tell you it's a pleasure to prepare foods for people who love to eat. My father-in-law Charlie Bruscato is probably the best person in the world to cook for. His palate is discriminating and he appreciates what goes into making special dishes. Just recently I fixed a new concoction of shrimp and pasta for him, and he liked it so much I decided to name the recipe after him. Try it!

1 1-lb. package #4 spaghetti (or elbow noodles)
2 tbsp. olive oil
4 cloves garlic, pressed
3 tbsp. finely chopped bell pepper
1 medium white onion, coarsely chopped
½ stick margarine
2 lbs. medium-size shrimp, peeled

½ tsp. oregano leaves
½ tsp. fennel seeds
salt and black pepper to taste
½ pt. heavy cream
1 cup shredded mozzarella cheese
3 tbsp. Romano cheese
1 cup coarsely chopped black olives

The first thing you do is break the spaghetti in half and drop it into boiling water. But *don't overcook it*—it should come out tender but firm. While the pasta is cooking, go ahead and prepare the shrimp.

Heat the olive oil in a skillet and sauté the garlic, bell pepper, and onion until they wilt. Then, on top of the vegetables, add the margarine, reduce the fire to *low*, and toss in the shrimp. Now here's what you do to the shrimp before adding it: coarsely *chop 1 pound, but leave 1 pound whole*. This will give you a really shrimpy flavor. As you're sautéing, gradually add the oregano, fennel seeds, salt and pepper, and heavy cream. Simmer the sauce for exactly 4 minutes on low (just to get a slow bubble).

When the shrimp are cooked just to the point where they are pink and tender, remove the skillet from the heat and set it aside. Then, when the spaghetti is cooked, drain it well and put it into a 1½-quart casserole dish. About *20 minutes* before you're ready to eat pour the shrimp and sauce over the spaghetti, add the mozzarella and the Romano, and mix everything together *quickly* (so the cheese doesn't stick together in one spot) and *evenly*. Then sprinkle the chopped olives over the top of the pasta, set the oven at 275 degrees, and heat to piping hot.

Hint: I suggest you serve this dish with crisp Italian salad, butter-basted breadsticks, and a nice white wine.

Corn-Shrimp Stew La Luzzianne

Served over rice, this is one recipe that hard-core gourmets will rave about for weeks at a time. It has been prepared numerous ways in New Orleans, but only by using all fresh ingredients do you capture the succulence that's true Louisiana!

6 ears fresh white corn on the cob	2 qts. water
1 stick margarine	salt and red pepper to taste
1 large white onion, minced	1 tbsp. flour
2 4-oz. cans Contadina tomato paste	2 lbs. medium-size shrimp, peeled and chopped
	4 hard-boiled eggs

Before you begin the dish, take a sharp knife and cut the kernels of corn off the cob and soak them briefly in cold water (for about 10 minutes). While they are soaking, melt the margarine in a skillet and sauté the onions and tomato paste. The best method is to fry the mixture until the paste starts to darken. Then, *a little at a time,* add the water and stir the mix until you get a smooth consistency. You can season with salt and pepper at this point, too. Increase the fire to *medium high* and bring the gravy to an easy boil.

Now sprinkle in the flour, stirring as you add it to keep it from getting lumpy. It should thicken the gravy a little. Then *add the corn* (which you've drained) *and the shrimp* (it should be chopped into segments), and cover the pot with a tight-fitting lid. Immediately reduce the heat to *simmer* and let the stew cook for about an hour and a half.

When you're ready to serve, chop up the hard-boiled eggs to the same consistency you'd use to make tuna salad, drop them into the gravy, and stir them in.

Hint: I'd spoon out the stew immediately after adding the chopped eggs, and I'd serve this recipe over buttered rice. Keep in mind that these ingredients produce a mild flavor that's great for feeding the kids, but if you want to increase the spiciness all you have to do is toss in a little garlic, a couple of bay leaves, maybe some bell pepper, and a generous helping of cayenne pepper.

Shrimp Casserole Chatelain

I was in the National Guard with a man named Norm Chatelain, who had the reputation of making the best shrimp casserole in Cajun Country. One Sunday afternoon while I was on K.P. duty I asked Norm if he would write down the recipe for me. He did, and you don't know how lucky you are that I put it in this book! This is a perfect example of perfection!

¼ cup melted margarine
4 tbsp. coarsely chopped white onions
4 tbsp. coarsely chopped celery
¼ cup coarsely chopped bell pepper
2 cups milk
2 cups toasted salad croutons

1 lb. boiled, unseasoned shrimp
1 cup steamed rice
½ cup sliced mushrooms
4 tbsp. chopped water chestnuts
3 eggs, beaten well
salt and red pepper to taste
1 cup shredded cheddar cheese

Melt the margarine in a pan and sauté the onions, celery, and bell pepper until they're wilted. Then stir in the milk gradually over low heat until the ingredients are well mixed. At this point toss in the croutons, being sure to work them into the mixture to soften them. Remove the pan from the fire.

Now put the shrimp, rice, mushrooms, and water chestnuts in a large mixing bowl and work everything into a uniform consistency. When it's all folded well, pour the sautéed vegetables and the softened croutons over the top and continue to mix. Then *gradually* add the eggs and mix everything all over again. You can also put in your salt and pepper.

Now you're ready to casserole the dish, so take a 1½-quart baking pan (or a 2-quart pan if you've made a little extra!), rub it with margarine, and begin spooning a thin layer of mix onto the bottom of the pan. Level it off smoothly and lightly sprinkle a layer of cheddar over the top. Then spoon out another layer of mix, followed by another layer of cheese, and so on until you've used all the ingredients. Save some cheese for the top and lightly sprinkle it over the casserole. Bake the dish in a 325-degree oven for about 45 minutes or until done. It's best if you leave it slightly moist. Serve with asparagus salad.

Louisiana Shrimp Dressing

You've probably fixed cornbread dressing, giblet dressing, rice dressing, and oyster dressing, but one of the best side dishes (which can also be a topping for broiled fish) you can serve with seafoods is *shrimp dressing*. Try this the next time you get tired of potatoes.

2 cups water
1 lb. coarsely chopped medium
   shrimp
1 stick butter
1 stalk celery, coarsely chopped
2 tbsp. minced carrots
1 clove garlic, pressed
1 medium onion, coarsely
   chopped

¼ cup chopped mushrooms
½ tbsp. lemon juice
¼ tsp. fresh nutmeg
1 tsp. parsley
salt and pepper to taste
1 cup toasted bread crumbs

In a skillet containing 2 cups of water, gently simmer the chopped shrimp until they turn pink. Immediately take them off the fire and let them sit for about an hour. This will give you a good stock, so keep the liquid to use as a moistening agent.

In a saucepan melt the butter and lightly sauté the celery, carrots, garlic, onions, and mushrooms. Don't overcook the vegetables because they'll lose the firmness you want in the stuffing. When they are tender but crisp, take the saucepan off the heat and stir in the lemon juice, nutmeg, parsley, salt, and pepper. At this point remove the chopped shrimp from the liquid, place them in a large mixing bowl along with the bread crumbs and the sautéed vegetables, and *mix everything together extremely well*. Here's where you can use the stock you made when boiling the shrimp: simply add about ¼ cup at a time (if you need it) until you get the consistency you desire. I suggest you don't make the stuffing too moist or it will taste gummy, but you don't want it *dried out* either!

Finally, place the mixture in a baking dish and cook in the oven only until it gets hot enough to serve (about 300 degrees). You can add a pat or two of butter while the mix is baking if you want your stuffing a little richer!

Bayou Country Shrimp Kabobs

Talk about a whole meal in one serving, there's none any better than what Calvin Boudreaux calls his Bayou Country Shrimp Kabobs. This stuff is so good, Calvin whips it up the night before, then wraps it in aluminum foil and takes it with him for lunch the next day on his trawling boat. You'll find it's a fun recipe, and a healthy one!

To make kabobs you'll need:
white onions
bell peppers
celery
zucchini
fresh mushroom buttons
carrots
cherry tomatoes
black olives
2 lbs. large shrimp, peeled

You'll also need:
½ cup olive oil
2 tbsp. soy sauce
¼ cup tarragon vinegar
1 tsp. salt
¼ tsp. garlic powder
dash black pepper

The first thing you need to do is fix your basting marinade. So blend together the olive oil, soy sauce, tarragon vinegar, salt, garlic powder, and pepper in a mixing bowl. Then set the mix aside for about a half-hour to "cure." Meanwhile cut the onions in quarters, the bell peppers in chunks, the zucchini in slices, the celery in 2-inch pieces, and the carrots in segments and toss all the ingredients, *including the shrimp*, in the marinade. Allow them to soak in the refrigerator for about an hour to pick up the seasonings.

Then alternate the ingredients on skewers: *shrimp*, then *onion*, then *bell pepper*, then *celery*, then *mushroom*, etc. To make your kabobs really "shrimpy," simply add a shrimp after each vegetable: *shrimp*, then *bell pepper*, then *shrimp*, then *onion*, then *shrimp*, and so on. Put your kabobs over a charcoal grill (or suspended over a baking dish in a 375-degree oven) and cook until tender—about 20 minutes. Keep basting with the marinade for extra flavor.

Deep-Fried Shrimp Drops

We're always talking about Acadian, Italian, and New Orleans specialty recipes for seafoods. But I've run into a recipe for shrimp that is probably more Oriental than Bayou Country Cajun. But who cares—it's delicious!

2 lbs. chopped shrimp
½ cup finely chopped water
  chestnuts
2 tbsp. cornstarch
¼ cup finely chopped bell
  peppers
2 eggs, slightly beaten
½ cup coarsely chopped celery
1 cup cornmeal, seasoned with
  salt and pepper
Crisco oil for frying

Sauce:
½ cup dry mustard
1½ cups boiling water
½ cup pineapple juice

First peel the shrimp and steam them (or cook them gently in a microwave oven) until they are pink and tender. Then chop them extra-fine—a food processor works great! What you want to end up with are shrimp in the form of very small *chips*. When they're processed enough, put them in a mixing bowl.

At this point add all the remaining ingredients except the cornmeal and the oil. Then get in there with your *hands* and mix everything together until it forms a blended paste. When it's mixed, shape small amounts into "drops" about an inch in diameter, something like meatballs. Then pour the cornmeal (seasoned with salt and pepper) on a sheet of waxed paper and lightly roll the drops in the meal until each one is sparsely coated. When they're all coated, set them on a tray, cover with waxed paper or Handi-Wrap, and let them "set."

Meanwhile, make a sauce with ½ cup dry mustard, 1½ cups boiling water, and ½ cup boiling pineapple juice. Mix together and cook slowly over low heat until the sauce is smooth and pasty. But watch it, *it's spicy!* When you're ready to eat, take the drops out of the refrigerator and deep fry them in Crisco oil at 375 degrees. Then serve them with the dipping sauce as a main dish with tomato salad and creamed potatoes.

Hint: The drops and sauce also make good hors d'oeuvres.

Stir-Fry Shrimp with Pea Pods

The Louisiana Cooperative Extension Service has come up with some really tasty recipes over the years. This one is among my favorites, because the natural juices of the shrimp are sealed in and the vegetables come out crisp, flavorful, and full of color. It not only tastes good, it *looks* good!

2 12-oz. packs frozen pea pods
1 8-oz. can water chestnuts
1 lb. shrimp, peeled
1 chicken bouillon cube dissolved
  in ½ cup water (or ½
  cup chicken stock)

¼ cup soy sauce
3 tbsp. dry white Chablis
2 tsp. minced fresh ginger
2 tbsp. cornstarch
¼ cup corn oil
3 green onions, coarsely cut

First, thaw the pea pods and slice the water chestnuts. Then peel the shrimp and cut them into bite-size pieces. Next, make a chicken broth using 1 bouillon cube to ½ cup of water (or take some homemade chicken stock out of the freezer). This takes care of the basics; now you're ready to start cooking.

Put the broth, soy sauce, wine, ginger, and cornstarch in a large bowl. Mix them around well. Take a pan (if you have a wok—a Chinese frying pan—use it; if not, use a large skillet), pour in the corn oil, *and get it hot.* Now here's where the technics come in: You're gonna cook these next ingredients *one at a time,* stir-frying rapidly for about 3 minutes each. First the pea pods. Drop them in the hot oil and swoosh them quickly. When they're done, put in the shrimp. When they're done, put in the onions. And finally, the water chestnuts. After each is cooked, remove it from the pan and put it in the bowl with the soy sauce, broth, ginger, wine, and cornstarch. But remember: *Cook one ingredient at a time.*

When all the ingredients are mixed together in the bowl, dump everything back into the frying pan or wok and stir-fry (and it's important to *keep stirring*) until the sauce thickens. Serve over steamed rice alongside a tossed green salad and you'll think you came to Louisiana by way of Singapore!

Claudia's Louisiana Shrimp Mold

You'll have to dig out the ol' double boiler to make this recipe, but it's worth the effort. Claudia Fowler created it, but I make this mold every chance I get, especially when I want something to serve at get-togethers. And it's delicious spread on a batch of chips or crackers.

1½ lbs. shrimp, boiled and
   seasoned
1 10¾-oz. can tomato soup
3 oz. Philadelphia cream cheese
pinch baking soda
2 ¼-oz. packs Knox gelatin

½ cup water
4 tbsp. chopped celery
½ cup chopped bell pepper
¼ cup chopped onion
1 cup real mayonnaise
salt and pepper to taste

The best way to put this recipe together is to start by boiling the shrimp in highly seasoned water—lots of lemon, salt, pepper, garlic, onions, and celery. After the shrimp are cooked, set them aside to cool.

Meanwhile, heat the soup and the Philadelphia cream cheese in the double boiler until they are melted and blended together. Then add the pinch of soda and stir it in. In a large bowl, dissolve the gelatin in a half-cup of water. Take the soup mix off the double boiler and add it slowly to the gelatin. Then set the mixture aside to cool to room temperature.

In a separate bowl mix the shrimp (and it's best to chop them up really fine first), the celery, the bell pepper, the onion, and the mayonnaise together. Pour the cooled soup-gelatin base into the shrimp mix. All that's left to do is to season the dish with the salt and pepper. Once that's done you put the whole concoction in your favorite mold, stash it in the refrigerator to ''set up,'' and decide what time you ought to have a party!

Hint: This mold is not only great when fixed with shrimp. It can also be prepared with crabmeat, crawfish tails, scallops, flaked fish, or whatever your taste dictates.

Pickled Shrimp a la Moody

Gourmet cookery involving seafoods is so important to Louisianians that even technologists with Ph.D.s often come up with unique concoctions. A perfect illustration of that statement is this spicy recipe, straight out of the laboratory of Dr. Mike Moody! And it probably would taste good served in a test tube—or a beaker . . .

½ gal. water
5 tbsp. salt
¼ tbsp. cayenne pepper
¼ tbsp. allspice
2 whole cloves
½ tbsp. mustard seeds
3 bay leaves
½ tbsp. Zatarain's liquid crab
    boil
2½ lbs. shrimp, peeled

Pickling Spices:
bay leaves
red peppers
cloves
Tabasco sauce
white vinegar
sugar

Mike says that the best way to prepare this dish is with the most scientific procedure—which means you throw all the ingredients *except the shrimp* into a large pot containing a half-gallon of water and simmer it well for a half-hour! That's easy enough, huh?

Then—scientifically—you bring the water to a rapid boil and add the shrimp. Now, it's going to take a while for the water to come back to a rapid boil, but once it does, *time it for 4 minutes*. This cooks your shrimp! Actually, the critters are ready to eat after this, and they're already delicious, but remember, we're making pickled shrimp. So set the pot in the refrigerator and let the shrimp and the water cool. Meanwhile, sterilize a couple of jars by boiling them for 10 minutes (mayonnaise jars work well) and put some spices in them—like a bay leaf, a few red peppers, a clove or two, and maybe a dash of Tabasco sauce. Then make a 50/50 solution of white vinegar (5% acid) and water. Now go to the refrigerator, get the shrimp, drain off the liquid, and start packing the cooled shrimp into the jars. When you're about an inch from the top, fill the jars to the brim with the vinegar solution. Add a pinch of sugar to the top, and give it one more dash of crab boil.

Finally, seal up the jars and stash them away for about 4 weeks in the refrigerator—until your next party! *Warning: It's spicy, folks.* So have the beer ready.

Fast and Easy Shrimp Salad

Here's an idea for using the leftovers from a shrimp boil. All it takes is about 10 minutes to whip up. Mrs. Jerald Horst says this creative dish makes a great hors d'oeuvre, a light summer entrée, or a suitable covered dish for a leisure-time gathering. And it's *gooooood!*

1 lb. seasoned boiled shrimp	1 tbsp. diced green onions
1 hard-boiled egg	2 tbsp. sweet pickle relish
1 rib celery, diced	1 cup real mayonnaise

If you have leftover shrimp from a seafood boil, just peel the meat from the tails and chop it into small pieces in a food processor. If you have to make the dish from scratch, boil your shrimp either in Zatarain's crab boil or in water containing 1 sliced lemon, 1 tablespoon salt, ½ tablespoon cayenne pepper, 1 clove garlic, and 1 small white onion.

Take the chopped shrimp, mix them well with a finely chopped boiled egg, and blend in smoothly all the remaining ingredients. *Do not whip the mixture into a paste.* It should have the texture of a heavy spread.

Serving Suggestions:
1. Serve chilled on snack crackers at parties.
2. Stuff into hollowed-out creole tomatoes and serve on a bed of crisp lettuce, dotted sparingly with Remoulade sauce.
3. Sandwich between two slices of trimmed toast.

PUT TOGETHER A QUICK COCKTAIL SAUCE FOR SHRIMP

Blend:

½ cup catsup	dash Tabasco sauce
2 tbsp. fresh lemon juice	¼ tsp. horseradish
½ tbsp. Worcestershire	dash garlic powder
sauce	

For best results, these ingredients should be stirred until they are uniformly mixed and then placed in a refrigerator to chill for about an hour.

Note: If you prefer, go on and double or triple the recipe, because the sauce can be stored for several weeks in the refrigerator in an airtight container.

Shrimp au Gratin Supreme

Food connoisseurs know "au gratin" usually means bubbly and hot. Another Jerald Horst concoction, this shrimp au gratin fits these criteria and is truly "supreme." But don't add up the calories!

1 lb. shrimp	½ tsp. salt
4 tbsp. melted butter, divided	¼ tsp. dry mustard
3 tbsp. chopped onions	dash black pepper
1½ cups whole milk	1 cup grated Velveeta cheese
¼ cup flour	¼ cup dry bread crumbs

First off, cut the shrimp into small pieces and simmer them lightly (in water) in a saucepan until they are pink. Then drain off the water and set the shrimp aside. While the shrimp are cooling, put 3 tablespoons of butter in a saucepan, add the chopped onions, and cook them until they are clear. Gradually add the milk to the saucepan and heat it; while the milk is heating mix together the flour, salt, dry mustard, and pepper.

When the milk is hot, slowly blend in the flour mix. You'll have to stir constantly so that it doesn't lump up. When the sauce has thickened, add all but ¼ cup of the Velveeta, and cook and stir the sauce until the cheese has melted completely. At this point add the shrimp and let them simmer for about 2 minutes. While the shrimp are heating go ahead and grease a casserole dish large enough to hold the contents. When the dish is ready, pour in the shrimp and sauce.

Finally, mix together the remaining cheese, all the bread crumbs, and the remaining tablespoon of butter and sprinkle the mix over the casserole. Bake in a 400-degree oven for about 15 minutes . . . and get ready for a feast!

Jerald's Shrimp and Mushroom Soup

This is another one of Jerald Horst's favorite recipes. And it will be one of yours too, especially if you like the taste of shrimp and mushrooms together. Jerald told me his secret in making this dish is to use equal parts shrimp and mushrooms. So be sure, if you plan to double the recipe, to keep the proportions equal.

1 lb. bite-size fresh shrimp	**salt to taste**
1 lb. sliced fresh mushrooms	**dash white pepper**
1 stick butter (not margarine)	**1 tbsp. flour**
3 cups chicken broth	**4 tbsp. water**
1 tsp. dry dill	**½ pt. heavy cream**

First, peel and chop up the shrimp and set them aside in a cool place. Slice the mushrooms and sauté them in the stick of butter until they are tender. Set them aside too.

Now you need to make the broth. If you don't have any broth prepared, the easiest way to do this is to take 3 cups of water in a saucepan, bring it to a rapid boil, and add 3 chicken bouillon cubes. Stir the cubes around until they are dissolved. Next, pour the mushrooms and butter into the broth and heat them. Gradually add the dill, the salt, and the white pepper, stirring constantly. While this is simmering, mix the flour and the 4 tbsp. of water to make a soupy paste. Then add the paste a little at a time to the broth until the stock reaches the texture you want. Go ahead and cook this mixture at medium heat for around 10 minutes.

Finally, add the shrimp and stir them in *briskly*. It will take about 4 minutes for the shrimp to become tender, so you should simmer the soup that long. When you're ready to serve, pour in the pint of heavy cream, reheat, and dish out the soup piping hot alongside a crisp salad topped with croutons. Jerald's Shrimp and Mushroom Soup is a terrific recipe to whip up any time, but it's exceptionally good right after a morning hunt out at the duck camp. Ummmmm–mmmmm!

Sicilian Shrimp Boats

You've heard it said: "There ain't nothing as good as a good, sloppy roast beef po-boy!" Well, that might not be true anymore, because this recipe gives a roast beef po-boy a run for its money. Some folks might even call this a real *gourmet sandwich*. But whatever you call it, serve it with a cold beer.

6 **French-style dinner buns
(Pee-Wee rolls are best)**
½ **stick corn-oil margarine**
2 **lbs. whole medium-size shrimp,
peeled**
½ **cup fresh mushroom stems
and pieces**
¼ **tsp. McCormick dried Italian
seasoning**
2 **tbsp. coarsely chopped white
onions**

pinch oregano
4 **tbsp. real mayonnaise**
1 **cup shredded mozzarella
cheese**
½ **cup coarsely chopped black
olives**
1 **cup diced fresh tomatoes**
1 **cup shredded lettuce**

The first thing you do is heat your oven to about 350 degrees and *lightly toast* the rolls. When they're starting to brown, remove them from the oven (but leave the oven on) and cut a deep wedge—lengthwise—out of each one. Keep the wedges and set the rolls aside.

Take a skillet, melt the margarine, and sauté the shrimp, mushrooms, Italian seasoning, onions, and oregano. Now don't cook these too long—just until the shrimp turns pink. Stir constantly while the shrimp are simmering to get even cooking. Remove them from the fire.

Okay, here's the gourmet part: When the sautéed shrimp and the seasonings have cooled, blend in the mayonnaise and the mozzarella cheese. *Don't add either,* though, until your basic sauté is cool, because if you do the cheese will melt before you want it to! Now take the rolls, place them on an ungreased pizza tin, and spoon in generous helpings of the sautéed shrimp mixture. Then put them back in the oven (still set at 350) and bake for about *5 minutes,* or until they're hot and bubbly!

Serve them open-face, with the black olives, diced tomatoes, and shredded lettuce sprinkled over the stuffing. If you want to you can put the wedges you removed from the rolls back on top. These are *good!*

Southern Shrimp Spread on Toast

This is one of the pages in the book that, in all probability, will end up completely dog-eared, because this recipe is so easy to fix and so tasty, you'll want to make it over and over again. It's versatile, too, equally suited to duty as a main dish and to party service. Take my advice and try it soon!

2 tbsp. butter
1 lb. small shrimp, peeled
1 cup chopped canned mushroom
stems and pieces
½ tsp. brown mustard
1 tsp. lemon juice
¼ tsp. garlic salt

1 small white onion, very
finely chopped
½ tsp. soy sauce
dash salt
dash cayenne pepper
1 cup large-curd cottage cheese
6 slices white bread

Gently melt the butter in a saucepan, *but don't let it burn*. Keep your heat on medium. Then, when the butter is hot enough to sauté, drop in the shrimp. Cook them about 3 minutes or until they are deep pink and tender. Then put the shrimp, butter, and mushrooms in your food processor (using the cutting blade) and very carefully *sliver* them until they almost become a paste. But keep in mind that you *do not* want a paste—*almost* a paste. It takes some watching, and a bit of patience.

When the shrimp and mushrooms are *just right,* change the cutting blade in the processor to the mixing blade and gently add all the remaining ingredients *except* the cottage cheese and the bread. At this point you want to blend together the seasonings, so do it gently with "start/stop" switching of the processor. Finally, add the cottage cheese to the processor and—*again with careful start/stop switching*—carefully blend in the curds. *Don't puree the mixture by being in a hurry*. The texture should remain stiff.

To serve, lightly toast the sliced white bread, then spread the mix evenly over the surface. When all the slices have been coated, cut them diagonally into triangles, put them on a cookie sheet, and place it in a 325-degree oven. Watch them closely. You don't want them to cook—just heat them nice and hot!

Suggestion: If you don't like cottage cheese you can substitute shredded farmer's cheese or monterey Jack instead.

Italian Eggplant Casserole-in-a-Dish

Louisianians have all kinds of ways of preparing eggplant and shrimp dishes, and many of them are included in this book. But for a fast and easy casserole, it's tough to beat this recipe.

2 lbs. medium-size shrimp
2 large eggplants, peeled but
  uncooked
½ stick margarine
½ cup chopped white onion
½ cup finely chopped celery
½ cup finely chopped shallots
4 cloves garlic, finely chopped

2 eggs
5 cups toasted bread crumbs
pinch parsley
2 tbsp. Parmesan cheese
salt and pepper to taste
2 tbsp. mozzarella cheese
  (optional)

The first thing you do is boil the shrimp in unseasoned water, peel them, and chop them into semicoarse pieces. Then you peel the eggplants and dice them into chunks about an inch square.

In a skillet, melt the margarine and sauté the eggplant, onion, celery, shallots, and garlic until they turn soft and tender. While everything is simmering together, crack the eggs over the bread crumbs and mix until you get a good blend. Then add the bread crumbs and eggs to the skillet and use a whisk to mix the sautéing ingredients together well. At this point fold in the chopped shrimp, toss in the pinch of parsley and the Parmesan cheese, and season with salt and pepper. If you feel you need a bit more moisture, add a few tablespoons of whole milk—*but do it sparingly*. You want it pasty.

Now take the well-blended stuffing and put it in a casserole pan that you've rubbed with oil. Bake it at 325 degrees for about 25 minutes.

Hint: If you want your casserole cheesy, you can add about 2 tablespoons of shredded mozzarella as a topping (sprinkle lightly over the dish about 10 minutes before you take it out of the oven). I recommend you serve this dish as a complementary vegetable with fried fish or fried oysters, or as a main dish alongside a large Italian green salad and garlic bread.

Mandy's Shrimp Broccoli Pop-Ups

Of all the exotic dishes I've put together in our kitchen at home, none got as big a rave from my 10-year-old daughter Mandy as this one. She didn't care if it was fancy or if it would qualify as gourmet fare. She liked the pop-ups because she could eat them while watching Boss Hogg and not make a mess on the sofa. There's a valid point there!

1 lb. medium-size shrimp, peeled	2 cups Bisquick mix
1 cup water plus 1 tbsp.	1 cup grated colby cheese
2 cups chopped frozen broccoli	4 tbsp. whole milk
3 tbsp. margarine	1 egg, well beaten

The first thing you do is poach the shrimp in just enough water to cook them; you can use a saucepan with half a cup of water in it. Then drain the shrimp well. When they're dry, cut them into small pieces. Next, simmer the broccoli in the margarine in a pan until it's *just cooked*. Be careful you don't overcook the broccoli—you want it crispy. Drain it, too, and set it aside.

At this point make your dough by putting the Bisquick into a mixing bowl and adding ½ cup of water to it. Use a fork to mold the Bisquick and water together into a firm ball. If the texture is too pasty and the dough sticks to your finger, add more Bisquick *2 tablespoons at a time*. Then knead the dough about a dozen times and, on a clean, well-floured dishcloth, roll it into a thin sheet. Start cutting individual squares 5 inches by 5 inches, and set them aside. Keep on rolling and cutting until all the Bisquick is used.

Now place the shrimp, broccoli, cheese, and milk in a bowl, and thoroughly mix everything together. When it's all well blended, start spooning the mix onto the Bisquick squares. Then fold each square into a *triangle* and mesh the edges together with a fork, as if you were making turnovers. Finally, place the pop-ups on an ungreased cookie sheet, mix the egg and 1 tablespoon of water together, and brush the mixture over each pop-up. Then bake 'em for about 20 minutes at 375 degrees (or until golden brown). And find out what channel "Dukes of Hazzard" is on.

Hint: If your TV fans are in a hurry you can substitute refrigerator biscuits. They cook up just as well.

Shrimp Boiled in Butter

On one of my radio shows I mentioned that I was collecting some unique recipes of Cajun origin that dealt with new ways of fixing shrimp. About two days later, this recipe came in the mail from a commercial fisherman in St. Bernard Parish. I've got to admit it's unique, but I also want you to know it's easy to fix and delicious! Try this real soon.

5 lbs. large shrimp, deheaded	3 tbsp. salt
1 lb. margarine	2 tbsp. liquid crab boil
3 medium onions, quartered	

There's nothing special about this recipe except *mixing everything together* and watching it cook, but you do have to mix well, and you do have to keep an eye on it.

All you need is a pot large enough to hold all the ingredients. Throw everything in at once, and turn up the fire to medium so that the butter will melt and the shrimp will cook. One of the reasons I said *mix well* is because until the margarine melts and the natural juices flow from the shrimp you'll have to keep stirring everything. Don't be too concerned that you have no juices at first, because as soon as the heat builds up a little they'll start to form. In fact, the combination of butter and shrimp juices will create a delicious sauce. And *do watch the shrimp* as they cook; you'll find out that with stirring it will take only about 15 minutes before you're ready to serve this recipe. You don't want to overcook because the shrimp will become *grainy*. Go ahead and sample occasionally. When your shrimp are pink, buttery, and tender, they're done.

The best way to eat this dish is to spoon generous helpings of shrimp and sauce into soup bowls. Then pick up the shrimp with your fingers, suck the juices out of the shells, and peel and eat the shrimp tails. If you want to make a special meal out of this dish, boil some tiny Irish potatoes in unseasoned stock and spoon them out into the bowls when you serve the shrimp. Put the bowls on the table with a good supply of French bread, though, because you'll want to do some sopping in the sauce, for sure. Oh—don't forget the tossed green salad!

Shrimp Stew Creole

Ever since the Cajuns came over from Nova Scotia, a good shrimp stew has been among the favorite dishes of Louisianians. From Monroe to Delacroix Island, a variety of versions has been put together, but the recipe listed here has got to be one of the best I've ever tasted. Try it and let me know what you think.

¼ cup flour
¼ cup Crisco oil
3 medium-size white onions,
 thinly sliced
4 cups water
1 cup tomato paste
3 cloves garlic, finely chopped
½ cup finely chopped bell pepper

¼ cup finely chopped celery
1 tbsp. lemon juice
2 tsp. salt
¼ tsp. cayenne pepper
¼ tsp. black pepper
2 lbs. shrimp, peeled
¼ cup sherry

In a large skillet, fry the flour in the oil until it turns a golden brown, then add the onions and fry them until they're tender. *You'll have to keep stirring so that the roux doesn't stick.* At this point, add half the water (2 cups) and stir everything together well. Then put in the tomato paste and simmer it for about 10 minutes. When the base is smooth, toss in the garlic, the bell pepper, the celery, and the lemon juice and let it simmer for about 10 minutes. If the base becomes too thick during simmering, *add a little water at a time.* When the vegetables are tender, add the remaining water and the salt and peppers and set the heat on medium low. Then cover the skillet with a tight-fitting lid and let the sauce cook for about 35 minutes. Note: You will have to stir everything around occasionally just to make sure the cooking is even.

Finally, about an hour before you're ready to serve the stew, drop in the shrimp and the sherry and reduce the heat to low. You want the stew to barely simmer and bubble for about 50 minutes, so watch that it doesn't cook too fast or your shrimp creole will become *too cooked.*

Hint: To make the stew spicy, add Tabasco to taste during the last 10 minutes of cooking time. Serve over steamed rice.

Cheesy Shrimp Muffins

For sandwich-type meals, there ain't nothing can beat a first-rate, fried shrimp po-boy! Right? Well, maybe this Cajun-style sandwich concoction comes close! One thing is for sure, your kids are gonna love it. And these make great TV snacks, too.

2 lbs. unseasoned boiled shrimp
½ cup grated colby cheese
2 tbsp. margarine
2 tbsp. flour
½ cup whole milk
2 tbsp. coarsely chopped white onion

1 tsp. salt
black pepper to taste
½ tsp. curry powder
1 cup finely ground bread crumbs
6 English muffins

The first thing to do is peel the shrimp and chop them into small pieces, about the size of raisins. Then set them aside on a paper towel. Next, take the colby cheese and grate it coarsely. Lay the cheese on the chopped shrimp on the paper towel.

At this point, get a skillet and melt the margarine. Don't let it boil and bubble—just melt it thoroughly. When it's melted, take it off the fire and, little by little, mix in the flour. When the mixture is smooth, return the skillet to the heat and slowly blend in the milk. Stir *constantly*. You want the base to *thicken*. The fire should be set on medium high. When the mixture is ready, take it off the stove and pour it into a large mixing bowl. One ingredient at a time, add the onion, the salt, the pepper, the curry powder, and enough bread crumbs to absorb the excess liquid. With everything blended well together, add the shrimp and cheese and get in there with your hands. Press all your ingredients into the shrimp and cheese, and continue to add bread crumbs until you can form *patties* that stick together well.

Finally, dust the patties with the remaining bread crumbs and panfry them at medium-high heat until they turn brown. Then toast the English muffins, spreading melted butter on one half, mayonnaise on the other half. Place the patty in the middle and garnish with lettuce and tomato.

Connie's Shrimp Italian

On one of the first fishing trips I ever made to Cocodrie, my host Stu Scheer, who runs Sportsman's Paradise Marina, told me to come down for supper and his wife would fix up a special dish for me to taste. Well, this recipe is what Connie Scheer concocted for that meal. And it's been at the top of my list of shrimp dishes ever since!

1 stick butter	1 small bell pepper, finely chopped
1 cup water	1 stalk celery, finely chopped
¼ tsp. rosemary	3 cloves garlic, finely chopped
3 bay leaves	2 shallots, finely chopped
¼ tsp. oregano	salt to taste
3 beef bouillon cubes	2 lbs. large shrimp, deheaded
10 small cloves	5 oz. white Chablis
1 tsp. McCormick lemon pepper	

Melt the butter in a large skillet and stir in the water over low heat. Then, stirring constantly, add the rosemary, bay leaves, oregano, bouillon cubes, cloves, lemon pepper, bell pepper, celery, garlic, and shallots. Take time and *simmer* these ingredients together well—about *20 minutes over low heat.* Taste the mix and add as much salt as you want. Then, when the base is cooked down well, add your shrimp to the stock in the skillet. Increase the heat to *medium,* pour in the white wine, and cook uncovered for another 10 minutes.

Finally, turn off the fire and let the dish sit for about 15 minutes so that the flavors are absorbed. Then spoon the shrimp and the juices into soup bowls and serve with buttered toast or French bread. This particular recipe should serve six . . . unless they're really hungry!

Hint: To make a full meal out of this recipe, boil some rice. After the shrimp are cooked, turn the fire back on low, remove the shrimp from the juices, and stir in some cornstarch until the sauce thickens to your taste. Then serve the sauce over the rice with the shrimp on the side. And have lots of buttered French bread handy to sop up the sauce! Oh, a cold, crisp lettuce salad goes well with it, too.

Leftover Shrimp Flambeaux

Here's a great recipe to prepare whenever you end up with some leftover boiled shrimp and cooked rice—if you ever have boiled shrimp left over! But even if you don't, it's really easy to whip up the ingredients and put this dish on your dinner table. It's perfect for buffet meals, too.

2 cups peeled boiled shrimp	4 cloves garlic, pressed
2 cups cooked rice	2 6-oz. cans tomato sauce
¼ cup Crisco oil	1 tbsp. red wine
1 medium-size white onion, finely chopped	½ tsp. cayenne pepper
½ bell pepper, coarsely chopped	salt and black pepper to taste

Before you begin working on the rest of the ingredients, cut your shrimp in pieces. I recommend you make the cuts at the segments. Then put the shrimp and the cooked rice in a bowl and mix them together with your hands. Then, in a skillet, panfry your onions, bell pepper, and garlic in the ¼ cup of Crisco until they are tender. It's best if you continue to stir while the vegetables are sautéing.

When your seasonings are cooked, add the tomato sauce to the skillet and fry it well. The best way to do this is to put the fire on medium low and continue to stir for about 10 minutes. Then pour the sauce into the bowl with the rice and the shrimp, and add the wine, cayenne, salt, and black pepper. Then *mix everything together* until you have an even consistency. You can't cook this dish properly unless you *taste* it, so taste *now* to make certain you have enough salt and pepper.

Finally, put the mixture into a buttered baking pan and cook in the oven (at about 350 degrees) for about 15 minutes. You want the dish to come out hot-hot and bubbly, so watch your oven. If the rice and shrimp are getting dried out, take it out right away.

Hint: I'd serve Shrimp Flambeaux with french-fried eggplant, glazed carrots, and a lettuce salad topped with French dressing. I'd also serve the wine you used in the dish.

Paul Arrigo's Oven-Italian Shrimp

The folks who work for the New Orleans Tourist and Convention Commission know where all the good eating places are in the Crescent City; it's part of the job. But if you ask them where the best Oven-Italian Shrimp come from, they'll be quick to tell you that you've got to go to Paul Arrigo's house just off Franklin Avenue. I did—and they're right!

4 lbs. large shrimp (with the heads on)	2 tbsp. dry barbecue spice
4 sticks melted margarine	3 tsp. Worcestershire sauce
¾ tbsp. cayenne pepper	2 tsp. paprika
2 tbsp. garlic powder	2 tbsp. black pepper

Wash the shrimp well under cold running water and allow them to drain. Then place them in a large casserole dish or a baking pan. Mix all the other ingredients in a bowl and allow them to sit for about 10 minutes until the flavorings blend.

When you're ready to cook—and this dish is best served right out of the oven—pour the mixture over the top of the shrimp and coat each shrimp really well. Then place the pan in a 300-degree oven and bake for 40 minutes, basting thoroughly every 10 minutes or so.

Paul says this shrimp dish is best served piping hot in soup bowls with the shrimp swimming in the basting sauce, accompanied by a bottle of your favorite wine, a big loaf of crisp French bread, and a spicy Italian salad. He also suggests that you wash your hands well before eating his Oven-Italian Shrimp, because you'll be licking your fingers a lot! Incidentally, Paul says this recipe should feed four "normal people" or *one really hungry Italian!*

Note: The leftover basting sauce from this dish (if there is any left over!) can be refrigerated and used as a topping for mashed potatoes, baked potatoes, steamed broccoli, or fried grits. It can also be used as a condiment for broiling oysters in the half shell (a couple of teaspoons in each shell), brushing over redfish on the barbecue grill, or whatever else strikes your creative fancy. So go ahead and create!

Shrimp Pilau

Virtually every recipe in this book originated in Louisiana (or was claimed for Louisiana by longtime residents). But there is one I want to include from a colleague in Florida—this one. It was compiled by an economist with the state fish and game department, and once you read through it you'll realize very quickly that the originator definitely knows how to cook. In Florida, this is referred to as Shrimp Perlo. It's a recipe that involves steaming, and it produces an unusual and unique taste.

1 lb. medium-size raw shrimp, peeled	¾ cup water
4 thin slices bacon	1 5-oz. pkg. yellow rice
1 cup chopped green pepper	1 tsp. salt
¼ cup chopped yellow onions	⅛ tsp. black pepper
1 16-oz. can whole tomatoes	⅛ tsp. thyme
	dash cayenne pepper

You can use either fresh or frozen shrimp for this recipe, and you should slice them in half *lengthwise* prior to preparing the dish. After the shrimp are sliced, take a 2-quart saucepan and sauté the bacon until it is super crisp. Remove the bacon from the pan and set it aside to drain well on paper towels. Then simmer the green peppers and onions in the bacon drippings until they are tender (it should take about 5 minutes). While the peppers and onions are cooking, pour your tomatoes into a bowl, break them up into small pieces, and remove all the tough centers. Then add the tomatoes and the water to the saucepan and bring the mixture to a boil. To blend the seasonings more uniformly, I suggest you allow the mixture to boil for about 3 or 4 minutes.

Then *gradually* stir in the yellow rice and the remaining seasonings (except for the bacon; do not put it in yet). When everything is well mixed, reduce the heat to low, cover the saucepan tightly, and simmer for about 20 minutes. When the grains of rice are half-cooked (7 minutes) toss in the sliced shrimp, mix them in evenly, cover again, and continue cooking for about 10 minutes more. When you're ready to serve the dish *gently fold in* the bacon. The flavor is enhanced if you crumble it really fine and allow the dish to "set up" for about 3 minutes before dishing it out.

Suggestion: This dish goes very well with a cold, crisp green salad; buttered dinner rolls; and a carafe of good Burgundy. Top it off with fried plantains (or bananas) sautéed in rum butter, and you've got a meal fit for a king!

Bayou-Style Shrimp-Pone Chowder

There are chowders and there are chowders. But one of the best chowders I've ever tasted was cooked up in a hurry while we scrubbed up a shrimp boat down in Yscloskey, just below New Orleans. Sadly, I don't even remember the name of the old Cajun who put it together, but I never lost his recipe, which I hurriedly jotted down on the inside liner of a Coca-Cola six-pack!

6 strips bacon
1 large onion, finely chopped
1 tbsp. minced shallots
¼ cup chopped celery
3 lbs. shrimp, peeled and
  chopped
½ stick butter
4 medium potatoes, boiled and
  mashed
pinch thyme
pinch sage
2½ cups whole milk, divided
2 tbsp. flour
1 3-oz. can BinB mushrooms
  (bits and pieces)
2 cups water
1 #303 can creamed corn
1 8-oz. can Petit Pois peas
salt and white pepper to taste
½ cup grated American cheese

In a frying pan, fry the strips of bacon until they become very crisp, and crumble them into small pieces on a paper towel. Then sauté your onions, shallots, and celery in the bacon drippings until they wilt. While the vegetables are cooking, sauté the chopped shrimp in the butter *until they turn pink*. Careful, now: Don't overcook them.

When the vegetables have wilted, add the mashed potatoes, the thyme, the sage, and half the milk. Stir well until the mixture is blended thoroughly. While continuing to stir, sprinkle in the flour and cook it in over medium heat, making sure that none of it lumps up. At this point you add the rest of the milk, the shrimp, the sautéing butter you cooked the shrimp in, the mushrooms, the water, the crumbled bacon bits, the cream-style corn, the green peas, and whatever salt and pepper you need to season. Then stir everything together over low heat for about 15 minutes. Just by way of a hint: If you want a *thinner* chowder, add extra milk; if you prefer a *thicker* chowder, just simmer the ingredients uncovered until enough liquid has evaporated.

When you're ready to serve, toss in the ½ cup of grated cheese and fold it into the mixture with a wire whisk *ever so lightly*. Then ladle out generous helpings in deep soup bowls, accompanied by hot-buttered French bread and a saucer of sliced creole tomatoes. This recipe should feed about six people.

Elaine's Egg-Shrimp Tarts

Several years ago I had the honor of being a judge in a cooking contest sponsored by those "Incredible Edible Egg" folks. You remember them? Well, we must have tasted 50 dishes that afternoon, but the one that stands out in my mind as being the most creative is this recipe by Elaine Naquin, who lives in Labadieville, Louisiana.

The Tart Pastry:

½ tsp. salt   ½ cup shortening
1⅓ cups all-purpose flour   3 tbsp. ice water

First mix the salt and the flour together and sift them several times into a medium bowl. Then, using a couple of knives, *cut* the ½ cup of shortening (I recommend Crisco) into the mixture. You want to keep blending until the mix takes on the texture of coarse cornmeal. When it reaches this point, quickly *sprinkle* in the ice water 1 tablespoon at a time. Don't put in too much water so that the dough becomes sticky; it should be just moist enough to hold together. Then wrap it up well in waxed paper, place it in the refrigerator for 1 hour, and let it "set up."

When the dough is properly chilled, prepare a floured surface and begin rolling out pieces small enough to fit into 2½-inch-diameter muffin cups. The recipe should give you enough dough for about 12 tarts if you roll them out right. Finally, put the cups in the muffin cups and bake at 400 degrees for about 10 minutes (or until they're nice and brown). When they're done, cool them on your counter top on a damp towel and remove them gently from the cups.

The Egg-Shrimp Filling:

6 hard-boiled eggs   1 tsp. finely chopped garlic
1 cup coarsely chopped boiled   ¼ tsp. finely chopped parsley
  shrimp   1 tbsp. sweet pickle relish
1 tbsp. finely chopped white   ¼ cup mayonnaise
  onion   salt and white pepper to taste

Peel the eggs and separate the whites from the yolks. Then chop the whites to a medium-fine consistency and toss them into a medium-size bowl. In a separate bowl mash the yolks to an extremely fine consistency and add them to the whites. Add your shrimp and all the vegetables. With a fork, blend everything together until it's fully mixed. Then fold in the relish, blending thoroughly. Finally, add the mayonnaise and blend it in well. If you want a really moist mix, add extra mayonnaise; for a drier mix, use less mayonnaise.

All that's left now is to season the concoction with salt and pepper and stuff it into the muffin pastries you baked earlier. For a pastry garnish, you can use your own creative flair—add a tiny cocktail onion, a thinly sliced piece of black olive, a strip of pimento, a butter-sautéed mushroom, a sprig of parsley, a sliver of butter-sautéed almonds, or thin crossed strips of American cheese. You can use just about anything. Note: If you'd rather serve these tarts as an entrée, they go great with a fresh vegetable mixture (broccoli, pea pods, carrots, and corn) *stir-fried* in butter.

Pontchartrain Shrimp Chowder

Mrs. Pat Armand is married to Mr. Pat Armand, whose favorite thing to do in the whole world is "eat good food." So I have Mr. Pat Armand's word for it that there ain't no better eating in the whole world than Mrs. Pat Armand's home-cooked Pontchartrain Shrimp Chowder. I tried it and I agree!

5 lbs. medium-size shrimp, peeled	**2 tbsp. butter**
6 large potatoes	**1 tbsp. finely chopped parsley**
2 10¾-oz. cans cream of shrimp soup	**¼ cup chopped green onion tops**
	salt and black pepper to taste

In a 4-quart Dutch oven, cover your shrimp with just enough water to boil them, *and not a half-inch more*. This concentrates the shrimp flavor and reduces cooking time to about 4 minutes from the time the water comes to a boil. When they're tender remove the shrimp from the water using a strainer, and set them aside to cool. Wash the potatoes well, put them in the shrimp water, and boil them until they're cooked. Go ahead and cut your shrimp in halves while you're waiting.

After the potatoes are boiled, remove them from the water with a strainer spoon and let them cool enough to peel, but save your shrimp water because it becomes your cooking stock base. Next, with the heat on medium, add the 2 cans of soup to the pot and stir gently. Don't let it boil. As the soup stock mixture is warming up, *mash* the potatoes to a fine consistency and add them to the pot, stirring the soup and potatoes together. At this point fold in the shrimp, the butter, the parsley, and the green onion tops. *Keep stirring*. You want the blend to be uniform. Increase the heat slightly, just until the chowder starts to bubble, and let everything simmer for about 10 minutes or so. The salt and pepper go in now, too. To vary the consistency you can either add some cream to thin the dish or cook it uncovered on low heat to thicken it. The dish should not be too watery.

Hint: Serve with a cucumber salad and melba toast!

Shrimp-Stuffed Cabbage Rolls

My wife always stuffed cabbage leaves with ground meat and topped them with tomato sauce—until one afternoon when we decided to experiment with shrimp. Well, need I say we no longer use ground meat? But I'm not going to say any more about this recipe. You have to taste it to know just how good it really is.

12 large raw cabbage leaves	1 tbsp. McCormick lemon
1 strip lean bacon	pepper
1 stick butter	1¼ tsp. salt
2 lbs. finely chopped shrimp	½ tsp. white pepper
½ cup chopped mushrooms	¼ tsp. cayenne pepper
1 cup chopped white onion	1 beaten egg
¼ tsp. powdered thyme	¼ cup grated Romano cheese
1 cup cooked long-grain rice	
2 cups barbecue sauce with onions	

Start off by boiling a pot of unsalted water and submerging the cabbage leaves until they are limp enough to roll without breaking. *It should take about 3 minutes to prepare the leaves*. Do not overcook; you want them *just pliable*. Set them aside to cool.

In a large 10- or 12-inch skillet, fry the bacon until it is super-crisp and set it on a paper towel to drain. When it hardens and cools, crumble it into very small pieces. Note that you want just a hint of bacon flavor in this recipe. Too much bacon will dominate the flavor, and that's undesirable. Next, add the stick of butter to the bacon drippings and melt it on medium-high heat (watch that it doesn't burn). As the butter melts, stir it into the bacon fat so that they are well blended. Add the raw shrimp, the chopped mushrooms (fresh is best), the chopped onions, and the thyme, and sauté everything together, stirring constantly, until each ingredient is tender (it usually takes about 5 minutes).

Then, with the skillet still over the flame, add the cooked rice and blend it in quickly. Also add *half* of the barbecue sauce, and blend again until the mix is a nice pinkish color. With the skillet still on the fire, mix in the lemon pepper, the salt, the white pepper, and the cayenne, and stir them around well. Then remove the skillet from the burner and let everything sit for about 3 minutes. You'll add the egg next, but get good and ready to do some rapid stirring! Pour it over the mix and literally whip it in as quickly as you can. You do not want it to cook into the rice; you want it to form a bonding agent to hold the mixture together. Keep that in mind—*and stir!* Then gently sprinkle in the crumbled bacon and lightly fold it into the mixture so that it only "dots" the ingredients. Take a break at this point and allow the filling to cool.

Then, using a large cookie sheet, lay out the cabbage leaves in front of you, and *separate the filling into 12 portions* so that the leaves can be stuffed equally. Place the portions in the leaves and begin rolling from the thicker part of the leaf to the thinner outer edge. The best stuffing method is to fold the sides over first, then roll lengthwise. This technique produces a nice rectangular bundle. When all the leaves are stuffed, place them side by side so that they touch each other in a baking pan. Take the remaining cup of barbecue sauce and lightly brush the tops of the rolls with the sauce, barely coating them. Then cover with a sheet of aluminum foil and bake in a 350-degree oven for a total of 35 minutes. At 10-minute intervals open the oven, remove the foil, and baste lightly with the sauce. Repeat the basting procedure 3 times. Don't worry if you don't use the whole cup!

Just before you're ready to serve the rolls, uncover the baking dish, brush once more with the sauce, and sprinkle the Romano cheese evenly over the cabbage bundles. Place them back in the oven for *no more than 5 minutes . . .* and they are ready, y'all!

Suggestion: These rolls go great with a side helping of crisp potato chips, a spoonful of baked beans (with the liquid drained off), and a cold salad of tomato slices served with a vinaigrette dressing. A nice, light rosé wine will also complement the meal.

AND WHEN IN DOUBT, MAKE A POTATO SALAD

Folks ask me all the time what makes a good side dish with seafoods. Well, as with anything else, your creativity (that word again) and taste will probably determine your personal answer to the question. But whenever in doubt, make a potato salad.

French fries, dirty rice, pasta, and a host of stir-fried vegetables all complement a good seafood meal. But for some reason or other nothing quite seems to hit the spot as well as a richly prepared *potato salad*.

Ol' Dominick's Shrimp and Crabmeat Baked Ditali

One of the first dishes I ever created to impress folks I put together decades ago with Dominick Delvechio, when we both were bachelors. We were going to entertain dates that evening, and we were going to do the cooking. But as fate would have it, the dates fell through, so Dom and I decided to cook anyway and drown our sorrows in food. When the cooking and the eating were over, we were glad they hadn't shown up—I mean, neither of us wanted to share anything that good with girls we weren't gonna marry!

2 cups ditali	½ tsp. ground oregano
½ stick butter	½ tsp. salt
2 cups chopped raw shrimp	1 tsp. white pepper
1 cup flaked crabmeat	3 tbsp. flour
4 tbsp. finely chopped onions	1½ cups half-and-half
1 tbsp. coarsely chopped garlic	1 egg yolk
2 tbsp. minced parsley	1 tbsp. lemon juice
¼ tsp. sweet basil	1 cup buttered bread crumbs

Measure out 2 cups of uncooked ditali and boil it in slightly salted water (a pinch or two of salt will do) until it is *just tender but not fully cooked*. (The secret to goodness in this dish is the firmness of the pasta, so watch the boiling process carefully.) Drain. Then take a 10-inch skillet, melt the butter over medium heat, and stir in the raw chopped shrimp and the cooked flaked crabmeat. With a wooden spoon, stir the two ingredients together until the mix is uniform and thoroughly sautéed in the butter. *Cook no more than 3 minutes.*

When your shrimp and crabmeat mix is ready, add the onions, the garlic, the parsley, the basil, the oregano, and the salt and pepper, and combine them rapidly, cooking for about 4 more minutes. At this point *sprinkle* the flour evenly over the mix and stir it in. Then pour in the cream. Stirring constantly, cook over medium heat until the mixture begins to thicken. Cook it well, because you want some body in this dish! When everything is well blended, take the skillet off the heat and *quickly* whip in the egg yolk. You'll have to do some mixing here; otherwise it will cook on the spot. Then pour the lemon juice into the mix and quickly whip it in.

Finally, take the ditali and fold it into the seafood mix so that each piece of pasta is coated with the sauce and the shrimp pieces and crab flakes are evenly distributed. Then put the mixture into a lightly buttered Pyrex casserole dish, top with buttered bread crumbs, and bake in a 350-degree oven for 20 minutes until the crumbs are moist and tender. If you want to add a little visual flair to the recipe, turn on the broiler element for a few minutes just before you serve it and toast the top of the dish.

Suggestion: On the day you make this recipe, I recommend you skip lunch—you just won't be able to quit eating this version of Italiana, and you won't want to, either. You'll probably want to look up Dominick and kiss him on the cheek!

Smitty's Shrimp Fondue

When Donald Smith sent me this recipe, the only note he attached to it was: "Frank—this is gonna blow your socks off!" Well, I've been barefootin' it ever since. You talk about tasty! And you can serve it hot, as a fondue; or cold, as a party dip; or at room temperature, as a salad dressing. Just serve it! And it's super simple.

3 lbs. chopped boiled shrimp	1 bunch shallots, minced
3 cups real mayonnaise	1 tsp. garlic puree
1 tsp. Zatarain's liquid crab boil	1 tbsp. lemon juice
	dash paprika
2 hard-boiled eggs, finely chopped	½ tsp. salt

I suggest you run the shrimp through the food processor to get the best texture for this dish, but if you don't have a processor just take the time to cut the shrimp really fine. (Incidentally, you should boil your shrimp for a few minutes, until they're just tender, in lightly salted water.) Once the shrimp are chopped, half of the work is done.

All that's left is to mix all the remaining ingredients together at once in a large bowl and fold in the chopped shrimp. I recommend you use a whisk instead of a spoon to do this—the results are better.

Hints:
1. Before serving the dish in any form (fondue, salad dressing, or dip), it is important to cover the mix and let it "set" in the refrigerator for at least 10 hours to allow the richness to develop.
2. If you serve it as a fondue, put it in a chafing dish and get it nice and bubbly before it is to be eaten. Skewered croutons, oyster-flavored crackers, Wheat Thins, Ritz crackers, and Italian breadsticks go great with the hot mix.
3. If you serve it as a salad dressing, Don recommends you let it reach room temperature before spreading it over sliced tomatoes, lettuce wedges, and other trimmings. Like a fine wine, its flavor is more intense at room temperature.
4. And if you serve it as a dip, well, the choice is yours. Hot, room temp., or cold: it's delicious with Doritos, Ruffles, Fritos, whatever.

Grandma's Favorite Shrimpy Spaghetti

On my grandmother's side of the family I'm Italian, as my temper and appetite will attest. And while I'll eat the heck out of pasta and tomato gravy, I still prefer fresh-boiled, *al dente* spaghetti covered with a rich, white, cream topping, Sicilian style. When you toss in some butterflied shrimp to spice it up, that's an offer I can't refuse!

1 16-oz. pkg. No. 4 spaghetti	1 pt. heavy cream
1 tbsp. olive oil	¼ tsp. McCormick Italian
1 stick unsalted butter plus 1	seasoning
tbsp.	⅛ tsp. oregano
3 strips bacon	1 tsp. salt
½ lb. fresh sliced mushrooms	1 tsp. white pepper
2 lbs. peeled, butterflied shrimp	1 hard-boiled egg, finely chopped
(sliced down the back)	

The first thing you do is boil the spaghetti in lightly salted water containing about a tablespoon of pure olive oil. But *do not overcook it*. It should be cooked, but firm and chewable, not mushy. When it's boiled just right (about 14 minutes at a rapid boil), pour the spaghetti into a colander and drain it. If you stir in a tablespoon of butter as it drains, the spaghetti will never stick together!

Next, make your sauce. You start by frying the bacon strips in a 2¾-quart sautéing pan until they are super-crispy, setting them on a paper towel to drain, and pouring out the excess drippings. But do *not wash the pan;* leave a light coating of the bacon fat on the bottom, put the pan back on the burner, turn the heat to high, and stir in the sliced mushrooms. Fry them hot and quick until they are *seared* (browned on the edges). (It should take about 4 minutes.)

At this point add the stick of butter to the pan and melt it. Keep in mind, however, that you must reduce the heat immediately to medium to prevent the butter from burning. Then stir in the butterflied shrimp and simmer them for about *5 minutes* or until they're nice and pink and tender. When they are ready, remove them from the pan and place them in a bowl with the bacon, which should now be crumbled up. Let the shrimp cool.

Reheat the butter to medium high and stir in the heavy cream. And I do mean *stir:* Keep it moving constantly so that it will cook thoroughly and thicken. This should take about *8 minutes,* and the sauce should come out nice and smooth. Also stir in the Italian seasoning, oregano, salt, and white pepper, and blend evenly. Then peel the egg, chop both the yolk and the white, and add them to the cream along with the crumbled bacon and the shrimp. When it's all well mixed and heated to piping hot, spoon the sauce over the spaghetti. Delicioso!

Stuffed Mirliton, Eggplant, or Bell Pepper

Rather than list three different recipes all utilizing the same ingredients (because I stuff all three the same way), I've combined the three major shrimp-stuffed vegetables—mirlitons, eggplants, and bell peppers—into one presentation. If you follow the directions here, you'll have some good eating regardless of what you stuff.

The Stuffing Mix

3 tbsp. butter
1 large white onion, finely
  chopped
3 cloves garlic, finely chopped
1 tbsp. finely chopped bell
  pepper
½ cup coarsely chopped
  mushrooms
1 lb. peeled, coarsely chopped
  raw shrimp
¼ cup finely chopped celery
1 tsp. finely chopped parsley

¼ tsp. thyme
¼ tsp. rosemary
1 tsp. salt
¼ tsp. cayenne pepper
½ tsp. black pepper
1 cup dry unseasoned bread
  crumbs
1 egg, beaten well
whole milk (optional)
½ cup buttered bread crumbs
appropriate vegetable pulps as
  indicated

For Stuffed Bell Peppers:

Take 6 medium-size bell peppers and prepare them for parboiling: cut off the tops and remove the seeds. Then submerge them for about *4 minutes* in rapidly boiling water. When the peppers are tender, remove them from the pot and drain them in the sink, taking care to wipe the outsides thoroughly.

In a large skillet (or as I prefer, a 4½-quart Dutch oven made of black cast iron), melt the butter over medium heat and sauté the onion, garlic, bell pepper, and mushrooms until they wilt (about 5 minutes). At this point toss in the chopped shrimp and rapidly stir them into the seasoning mixture for about 3 minutes until they turn pink. Then stir in the celery, parsley, thyme, rosemary, salt, and peppers. Before taking the mixture off the heat, be sure all the ingredients are evenly blended. Then cool the mix for about 5 minutes.

Begin stirring in the dry bread crumbs, a little at a time. When you have those mixed in, very quickly whip in the beaten egg (do it quickly so that it becomes a bonding agent and doesn't cook on the spot). Suggestion: If your mix is too dry—*and it should be pasty, not wet or crumbly*—add a few tablespoons of whole milk to moisten the mix. *But do not add too much;* the stuffing will become watery after it bakes if you do.

Finally, stuff the mix into the hollowed bell pepper so that the stuffing *rounds out* on top. Then cap the peppers with a sprinkling of buttered bread crumbs and bake in a 300-degree oven for about 20 minutes. Serve with creamed peas, buttered carrots, a crisp lettuce salad topped with French dressing, and a bottle of chilled Chenin Blanc.

For Stuffed Mirlitons:

Take 6 medium-size mirlitons and boil them in lightly salted water until a testing fork will pierce them all the way through (without using excessive force). Then remove them from the water and set them aside to cool.

In a 4½-quart cast-iron Dutch oven, melt the butter over medium heat and sauté the onions, garlic, bell pepper, celery, and mushrooms until they are tender (about 5 minutes). Reduce your fire about 2 minutes into the sautéing process, and, while the vegetables are simmering on low heat, slice the mirlitons in halves lengthwise and remove the center seed pod. With a tablespoon, *gently* scrape out the mirliton pulp to within about ¼-inch of the outer skin. *Be careful not to break the outer skin.* With a sharp knife, dice up your pulp into small pieces.

At this point turn up the fire to high and toss in the pulp. Stirring constantly for 10 to 15 minutes, cook the pulp and the vegetable seasonings together until a paste forms (it will be slightly watery, but don't worry about it). About three-quarters of the way through this portion of the cooking process, add the raw shrimp and stir them around. The shrimp will turn pink in about 2 minutes, which is exactly how you want it. Remove the pot from the fire. Now's the time to add the spices and herbs—the parsley, thyme, rosemary, salt, and peppers. Blend them well into the pulp mix, so that you have no "potent" spots. Then begin stirring in the dry bread crumbs a little at a time. When all the dry crumbs are added, you should wind up with a rather dry paste that tends to stick to the spoon. If it is still too moist, add a few extra crumbs, because if the mixture is too wet it will "run" during the baking process. Now stir in the egg!

Finally, stuff the mix into the cooled mirliton halves so that the stuffing domes at the top (in other words, almost overstuff). Then sprinkle the tops with the buttered bread crumbs, place the halves on a flat cookie sheet (or a Pyrex baking dish), and bake in a 275-degree oven for about 25 minutes. For extra enhancement, sprinkle liberally with grated Romano cheese when serving.

Hint: The side dishes I suggested with the bell peppers also go well with mirlitons.

For Stuffed Eggplants:

Take 3 medium-size eggplants and boil them in lightly salted water until a testing fork will pierce them all the way through (without using excessive force). Then remove them from the water and set them aside to cool.

In a 4½-quart cast-iron Dutch oven, melt the butter over medium heat and sauté the onions, garlic, bell pepper, celery, and mushrooms until they are tender (about 5 minutes). Reduce your fire about 2 minutes into the sautéing process. While the vegetables are simmering, slice the eggplants into halves lengthwise, and begin gently scraping out the eggplant pulp with a tablespoon. You want to come within about ¼-*inch* of the outer skin, but be careful not to put a hole in the skin. Dice up the pulp into small pieces.

At this point, turn the fire up to high and toss the pulp into the Dutch oven with the vegetable mixture. Then cook all the ingredients for about 15 minutes, stirring constantly. As with the mirliton stuffing, you want the resulting mix to be rather stiff instead of watery, but it will appear watery at the outset. Don't be too concerned about the texture at this time, since the bread crumbs will probably absorb just the proper amount of moisture. About 12 minutes into the cooking process, toss in the shrimp and stir them around uniformly. The shrimp will turn pink in about 2 minutes. Then remove the pot from the fire and set the mixture aside to cool slightly.

Now add the spices and herbs—the parsley, thyme, rosemary, salt, and peppers. Blend them into the pulp well, so that you don't have any "potent" spots. At this point, too, whip in the raw egg; whip it in quickly so that it doesn't cook on the spot. Then begin adding the dry bread crumbs a little at a time, blending after each spoonful for uniformity. Like the mirliton stuffing, the eggplant mixture should stiffen up and have the tendency to stick to the spoon.

Finally, stuff the mix into the eggplant halves so that the stuffing forms a rounded peak (you can almost overstuff). Then sprinkle the buttered bread crumbs over the tops of the eggplant halves and bake them in a casserole dish at 300 degrees for 25 minutes. I also suggest you top your eggplants liberally with grated Romano before serving.

A Couple of Short-Cuts:
If you would rather not scrape out the pulp from the mirlitons and eggplants and restuff them, some equally fine dishes can be made using the same ingredients and procedures in casseroles. (This is especially useful in northern states where mirlitons may not be available and where zucchini and other squashes may be substituted.) In other words, rather than stuff the mixture into the vegetable halves, just spoon everything into a buttered Pyrex casserole dish and bake for

the indicated time in each recipe. One-dish casseroles are excellent ways of serving mirlitons, eggplants, and squash at parties and get-togethers as complements to other seafood entrées.

As casseroles, they can be garnished differently, too. Top them with sliced mushrooms, slivered and toasted almonds, parsley sprigs, black olive rings— you name it—they all produce tasty creations with extra eye appeal. Use some flair!

Frank's Shrimp-Stuffed Manicotti

Nothing tantalizes my taste buds more than a rich shrimp stuffing packed solidly into a tender manicotti noodle and topped with a succulent white Italian sauce. Tempts you? Well, this recipe tells you how to do it from start to delicious finish. If you want to wallow in culinary praise, fix this dish for a party. You talk about popularity! Everyone will want to take you home!

The Stuffing:

1 8-oz. pkg. manicotti (14 pieces)
1 stick butter
3 lbs. coarsely chopped raw shrimp
2 ribs celery, coarsely chopped
2 medium-size onions, coarsely chopped
1 clove garlic, finely chopped
1 cup coarsely chopped fresh carrots
¼ tsp. oregano

½ tsp. basil
⅛ tsp. fennel seed
½ cup grated mozzarella cheese
½ cup grated mild cheddar cheese
½ cup large-curd, low-fat cottage cheese
½ cup Italian seasoned bread crumbs
3 hard-boiled eggs

Start off by boiling the manicotti in lightly salted water until each piece is "just tender"; you don't want to get them too soft because they will become fully tender when baked in the sauce. When they're cooked, remove them gently from the pot with a strainer ladle and place them in the sink in cold water to keep the pieces from sticking together.

In a 10-inch stainless-steel sauté pan, melt the stick of butter over medium heat and gently stir in the chopped shrimp. Cook them uncovered, stirring constantly, for about *3 minutes* (until they turn pink). Then remove one-third of the shrimp and set them aside in a bowl. With the pan still on medium heat, toss in the celery, onions, garlic, carrots, oregano, basil, and fennel seed. Stir everything together well, then *remove the pan from the fire*. The vegetables *should not* be wilted at this point, but still crisp and crunchy. Allow the mixture to cool enough so that the cheeses will not fully melt when added, *about 15 minutes*.

When it's cool, add the mozzarella, cheddar, and cottage cheeses, along with the bread crumbs. Then *very gently* fold the cheeses and bread crumbs into the shrimp-vegetable mixture. Pause for a moment, peel the hard-boiled eggs, chop them; and distribute them evenly over the top of the mix. At this point let the mixture "set" while you prepare the sauce.

The Cream Sauce:

2 sticks butter
1 pt. heavy cream
1½ tsp. salt
½ tsp. white pepper
¼ tsp. cayenne pepper

¼ cup grated Parmesan cheese
dash thyme
1 3-oz. can Durkee French Fried Onions

In a 1½-quart saucepan, melt the butter over medium heat and gently stir in the shrimp you saved from the stuffing portion of the recipe. When the shrimp chunks and the butter are the same temperature, gradually begin adding the heavy cream a little at a time, *stirring constantly*. Then reduce the heat to *medium low* and continue cooking until the cream begins to thicken.

As the sauce simmers, remove the manicotti shells from the cold water in the sink and begin stuffing them with the shrimp-and-cheese mix. (If you hold the pasta in your left hand, insert your index finger into one end, and fill the opposite end with a teaspoon, the procedure is rather simple.) When they are all stuffed full (and stuff 'em tight!), place them in rows in a 13-inch Pyrex baking dish, so that they touch each other *but are not smashed together*. Set them aside momentarily, and check your topping sauce. By this time it should be nice and thick and bubbly. Sprinkle on the salt and peppers, and stir them into the mixture. And then slowly stir in the Parmesan cheese and the thyme. The cheese should melt quickly; as soon as it does, the sauce is ready to add to the main dish.

Just spoon it liberally over the top of the manicotti until every single square inch is covered with the chunked-shrimp sauce. Then top with a light coating of Durkee French Fried Onions. And when you're ready to eat, place the dish in the oven and bake uncovered at 325 degrees for about 20 minutes or until it's hot and bubbly.

Suggestion: Serve with buttered green beans, a sliced beet and onion salad, and a big chunk of garlic bread. And don't forget the chilled wine—a glass of Lambrusco would go nicely with this entrée.

Frank's Succulent-Fried Butterflied Shrimp

Just about everyone at one time or another has fried shrimp, but if you want to taste some of the most tender, delicately flavored, and extremely light shrimp ever dropped into hot oil, then fix this recipe. But be warned—you may like it so much you won't want to go back to your old style of cooking shrimp!

4 lbs. shrimp, peeled	1 tsp. black pepper
2 cups whole milk	½ tsp. cayenne pepper
1 cup corn flour (or Zatarain's Fish-Fri)	½ tsp. white pepper
1 cup corn meal	2 eggs, well beaten
2 tsp. salt	Crisco oil for frying

Start off by washing the shrimp well and placing them in a large bowl. Then grasp each shrimp between your thumb and index finger with the dorsal (back) side facing up. With a sharp paring knife slice about *three-quarters of the way* through the body from head to tail, laying the shrimp open in a butterfly-wing configuration. When you've butterflied them all, place them back in the sink and wash them again several times. The vein will come out of the shrimp during the wash period, so you will have no need for deveining as such. Then place the shrimp back in the bowl, pour the 2 cups of milk over them, and mix the milk in well so that each shrimp is coated. Cover the bowl with Saran Wrap and place it in the refrigerator for no less than *6 hours*.

To make your coating mix, stir together the corn flour, the cornmeal, the salt, and the 3 kinds of pepper with a whisk. Incidentally, if your mix doesn't get too wet during the coating process, you can bag what's left and freeze it for later use. Then, when you're ready to fry your shrimp, dump them into a colander and rinse the milk away with cold water. *But do not let them sit in the water.* You want to do this rinsing quickly so that they are still cold when you fry them.

Using two large Ziploc freezer bags, put half of the coating mix into one bag and half into the other, with the bowl containing the beaten eggs between the two. Then pour all the shrimp into the first bag, seal it up, and shake the shrimp briskly (turning the bag over and over) until they are coated. At this point pick them out of the mix and shake off the excess coating. Incidentally, while you are doing this, heat up your deep fryer (I recommend using Crisco oil) to 400 to 425 degrees. And if you are going to use a basket in the fryer, put the basket into the oil now. Then run each shrimp through the egg wash and, after they are dipped, set all the shrimp together in a bowl. Allow the excess egg to drain off, then separate the shrimp into "batches"—just the amount you will fry in each batch (for 2 pounds of shrimp, there should be 3 batches—and coat and fry each batch separately. In other words, take the first batch, recoat the shrimp in the *second bag* of mix, and immediately drop them into the fryer. *Do not take the basket out of the oil.* Drop the shrimp one at a time into the oil, with the basket submerged. But you must do this quickly. In fact, while this may sound like a lengthy process, it really isn't. From the first coating bag to the egg to the second coating bag to the oil should take only a minute or two.

After the shrimp are in the oil, agitate the basket several times to move them around. Then, at the first indication that they are *floating* (and turning brown, which won't take long at 425 degrees!), lift the basket and drain the shrimp. Actual frying time should be something like *2 or 3 minutes, maybe less.* Right away you will notice the greasy appearance disappear, and the coating on the shrimp will come out light, not thick and heavy-battered, yet crisp. Repeat the process for the next two batches and you will have some of the most succulent fried shrimp ever!

Just one note: *Allow several minutes between batches, for two reasons: (1) you want to replace the basket in the oil so that it will be at the same temperature as the oil, and (2) you will want the oil to reheat to 425 degrees so that all of your shrimp will come out uniformly fried. It is really a simple process, and after preparing your fried shrimp this way a couple of times you'll get the hang of it. Whether you follow this recipe, though, or any other, do yourself a taste favor and always butterfly your shrimp. There is no better way to get them tender!*

WHEN TO BUY FRESH SHRIMP

If you live along the coastline of the Gulf of Mexico, you will be able to obtain fresh-from-the-water shrimp virtually all year long. But some times of the year are better than others because you'll save money!

Keep in mind that Louisiana and most other coastal states have two major *shrimp seasons:* (1) the spring brown-shrimp season that usually starts in late May or early June, and (2) the white-shrimp season that begins the third Monday in August. If you buy the bulk of your shrimp during the early parts of these two seasons and freeze them, you will save considerable amounts of money per pound. Early-season shrimp are smaller, but they're excellent for cooking hundreds of dishes.

Shrimp and Chokes

For eons stuffed artichokes have been as important a part of New Orleans cuisine as pickled onions in red beans and hog's head cheese on saltine crackers. And just about every Ninth Warder knows how to stuff the leaves Italian-style so that they'll bring tears to your eyes! But I've taken the fantastic New Orleans concoction one step further, adding the succulent flavor of Gulf of Mexico shrimp to the steamed uniqueness of the artichoke. You've got to try this one, y'all!

4 fresh artichokes
2 cups Italian seasoned bread crumbs
¼ cup Parmesan cheese
¼ cup Romano cheese
1 tsp. McCormick lemon pepper

1 tsp. garlic powder
½ tsp. onion powder
½ cup imported olive oil
2 lbs. small raw shrimp (50 count)

The first thing you do is place the artichokes on their sides and trim off *the tops* (so that the top is now flat, and the inner leaves are exposed) and *the stems* (so that the chokes will sit upright in the pan during steaming). Then wash them well in clear tap water and set them upside down to drain thoroughly. While they are draining, take a large bowl and combine the bread crumbs, Parmesan and Romano cheeses, lemon pepper, garlic powder, and onion powder. These *must* be mixed together well. Then, in a 10-inch sautéing pan, heat the olive oil to medium high and stir in the shrimp, frying them until they turn pink (about 4 minutes). Now here's where the extra effort comes in: (1) when the shrimp are cooked, remove them from the oil and drain them completely on several layers of paper towels—*you want them as greaseless as possible;* (2) set the oil off to the side to cool—you'll baste the artichokes with it later; (3) after the shrimp are drained, either chop them with a chef's knife or run them through the fine blade of a grinder or food processor until they are transformed into tiny "chips"; and then (4) add the shrimp to the cheese–bread crumb mixture and again blend everything together well.

All that's left, then, is to stuff the chokes. The best way is to set them on a piece of waxed paper and apply handfuls of the mix on top of the flat cut, gently working the stuffing into each leaf space with your fingertips. Take time to make certain that *every leaf* contains some filling. When they are all stuffed, set them down inside a 6-quart stainless-steel Dutch oven with a tight-fitting lid. Then add about a half-inch of water to the bottom of the pot, bring the water to a boil, reduce the heat to low, cover the artichokes, and begin steaming them. About every 10 minutes check the water in the pot, and baste spoonful after spoonful of the olive oil in which you sautéed the shrimp over the top of the artichokes. The basting works best if the oil is dribbled on every time you check the water level.

Steaming time (depending upon the temperature of your stove) should range from 45 minutes to 2 hours—perhaps somewhere in between if the lid fits tightly and the steam stays in the pot. I don't recommend that you *time* the process, though. Instead, whenever you check the pot for the water level, test the artichokes with a fork; if your fork pierces the entire artichoke through and through with ease, the choke is done. It's that easy.

Suggestion: Artichokes stuffed in this manner always taste best when served at room temperature. You will also find that the ground shrimp suspended between the leaves gives the vegetable a unique, savory flavor that will please the most discriminating connoisseur.

MICROWAVE BUTTER SHRIMP

For a super-quick seafood snack to nibble on with crackers during a ball game or soap opera, try this: Peel about a dozen shrimp and lightly salt and pepper them. Place them in a soup bowl and cover them with 4 or 5 pats of butter and sprinkle a little dab of onion powder over the butter.

Then stick the bowl in the microwave oven and cook the shrimp, stirring every 30 seconds or so, until they turn pink and tender and a shrimpy sauce forms. You talk about good?

ROCK SHRIMP, A SEAFOOD TREAT FROM FLORIDA

There is a seafood that's been popping up lately on a lot of Louisiana tables that is not native to Louisiana waters. But because of its flavor, because it resembles the texture of lobster, and because it has been relatively inexpensive, it is rapidly gaining in popularity among southern seafood lovers. I'm talking about **rock shrimp**.

According to the experts at the Gulf South and Atlantic Fisheries Development Foundation (GSAFDF), rock shrimp, imported from Florida, get their name from the extremely tough and rigid shell that covers the succulent tail meat. For centuries they were prized critters among fishermen who kept them for their own use, but they weren't well known to the public. All that, of course, has changed now, and the little crustaceans are being quick-frozen and shipped all over the South.

They are uniquely delicious when prepared properly, but they *must* be prepared *properly*. Unlike brown or white shrimp, rock shrimp have a significant sand vein that runs down the back, and unless it is totally removed dining on rock shrimp is like chewing wads of sandpaper! Fortunately, removing the vein is a snap; I'll tell you how to do it in a minute. But first, a couple of notes:

1. Rock shrimp are marketed raw and frozen, either whole or as split tails. The whole tails you've got to clean. The split tails are already cleaned for you.

2. They are definitely members of the shrimp family, so they can be fixed in almost any standard shrimp dish once they are cleaned. Of course, the flavor will be more delicate than that of white or brown shrimp.

3. The texture of the meat is like lobster, which means rock shrimp can be easily fashioned into Newburgs and Thermidors.

4. The flavor of the meat is a pleasing cross between shrimp and lobster, somewhat milder than shrimp, but more robust than lobster.

5. While generally it is accepted that shrimp products are best when purchased fresh, the GSAFDF experts agree that rock shrimp are equally good—and perhaps better—when purchased frozen. I've eaten them both ways and found them equally good.

6. Like white and brown shrimp, rock shrimp are sold by *count* (the number of shrimp to the pound), with the largest ones generally running 21–25s. The larger ones, naturally, are easier to work with. But, like Louisiana shrimp, the medium-size critters seem to have more flavor.

7. As you can with Louisiana shrimp, you can determine if rock shrimp are fresh by their appearance and odor: the flesh will be clear or transparent without discoloration, and the odor will be mild with absolutely no "fishy" aroma. So if they don't fit this description when you go to purchase yours, leave them in the seafood market bin.

8. Rock shrimp are far more perishable than either type of Louisiana shrimp. So keep them under refrigeration at all times, and cook them as soon as possible after you buy them.

9. Cooked rock shrimp will stay fresh in the refrigerator for up to 3 days. I suggest you keep them covered, too.

10. Finally, it is helpful to remember that, when properly cleaned and cooked, rock shrimp will weigh about 50 percent of the weight of the raw, uncooked product. In other words, *2 pounds* of green tails will give you *1 pound* of cooked, peeled, deveined rock shrimp, which, unless one is a gourmand, will feed about four persons.

Cleaning the Tails for Simmering

Hold the tail section in one hand with the swimmerettes down toward the palm of the hand. Using kitchen shears, insert one blade of the scissors in the sand vein opening and cut through the shell along the outer (back) curve to the end of the tail.

Then pull the sides apart and remove the meat. Wash it thoroughly in cold, running water and strip out every bit of the sand vein (it comes out rather easily). And that's all there is to it.

Cleaning the Tails for Broiling

Rock shrimp are delicious broiled in their own shells. But the cleaning instructions are different for this method of cooking. Here's how it's done:

Place the tail on a cutting board so that the shrimp is on its back and the swimmerettes are facing up. Then, with a sharp knife (a paring knife works well), make a cut between the swimmerettes through the meat to the hard shell. Go ahead and spread the shell open until it lies flat. The tail meat should clearly be in two halves, left and right.

At this point wash the tails thoroughly in cold running water and remove the sand veins completely. Then set them in a colander to drain.

To Simmer:

Rock shrimp are different from other shrimp in that they cook *extremely* fast, so they require very close attention to prevent overcooking. In fact, overcooked rock shrimp lose all flavor and the texture of the meat becomes rubbery. The best method to prepare them for simmering is as follows:

To *1 quart* of rapidly boiling water containing *2 tablespoons of salt*, add 1½ pounds of raw, peeled, deveined rock shrimp tails and *simmer for 30 to 45 seconds*—no more.

Serve them with melted butter or sauce, or use them in recipes calling for cooked shrimp or lobster.

To Broil:

Lay the rock shrimp in their shells (shells down) in a shallow baking pan, making sure the tail meat is exposed to the overhead heat source. Then brush the tails with melted butter, dribble on a drop or two of lemon juice, and lightly sprinkle with garlic powder and paprika. Slide the pan under the broiler (no more than *4 inches* from the heat source) and cook for about *2 minutes* or until the tails turn upward. Serve immediately with a drawn-butter dip as you would lobster. Excellent!

To Fry:

You can fry rock shrimp, *but watch your cooking time*. They should not go beyond the point of being *lightly* browned, and the cooking time should not be more than *30 seconds*. I do not recommend frying rock shrimp!

As mentioned earlier, rock shrimp can be used in just about any conventional shrimp dish in this cookbook. All you have to do is reduce the cooking time to keep the shrimp tender and juicy. I recommend you make the substitution occasionally just to experiment with variations in taste and texture. You'll be amazed at the results you'll be able to get.

There are, however, several specialty recipes the food scientists in Florida have come up with specifically for rock shrimp. Naturally I've doctored them up a little to fit the cooking style of spice-loving Louisiana, but you might want to try them and make your own changes here and there.

Rock Shrimp Royale

24 fresh steamed asparagus spears	**2 tbsp. finely chopped shallots**
1 lb. cooked, peeled, deveined rock shrimp	**dash cayenne pepper**
	dash garlic powder
4 hard-boiled eggs, sliced	**½ cup sour cream**
2 tbsp. melted butter	**¾ cup soft bread crumbs**
	1 tbsp. grated Parmesan cheese

Arrange the asparagus spears in the bottom of a buttered 12-by-8-by-2-inch baking pan and place the rock shrimp evenly over the top of the spears. Then arrange the sliced eggs over the spears and shrimp.

In a sautéing pan, heat the butter over medium heat and gently fry the shallots. Stir in the cayenne pepper and garlic powder. Add the sour cream and stir it into the butter-onion mixture until everything is blended and the sauce is nice and bubbly. Pour it over the shrimp, eggs, and asparagus. Then combine the bread crumbs and the Parmesan cheese in a bowl and evenly sprinkle all of the mixture over the sauce. At this point put the dish in the oven and bake it at 350 degrees for 15 minutes, until the crumbs are toasted brown. Serve immediately.

Hint: Instead of sour cream, try this with Hollandaise sauce.

Sweet-and-Sour Rock Shrimp Tails

1 lb. cooked, peeled, deveined
rock shrimp
¼ cup melted butter
1 medium onion, thinly sliced
1 small bell pepper, diced in
chunks
2 8¼-oz. cans pineapple chunks
in heavy syrup
½ cup white vinegar

¼ cup granulated sugar
2 tbsp. cornstarch
1 tbsp. soy sauce
½ tsp. dry mustard
1 tsp. white pepper
¼ tsp. salt
½ cup toasted, slivered almonds
3 cups hot, cooked rice

Cut the large shrimp in half and set them aside momentarily. In a stainless-steel skillet, heat the butter over a medium fire and cook the onion and bell pepper until they are tender but not brown.

While the seasonings are simmering, drain the pineapple chunks in a strainer (but keep the syrup—you'll need it). Set the pieces aside. In a heavy bowl, use a whisk to thoroughly blend together the pineapple syrup, vinegar, sugar, cornstarch, soy sauce, dry mustard, pepper, and salt. Make sure this is well mixed. Pay particularly close attention to the cornstarch and dry mustard—you don't want lumps in the mixture. When it's just right, stir it into the sautéing vegetables, and cook until the sauce thickens and turns clear. At this point gently stir in the pineapple chunks and shrimp and heat everything to piping hot. While it's heating, mix the almonds into the rice. Then, when you're ready to eat, generously spoon the sauce over the rice. It really comes out great!

For really Chinese robustness, make the recipe as indicated and toss in extra onion chunks, snow peas, mushrooms, and bamboo shoots when you sauté the vegetables. And serve it with side dishes of steamed broccoli and fresh-steamed carrots, dabbed with a touch or two of the pineapple sauce. Be daring.

Note: Oriental-style dishes like this one are a lot easier to prepare if you fix them in a wok. The deep, sloping sides help to keep vegetables crisper (because of the principles of stir-frying) and the heat concentration on the bottom of the wok produces excellent cooking effects.

Golden Rock Shrimp Stew

More than any other way, I like to have my rock shrimp broiled in their shells and dipped in drawn butter. But if there has to be a close second, I've got to admit that this recipe is my choice. It's better than a tax refund!

¼ cup butter
½ cup chopped onion
½ cup sliced celery
2 cups sliced fresh mushrooms
2 tbsp. all-purpose flour
1 tsp. salt
black pepper to taste
1 tsp. Tabasco sauce
2 cups whole milk

1 10¾-oz. can cream of potato soup
1½ cups grated sharp cheddar cheese
2 tbsp. finely chopped parsley
2 lbs. cooked, peeled, deveined rock shrimp
1 2-oz. jar diced pimentos

In a 10-inch stainless-steel skillet, heat the butter over a medium flame and gently sauté the onion, celery, and mushrooms until they are tender. Then reduce the heat to low and stir in the flour, salt, pepper, and Tabasco, mixing well until everything is fully blended. At this point gradually begin stirring in the milk (remember to keep the fire on low and to stir constantly). When all the milk is added, gradually stir in the potato soup. Then turn the heat back up to medium and cook and stir until the milk-soup mixture *thickens*. It should take only a few minutes, but don't leave the skillet unattended; the milk and cream will burn if you do.

Now is the time to taste the liquid for seasoning adjustments: does it need more pepper for your taste . . . or more salt? Do you want the mixture thinner (add a little more milk) or thicker (increase the heat slightly and stir until some of the moisture evaporates)? Make your adjustments at this point. The next step leaves you just seconds away from serving.

When you're ready to eat, pour in the grated cheese, the parsley, and the rock shrimp, *but stir them only slightly, just enough to cover them in the sauce.* Then immediately cover the pot and heat for *3 minutes* on *medium high.* Finally, uncover, swirl the shrimp and cheese around once more, and spoon generous helpings of the stew into large soup bowls, topping each bowl with a sprinkling of pimento. Then go to it with crackers, French bread, or croutons— and serve with a chilled bottle of Chablis. Aaaaa-eeee!

CHAPTER TWELVE

Mixed Seafood Lagniappe

Cajun Deviled Clams

Not until 1978 did Louisiana develop a fishery around clams, and it was several months into that year before the first perfected recipes for the Louisiana quahogs started to circulate. But wouldn't you know it, none of them looked anything like the traditional clambake. Because the first ingredients listed in the recipes were those spicy Cajun herbs! Bon appetit!

4 tbsp. butter (not margarine)	1 cup half-and-half
1 large white onion, chopped	4 egg yolks, well beaten
2 stalks celery, coarsely chopped	5 tbsp. chopped chives
1 tbsp. chopped bell pepper	¼ cup toasted bread crumbs
2 lbs. minced Louisiana clams	

In a large saucepan melt the butter gently over low heat and sauté the onions, celery, and bell pepper until they are tender. *Be careful, though, that the butter does not burn.* Add the clams a little at a time, stirring constantly. After they're all in the sauté, increase the heat to about medium and simmer. The best way to do this is to put the pan on the fire until it sizzles, then take it off the fire and stir rapidly. After about 3 minutes of stirring and simmering, again reduce the heat to low, and put the saucepan back on the range.

Now is the time to stir in the cream. Add it slowly and stir it so that the sautéed clams are mixed well in the liquid. *Bring the whole thing to a boil,* but as soon as the liquid bubbles take it off the fire. Then *rapidly* beat in the egg yolks. You must do this quickly or they'll cook hard.

Add the chives, stirring them to mix them in well, and add enough bread crumbs to give the dish the body you want. Finally, spoon out the mixture into ramekins, sprinkle the tops with the remaining bread crumbs, and bake them in a 375-degree oven for about 20 minutes.

Serving Suggestion: Goes great with a tossed green salad and candied Louisiana yams!

Cajun Okra Jambalaya

When I'm not pounding out books at my typewriter, I'm laying out the format for my radio shows on WWL. One of the features that has become regular fare is the inclusion of a popular seafood recipe or two. Of all the recipes I've done over the years, none has gotten more requests for copies than Cajun Okra Jambalaya. Here's how you put it together:

4 tbsp. Crisco oil
6 #303 cans okra (or 4 10-oz.
    pkg. frozen okra)
1 tbsp. vinegar
¼ cup chicken stock
2 tbsp. flour
2 medium-size yellow onions,
    minced
1 large bell pepper, finely
    chopped
3 cups diced tomatoes

2 cloves garlic, crushed
3 cups water
1½ tsp. salt
½ tsp. thyme
¼ cup basil
1 tsp. cayenne pepper
½ tsp. black pepper
2 cups raw rice, washed
1 tbsp. minced shallots
2 tbsp. minced parsley

First heat the Crisco in a heavy black pot (a Dutch oven is best if you've got it seasoned well) and fry the okra until it becomes tender. If the okra is rather gooey and slimy, add *1 tablespoon of vinegar* and fry until the gooiness disappears. The vinegar cuts the slime in a matter of minutes. Fry the okra for about 20 minutes.

Remove as much of the okra as you can and put the chicken stock in the pot. Heat it to almost bubbling, then add the flour (stirring all the while) and cook it for about 3 or 4 minutes, until well blended. Next, put in the onions, bell pepper, tomatoes, garlic, *and the okra,* and cook it all down well (about 5 minutes on medium heat). Keep stirring.

When the ingredients look mixed, add the 3 cups of water, the salt, the thyme, the basil, the peppers (both the cayenne and the black), and bring the mixture to a *boil.* Keep stirring everything around well. When the water boils, stir in the rice and let the water come to a boil again. Then stir again to make sure the rice is well mixed with the other ingredients. Cover the pot tightly, reduce the heat to simmer, and cook until the rice is tender (usually about 20 to 30 minutes, depending upon your stove).

When everything is cooked—and about *5 minutes* before you're ready to serve the jambalaya—toss in the shallots and the parsley, cover the pot for another 5 minutes, and simmer on low heat.

If you want to add shrimp or crabmeat to your okra, just simmer the seafood lightly in butter (not margarine!) in a sautéing pan, and fold it into the rice about a minute or two before you serve the dish. I suggest you use a half-stick of butter for every pound of seafood.

And that, m'frien', is okra jambalaya, Cajun style!

Just a few notes, here:

1. Under no circumstances should you cook the parsley into the jambalaya. Add it only at the very end of the cooking process; otherwise it will impart a bitter taste to the entire dish.

2. Make certain that if you use a black cast-iron Dutch oven you have it seasoned well, and be certain that there are no rust spots inside the pot. The rust will "flavor" the rice for you during simmering and your jambalaya will come out bitter-tasting.

3. Leftover jambalaya can be frozen in Corning Ware casseroles and reheated in the oven without losing too much quality.

Duffy's Turtle Soup

I got this recipe from my old friend McFadden Duffy, who isn't just a good writer, but a good cook as well. Mac says the dish, prepared according to the steps listed here, will give you a full-bodied turtle soup that has the consistency of gumbo. I tried it, and he's right; it's delicious. Oh, the recipe makes 3 quarts.

3 lbs. snapping turtle meat	1 cup finely chopped celery
3 qt. water	1 tbsp. finely chopped parsley
½ cup flour	1 tbsp. salt
4 tbsp. cooking oil	1 tsp. black pepper
3 cups finely chopped white onions	1 oz. dry sherry per serving
	4 hard-boiled eggs
1 cup finely chopped green pepper	½ cup minced shallots

First, boil the turtle meat in the water until the meat is tender. Then drain off the water and let the meat cool. *But keep the water*—this is your cooking stock!

Next, brown the flour in the cooking oil and make a gravy by pouring into the browned flour *a full quart* of the water you used to boil the turtle meat. Stir well until the flour is completely cooked into the mixture. Then stir in the onions, pepper, celery, parsley, salt, and pepper. Simmer the mixture at a "low bubble" for an hour (or until the ingredients are tender to the taste). If the liquid becomes thicker than heavy cream, just add more of the cooking stock. When everything is cooked well, pour in the remaining stock, simmer for another 10 minutes, and add the cooked turtle meat. The meat should be diced into half-inch cubes. Some of it might shred while you're cutting, but add the shredded meat, too.

Finally, simmer for another 15 minutes. If the soup is too thin, simmer with a tablespoon of arrowroot. When you are ready to serve, pour the soup into individual bowls, add an ounce of sherry to each bowl, and garnish with chopped eggs and a *pinch* of shallots.

Baked Seafood d'Orleans

Nobody seems to know for sure where this recipe originated. But rumor has it that an old weather-beaten fisherman who lived near New Orleans at a place called Bucktown fixed the dish regularly with the leftover fish and crabs that he couldn't peddle to his customers. That may or may not be the case, but one thing is for certain: This is good!

1 tbsp. cooking oil	1½ cup real mayonnaise
2 lbs. unseasoned crabmeat, cooked	6 tbsp. lemon juice
	2 tbsp. dry sherry
2 lbs. boiled shrimp, coarsely cut	2 tsp. Tabasco sauce
1 cup finely chopped bell pepper	4 tbsp. Worcestershire sauce
1 cup finely chopped white onion	salt and black pepper to taste
	½ cup bread crumbs
2 cups coarsely cut celery	2 tbsp. melted butter

This is one of the easiest and tastiest recipes in this collection. In fact, you can probably put the whole dish together in less than 15 minutes. Here's how to do it:

Take a medium-size baking pan and rub it down with cooking oil to keep the food from sticking. Then mix the crabmeat and the chopped shrimp together and spread them evenly across the bottom of the pan. At this point add the bell pepper, the onions, and the celery, spreading each *evenly* in layers, much as you would if you were making a pizza.

Then place the mayonnaise in the middle of the baking pan, pour the lemon juice, sherry, Tabasco, Worcestershire sauce, and salt and pepper on top of the mayonnaise, and begin folding all the ingredients together until you get a uniform mixture. Don't worry about keeping layers together. The only reason you layer is to distribute the ingredients properly.

Finally, smooth out the mixture in the baking dish, making sure you have about an inch of *free space* at the top because everything will bubble while it cooks. Then sprinkle the top with bread crumbs, dribble the melted butter over the surface, and bake in the center of the oven at about 375 degrees for 20 minutes.

Serving suggestion: This goes well with a tossed salad.

Dutch Oven Seafood with Rice

I was sitting in a restaurant in Lake Charles one morning having breakfast with Cajun comedian Justin Wilson and Bob Dennie, and the conversation got around to cooking. An excellent chef himself, Justin was explaining some of the old French techniques when he said something to the effect of "Some of the best dishes you ever ate, m'frien, were cooked in a black iron pot!" The statement couldn't be more accurate, and this recipe proves it.

1 tbsp. Crisco oil
1 tbsp. flour
5 cups water
½ cup finely chopped shallots
1 clove fresh garlic, minced
2 tbsp. minced bell pepper
2 bay leaves
½ cup minced celery
¼ tsp. cayenne pepper
1 tsp. thyme
1 doz. raw oysters, drained

1 lb. coarsely chopped raw shrimp
1 lb. lump crabmeat
1 cup mushrooms stems and pieces
1 tsp. salt
1 cup uncooked rice
1 tsp. minced parsley
½ cup sharp Cracker Barrel cheese

In a black iron pot, pour the Crisco and the flour and make a dark roux. You want it to brown well, but *don't let it burn*. When it's deep brown, add about a cup of the water and stir the mixture well. Then add the shallots, the garlic, the bell pepper, bay leaves, celery, cayenne, and thyme. Continue to stir as you add these ingredients; and if the ingredients get too dry and you need a little more water, *add it!* Cook these seasonings for about 5 minutes, then toss in the oysters, shrimp, and crabmeat. Continue to cook for about 2 minutes, then add the mushrooms. You want to reduce the heat at this point and simmer everything for about 5 minutes.

When the mixture in the pot is bubbling well, it's time to add the remaining water and bring it to a boil. Then add the salt and the uncooked rice, stir around until they're blended, reduce the heat to low (just enough to keep it bubbling), and cover the black pot tightly. Unless the lid fits snugly the steam and heat won't cook the rice. And don't keep uncovering the pot to see if it's cooking. *It is!*

About 20 minutes after you've sealed the pot (it's best to use a timer), take the cover off and stir everything well. The rice should be beginning to "puff" and should be getting soft at this point, but if it's not increase the heat slightly and add a little more water (no more than ¼ cup) if needed. You don't want this recipe soupy—*it should be semidry*. Oh, before you re-cover the pot, mix in the parsley.

As soon as the rice is done the dish is ready to serve. But before you spoon it out, grate the Cracker Barrel and sprinkle it over the top. You can stir it in if you want uniform cheese flavoring, or you can leave it as a topping, it's up to you.

Serving Suggestion: I recommend you serve this seafood steaming hot alongside a very cold sliced tomato and cucumber salad. Green peas or sautéed broccoli will balance the meal. And don't forget the Chablis!

Seafood Acadienne

This recipe comes from the bayou country around Abbeville. It exemplifies what you can do with small quantities of seafoods mixed together. While it is primarily French in origin, it does have a few local adaptations which have given it added taste appeal. This is one recipe you want to make when you have to bring a covered dish to a party!

½ lb. coarsely cut uncooked shrimp	2 tbsp. capers
2 8-oz. fish fillets (lean to medium oily)	2 tsp. lemon juice
	1 tsp. Coleman's dry mustard
½ lb. flaked crabmeat	2 cups stale French bread
½ cup real mayonnaise	1½ tsp. chopped fresh parsley
1 medium onion, finely chopped	dash Worcestershire sauce
1 stalk celery, finely chopped	dash Tabasco sauce
3 tsp. pimentos	pinch sage

The crabmeat should be picked from crabs boiled in lightly salted water with no other seasonings, but if you can't get fresh crabs you can use a couple of 8-oz. cans of processed claw meat. If you use canned crabmeat, drain it well.

To prepare this dish, boil the shrimp and the fish fillets in just enough water to cover them for about 3 minutes. Then drain the seafood, saving the boiling liquor. Take a large bowl and put in the boiled shrimp, fish, crabmeat, and all the other ingredients and mix *extremely well*. This is important. Now put the bowl in the refrigerator for 2 hours until the spices have had a chance to blend.

Remember the liquor you saved when you boiled the seafood? Well, now you use it. Take the bowl from the refrigerator, add the seafood liquor slowly as you stir, and mix all the ingredients again until everything is moist. You should need about half a cup or so.

Finally, put the mixture in a 1½-quart casserole dish, set the oven at 350 degrees, and let it bake for an hour.

Frank's Shrimp and Oyster Pillows

Bored to death with eating the same old party snacks? You can get pretty burned out on potato chips, wheat crackers, and pitted olives! I decided to come up with something else that was tasty and creative. So I started experimenting, and would you believe I've made a hit with this recipe? It doesn't take a lot of effort to put together, and it's *good*.

1 lb. small uncooked shrimp	1 stalk celery, coarsely chopped
1 doz. fresh oysters	¼ tsp. dry mustard
1 cup coarsely chopped bell	1 tsp. cayenne pepper
pepper	1 tsp. salt
1 small white onion, coarsely	dash allspice
chopped	1 pkg. egg-roll wrappers

The first thing you do is peel the shrimp and chop them and the oysters into *small* pieces. Put them in a colander to drain (you don't want excessive moisture in these ingredients, especially in the oysters). While the shrimp and oysters are drying, cut up your bell pepper, onion, and celery, but don't cut too finely because if you do your pillows won't come out crunchy. When everything is cut, mix the vegetables and the shrimp and oysters together in a bowl, along with the spices. (*Hint: If you didn't drain the oysters well enough and your mix is still wet, toss in half a handful of bread crumbs, but not too much!*) *Let the mixture sit for a minute or two.*

Now here's where the recipe gets creative. Cut the egg-roll wrappers (which you can buy in the freezer section of most supermarkets) so that you end up with 3-inch-by-4-inch pieces. Lay these out flat, then spoon enough of the mix into the center of the pieces so that you'll be able to wrap them tightly. *Seal the edges well,* and *don't overstuff* 'em! (If you have egg-roll wrappers left over, you can refreeze them.) When you're ready to serve (and you should keep them chilled until then), simply drop them *one at a time* into a deep fryer set at 350 degrees. For consistent cooking, pierce a hole in the side of the wrapper with a toothpick. Fry until they're golden brown, because you have to fry the shrimp and oysters inside the wrapper!

It may take you a few batches to get the hang of it, but once you do it's simple. Oh, you'll probably have to keep right on cooking, because they seem to disappear fast.

Bayou Terrebonne Chowder

In the shrimp-boat country that lies below Houma, there is a recipe that many of the Cajun fishermen cook up, pack into tall Thermos bottles, and carry aboard the gulf trawlers so that they'll have a hot meal that will stick to their ribs while the nets are overboard. This is the recipe, and it tastes every bit as good at home as it does on the deck of the boat. You'll see!

1 lb. smoked sausage
¼ cup butter
½ cup chopped white onion
4 large potatoes, diced
2 lbs. coarsely cut shrimp
1 lb. crabmeat
2 lbs. coarsely chopped fish
  fillets
1 tsp. salt

4 cups milk
2 cups water plus some for
  boiling
2 cups light cream
1 tsp. celery salt
½ tsp. Zatarain's crab boil
4 hard-boiled eggs
½ tbsp. parsley

Before you start preparing the rest of the ingredients, boil the sausage in a small amount of water for about 4 minutes, drain off the water, and let the sausage cool. Then cut it up really fine by hand, or run it through a food processor. Set it aside.

In a saucepan—you'll need a large one—melt the butter and sauté the onions, potatoes, shrimp, and crabmeat. This will take about 4 minutes; all you want to do is heat everything up. Then add the cut-up fish and stir it around until it turns white. As it cooks, sprinkle in the salt. At this point turn up the heat to medium high and pour in the milk, water, and cream. Stir constantly and make sure the mixture just bubbles; it shouldn't really boil. When it's hot and steamy, stir in the celery salt, the crab boil, and the chopped sausage. Then reduce the heat so that it just stays hot.

Finally, chop up the hard-boiled eggs, add them to the chowder along with the parsley, and cook the dish on *low* for about 15 minutes. The flavor is distinctive, full-bodied, and rich!

Louisiana Seafood Okra Gumbo Classique

There must be a ton of recipes for every kind of gumbo: chicken gumbo, oyster gumbo, andouille gumbo—the list goes on and on and on. But in this section you get *just one* recipe for gumbo. That's because in all the years I've been cooking, I believe I've tried them all, and none compares in richness with the one outlined below. So fix this one, and what you have left you can put in your freezer!

8 #303 cans okra (or 4 10-oz. pkg. frozen okra)	3 tsp. garlic powder
8 1¼-oz. pkg. sun-dried shrimp (optional)	2 tbsp. liquid crab boil
	3 tsp. thyme
1 doz. raw crabs, cleaned and quartered	2 lbs. raw shrimp, cut small
	1 lb. picked crabmeat
1 lb. diced smoked sausage	8 bay leaves
12 tbsp. Crisco oil	½ cup finely chopped parsley
8 qt. water	1 16-oz. can tomato sauce
2 sticks corn-oil margarine	2 tbsp. salt
6 tbsp. flour	3 lbs. whole raw shrimp
3 large onions, finely chopped	4 cups steamed rice

Experience has taught me that this gumbo comes together best when everything is prepared in advance. For instance, you should drain the okra in a colander, unpackage the dried shrimp, clean and wash the crabs, and cut up the sausage before you ever put a skillet on the stove top. Doing this will keep you from rushing around while you're building up the gumbo.

Okay. Assuming you've got everything ready, the first thing you want to do is select the right size pot. It should be nothing less than 10 quarts in capacity. A big spaghetti cooker or a canner is ideal because it gives you room to stir the ingredients without crowding them.

One more thing. Procedure is important in making this gumbo. So to get quality, *don't skip any of the steps*. Ready?

First off, put the pot on a high fire, add 6 tablespoons of cooking oil, and toss in the smoked sausage. Fry this really well. It's the base for browning the okra. Next, without removing the sausage, add all the okra and fry it well, too. Canned okra doesn't have nearly as much "rope" (the sticky stuff) as fresh okra, so it should cook well in about 20 minutes. But note: When you add the okra, reduce the heat to medium so the vegetable won't burn. When the okra is cooked, pour in *1 quart* of water and let the contents simmer on low heat. Cover the pot!

At this point take a small saucepan, put in the extra 6 tablespoons of oil, the *2 sticks* of margarine, and the *6 tablespoons* of flour and cook the flour into a roux (you want it to brown well without burning). When it's brown, add the onions, garlic powder, crab boil, and thyme and stir the mix around briskly until the onions get tender. Keep a close eye on the heat—*don't let the roux burn*. When it has cooked enough (about 4 minutes), pour it into the okra in the big pot and blend everything together well. *Now add the remainder of the water* and simmer on low heat, stirring constantly, for about 10 minutes.

All the remaining ingredients *except the whole shrimp and the rice* go in next—the sun-dried shrimp, the cut shrimp, the quartered crabs, the crabmeat, the bay leaves, the parsley, the tomato sauce, and the salt. Stir everything in well; you want all the ingredients in the pot to blend together. At this point the gumbo liquid should be *brownish with a reddish tinge,* and the okra should be broken up and suspended in the solution. Now cover the pot and simmer on low heat for about 25 to 30 minutes. During this period stir the liquid about 3 times to keep the contents uniformly mixed. After the cooking time has lapsed, uncover the pot and toss in the 3 pounds of *whole shrimp*. It's important to turn the heat up to high when the shrimp are added because you want them to cook quickly so they won't turn soft. And stir . . . keep stirring! It's gonna take about 5 minutes for the whole shrimp to cook through.

When the shrimp are done, take the pot off the fire and set it aside, but leave the cover on *for 20 more minutes*. This will allow the seasonings to blend fully; the gumbo won't taste "creole" unless you let it "set." Finally, after the gumbo has cooled slightly, toss in the steamed rice and stir it in well. Once again, cover the pot and let the rice "swell" for at least 30 minutes to pick up the flavors. Then reheat . . . and eat! That's *gumbo!*

McSeafood Burgers Rosina

All New Orleans knows about codfish cakes. They were the main dishes of post-Depression cuisine, glorified by cooks on a tight budget who still wanted their families to get nutritious meals. My mother, bless her heart, was a staunch believer in codfish cakes. I think she held stock in the fish flake company! At least once or twice a week she'd fix the things—she used to call them codfish *balls,* even though they were flattened out! But we ate well, and we got full. So in tribute to her I've turned the old standby recipe into gourmet fare and named it after her. Who knows—maybe she'll read this recipe, fix up a batch, and invite me over to dinner!

4 tbsp. butter (not margarine)	1 medium onion, coarsely
1 lb. shrimp, peeled and	chopped
chopped	2 tbsp. chopped bell pepper
½ lb. lump crabmeat, flaked	6 cups boiled, chopped potatoes
1 doz. fresh oysters, chopped	2 raw eggs
and drained	½ pt. heavy cream, divided
1 rib celery, finely chopped	salt and pepper to taste
2 cloves garlic, minced	

In a 10-inch saucepan, melt the butter over medium-low heat and lightly sauté the shrimp, crabmeat, and oysters until they are tender (just a few minutes will do it—do not overcook). Then toss in the celery, garlic, onion, and bell pepper and stir-fry them for about *2 minutes,* no longer.

Then, in a large bowl to which you have added the boiled potatoes, pour in the seafoods and vegetables and mix together well. Also add the raw eggs, *half* of the cream, and salt and pepper to taste. Be sure everything is well mixed. Moisten your hands and form patties large enough to cover the bottom half of a hamburger bun. Set them aside.

While they are "drying" (a sheen will form on the outside of the patties after about 15 minutes), whip up your sauce. You'll need:

3 slices bacon	½ tsp. white pepper
½ stick unsalted butter	2 tbsp. Parmesan cheese
the remaining heavy cream	1 pkg. hamburger buns
½ tsp. salt	

Fry the bacon in a skillet until it is crisp and drain off the drippings. Set the bacon to cool and melt the butter in the residual drippings still in the pan. Then pour in the cream, reduce the heat to medium, add the salt and pepper, and cook for about 5 minutes until the cream thickens. When it reaches the consistency of pancake batter, crumble the bacon, toss it in with the cheese, and reduce the heat to simmer to allow the flavors to blend.

In a skillet (rubbed lightly with corn oil), brown the patties on both sides. When they are hot, ladle some of the sauce over half of a hamburger bun, place the patty on the sauce, and ladle some more sauce over the top of the patty; you'll serve it open-face. And that's a McSeafood Burger Rosina, gourmet style!

Note: You can make a large batch of patties and store them in your freezer for instant access. All you need to make is the sauce. To keep them from sticking together, separate the patties with sheets of waxed paper. They're great for school lunch boxes, late-night snacks, and other occasions when you get the urge to eat. And they're delicious, y'all! They go great with steamed broccoli and buttered carrots, plus a sliced tomato salad and a light white wine or iced tea.

A NOTE ABOUT BAKING SEAFOODS RIGHT

Good cooks always recommend that you preheat your oven before baking any kind of seafood. Getting an oven to the *right cooking temperature* will begin the actual *cooking* process immediately. Waiting for the right temperature to *build up* will often dry out seafoods, which leaves you with poor taste, rubbery texture, and a lack of body.

As a rule of thumb, *always preheat.*

Shrimp and Crab Creamed Bisque

I first tasted this succulent stew-type dish at a fishing camp built on the marsh near the mouth of the Mississippi River. It was prepared by an old Frenchman who had been shrimping commercially most of his life. Ever since then, it's been one of my favorite mixed seafood recipes.

1 10¾-oz. can cream of shrimp soup	1 stalk celery, coarsely chopped
1 10¾-oz. can cream of mushroom soup	1 cup green peas
	½ cup mushroom buttons
2 cups water	¼ tsp. garlic powder
1½ sticks margarine	3 tbsp. sherry
½ cup coarsely chopped bell pepper	½ tsp. dry mustard
	salt and red pepper to taste
2 cups diced carrots	1 lb. chopped medium shrimp
¼ cup finely chopped white onions	1 lb. flaked crabmeat

Before you get started, remember that this is a full-bodied dish that can be prepared with any consistency you desire. So if this recipe comes out too thick for your taste, simply add a little more water and simmer it in. Personally, I prefer it "stewy" rather than "soupy." So, with that in mind, set the stove at medium. Take a large skillet, and put in the 2 cans of soup and the 2 cups of water, stirring until the mixture becomes smooth. Then add the margarine, cover the pan, and allow the mixture to simmer for about 10 minutes.

Next—and look how simple this is—add everything else on the ingredient list *except* the shrimp and the crabmeat, and spend about 5 minutes stirring the ingredients into the soup over a *medium fire*. Then cover the skillet, reduce the heat to simmer, and let the base cook for 30 minutes.

Finally, add the chopped raw shrimp and the flaked crabmeat and stir them in well. Then re-cover the skillet and let the bisque simmer for about 10 more minutes or until your shrimp turn pink and tender.

Hint: Serve the bisque in a soup bowl alongside a tossed green salad and a plate of buttered, homemade biscuits. That's down-home!

An Open Invitation, Y'all

Makes no difference how complete you try to be, seems like you always end up leaving something out when you create a project like a cookbook. Well, I don't want that to happen.

If, for any reason whatsoever, you have questions you can't find answers to in the text; if you need information on seafoods not included in this book; or if you just want to drop a line to pass along some new recipe you may have created—*write me!* I'm always happy to hear from folks who cook.

The address is:

> **Frank Davis**
> **c/o Pelican Publishing Company**
> **P.O. Box 189**
> **Gretna, LA 70054**

Or you can call me on the air any weekend on my radio shows on WWL—Newsradio 87 and talk cooking with gourmets from all over the country. The number is (504) 524–8700.

Seafood Connoisseur's Bulletin

If you're still having difficulty getting your dishes to taste "authentically Louisiana" after reading this cookbook and trying the recipes, don't fret! It takes practice to learn to blend herbs and spices in the right proportions to achieve this special flavor. As an alternative while you continue to practice, I've made arrangements with Chef Paul Prudhomme to have his Cajun Magic seasonings available to be shipped directly to your kitchen. How's that for service? There are four varieties, so make sure you indicate which blend you want to order: Cajun Magic for poultry, Cajun Magic for meat, Cajun Magic for fish, and Cajun Magic for Blackened Redfish. And they're all excellent! The cost per bottle is $3.50 postpaid. To order write Chef Paul Prudhomme, c/o Cajun Magic, Inc., 406 Chartres Street, Suite 2, New Orleans, LA 70130.

That's not all, cher—if you're also having trouble finding quality seafood products or suitable substitutions, I've taken care of this problem too! Harlon Pierce, president of Harlon's Old New Orleans Seafood House (what else, huh?), will ship fresh Louisiana-style seafood to you. You can call him at (504) 831–4592. Harlon will ship anything that swims! Your order will be mailed the same day if possible, and all major credit cards are accepted. If you want to write for more information, the address is Harlon's Old New Orleans Seafood House, 128 Airline Highway, Metairie, LA 70001. (Incidentally, the Seafood House is one of the most reputable distributorships in Louisiana; I get a lot of my seafood from them.)

I want y'all to really enjoy preparing the fabulous foods of the Bayou State, and I don't want a scarcity of products to prevent anyone from exercising creativity in the kitchen.

Bon appétit!

Index